THE DUTCH DIAMOND ?
THE USEFULNESS OF PORTER
IN ANALYZING SMALL COUNTRIES

Lismo

P.R. Beije & H.O. Nuys (Eds.)

The Dutch Diamond ?
The Usefulness of Porter
in Analyzing Small Countries

Garant

Leuven-Apeldoorn

P.R. Beije & H.O Nuys
The Dutch Diamond ?
The Usefulness of Porter in Analyzing Small Countries
Leuven / Apeldoorn
Garant, 1995 - First edition
280 p. - 24 cm.
D/1995/5779/105
ISBN 90-5350-460-5
NUGI 681

Cover : Fred de Wit

Garant
Tiensesteenweg 83, 3010 Leuven-Kessel-Lo (België)
Koninginnelaan 96, 7315 EB - Apeldoorn (Nederland)

CONTENTS

CHAPTER 3
Competitiveness of industries and the economics of innovation   87
P.R. Beije

CHAPTER 4
The Dutch dairy sector in a European perspective   105
D.J.F. Kamann. D. Strijker

CHAPTER 5
Industry competitive analysis in the Netherlands.   155
A practitioner's view
J. Kuijper, S.R. Maltha

CHAPTER 8
Conclusions   257
P.R. Beije, H.O. Nuys

PREFACE

Introduction

In the by now well-known book *The Competitive Advantage of Nations* (Porter, 1990) a framework has been developed which offers an explanation for the competitiveness of (clusters of) industries in a country. The main indicator of competitiveness in this diamond-framework is a domestic industry's share in total world export of the industry. The 'diamond' is derived from the insights gained from existing theory, especially the new trade theory, and from studying a large number of industries in ten countries: Denmark, Germany, Italy, Japan, Korea, Singapore, Sweden, Switzerland, the United Kingdom and the United States.

The aim of the current book is to examine whether the 'diamond' model is useful in explaining the competitiveness of various industries in an open small economy. Dutch case-studies are used as an illustration. More specifically, the book examines theoretical issues on the measurement of competitiveness, and on factors specific to the Netherlands. Additionally there are other theories about elements present in the 'diamond', such as innovation, history and institutions. While the case-studies also address some of these questions, they by definition add case-specific factors and come up with problems of operationalisation. In such a way a fruitful 'interplay' between theoretical and empirical research is established. The book can therefore be said to offer new insight into the matter of how and to what extent the Porter concept can be used to analyze a small open country's competitiveness with respect to its exporting industries.

The organisation of the book is as follows. In chapter 1 the most relevant elements of the Porter concept are discussed followed by a presentation of the main results of the 'Dutch Porter study', which was published in 1990. In addition, a brief overview is given of specifically Dutch factors and reference is made to some other theoretical elements which may be used in addition to or instead of the 'diamond'. The main conclusions of the Dutch study are that the country is mainly strong in agriculture and related manufacturing industries and to a lesser extent in transport services, while no real strength in other manufacturing industries exists. Related to this, a lack of innovativeness is seen as the main explanation for the weak export performance of Dutch manufacturing industries.

Chapter 2 discusses how precisely export performance is used in the Porter studies to determine strong and weak industries. Alternatively, a new export measure is discusses and applied to OECD countries. Other results than those in the Porter study come up. The use of this alternative measure shows just how sensitive results of empirical analysis on the strengths and weaknesses of a nation's industries may be to specific procedures followed to measure competitiveness and more specifically, export performance.

Chapter 3 picks up on one of the main conclusions from the first chapter, namely that a lack of innovativeness is the main reason for the weak export performance of most Dutch manufacturing industries. First examined is how 'the diamond' sees innovation, followed by an overview of innovation theories from 'the economics of innovation' explaining export performance of industries and their main empirical results. Specific attention is paid to the distinction between incremental and radical innovations and the question whether the 'diamond' can explain both. The chapter ends with a discussion on technology policy.

The remaining four chapters before the conclusion contain specific Dutch case-studies. Chapters 4 and 5 are concerned with an explanation of the competitiveness of specific industries (clusters). The four cases presented in these chapters all take the Porter framework as a starting point, but add some other 'explanatory variables' when deemed necessary. In chapter 4 the Dutch dairy industry is analysed. Until quite recently, this industry was one of the success stories of the Dutch economy. It is considered to what extent the 'diamond' can explain the original strength and the current signs of weakness of the sector. This chapter corresponds to another main conclusions from chapter 1, namely that the Netherlands is (only) strong in agriculture and related industries. A distinction made between dairy industry appears to be instrumental in understanding the competitiveness of this agricultural cluster. A particularly interesting point is the role of (public) institutions in this sector. Chapter 5 analyses three industries simultaneously: dredging, telecommunication, and plastics processing. This opens up the possibility of comparing several 'Porter-like' cases and to see whether industry and country-specific conditions determine competitiveness in addition to the 'diamond' factors. An interesting element in this chapter is a classification of industries according to the size and location of the relevant market - Porter's exporting sectors appear to be only one of the classes. This implies that the 'diamond' concept may only be relevant for a limited number of industries.

Chapters 6 and 7 focus on the competitiveness of regions. One of the most striking statements in the Porter book is that, in many cases, the region is the best level of analysis to explain a domestic industry's competitiveness using the 'diamond'. Chapter 6 begins by exploring this statement further. It then proceeds with a critical analysis of the 'diamond' concept in the light of theories of regional development available from regional economics and corporate geography. In discussing theoretical issues and empirical results of a study about regional competitiveness the authors assess the usefulness of the 'diamond' concept at the regional level. Chapter 7 also focuses on the application of the Porter concepts at the regional level. It presents an analysis of the competitiveness of a specific Dutch region, namely the eastern part of North Brabant. Although this region has been weakened considerably due to the 'down-sizing' of DAF Trucks, and the poor performance of Philips and some other larger firms, it has recently been seen as one of the most promising areas in the country, due to a new spirit of entrepreneurship in small and medium-size firms. This study relates to one of the points mentioned in chapters 1 and 3 concerning (technological) networks of firms. An important point here is the distinction between Porter's 'diamond' factors and the firms' ability to improve their competitive advantage by incorporating conditions of the environment in their strategy.

The concluding (chapter 8) summarises the findings of the previous chapters by concentrating on three points: First the explanatory value of the 'diamond'; second the importance of country and industry/region specific factors; third the need for additional theories to explain the competitiveness of Dutch industries and networks. In addition, some implications for industrial policy are presented.

The book contains studies of which most have been presented during a series of 'workshops' organised by the Studygroup for Industrial and Technology Policy (STIP) of SISWO - Netherlands' Universities Institute for Coordination of Research in Social Sciences.

Acknowledgements

First, we want to thank the authors of this book who made a valuable contribution to the ideas of Porter, especially by questioning the usefulness of Porter's diamond-framework in analyzing small countries such as the Netherlands. Secondly, we thank the English editor Lisa Chason who changed the manuscript into a very readable book. Finally, our thanks goes to Lidwien van Dartel who took on the assignment of preparing the articles for the publishers, suggesting several important substantive improvements in the lay-out.

STIP has been aided in publishing *'The Dutch Diamond? The Usefulness of Porter in Analyzing Small Countries'* by a subsidy from the Ministry of Economic Affairs, Directorate for General Technology Policy, and additional financing by SISWO.

October, 1995   PAUL BEIJE
Amsterdam   OTTO NUYS

Chapter 1

H.O. NUYS

A CRITICAL REVIEW OF PORTER'S 'DIAMOND' WITH REGARD TO SMALL COUNTRIES

1. Introduction

The purpose of this chapter is threefold. First, a brief and critical review is given of Porter's concept of competitive advantage of specific industries in a country, in the light of some particular specific characteristics of the Dutch economy such as size and openness. The purpose of this book is to analyse how, in various ways, the 'Dutch nation' influences its firms' ability to compete in specific industries and industry segments. In this chapter some attributes of the 'Dutch nation' are being presented. Second, the competitive strength of the Dutch industries at a given moment is analysed. For data we used among others an analysis of TNO/STB called 'The economic clout of the Netherlands' (Jacobs et al., 1990). Third, we go more into detail about the importance of institutional factors in shaping a nation's competitiveness. We pay special attention to the possibilities and restrictions of the Dutch national and local government(s) and the specific role of labour-management relations.

By posing a number of interesting questions Porter outlines the leitmotif of his study. Why does a nation become the home base for successful international competitors in an industry? Why are firms based in a particular nation able to create and sustain competitive advantage against the world's most successful competitors in an industry? Why is one nation often the home for so many of an industry's world leaders? Why is tiny Holland the home base for international leaders in the cut flower industry (Porter, 1990a, 1)[1]? One of the answers is that selective disadvantages (a cold, and grey climate) have led to innovations in this industry[2]. The Dutch success in upgrading its advantage in the cut flower industry has also heavily depended on the other determinants of the 'diamond' (strong home demand, active domestic rivalry, etc.)
Porter tries to explain the role played by a nation's economic environment, institutions, and policies in the competitive success of its firms in particular industries. In some chapters of the book we try to locate national attributes that foster competitive advantage in such industries, as dairy (chapter 4), dredging, telecommunications, and plastics (chapter 6). The Netherlands cannot be, in Porter's terms, competitive in (and a net exporter of) everything. Sometimes market positions in some segments

and industries must necessarily be lost if a national economy is to progress. Protection of those industries (e.g. RSV) slows down the upgrading
of the economy. For Porter, it is essential for nations like the Netherlands
to be able to compete in sophisticated industries and activities involving
high productivity in order to achieve economic prosperity. To sustain
competitive advantage in a particular industry(segment), Dutch firms must
achieve more sophisticated advantages in the long run, through providing
higher quality products and services or producing more efficiently. Access
to abundant factors of production is no longer important, what counts is
that most factors become in Porter's terms fleeting advantages. Any
advantage of today can be a disadvantage tomorrow. It depends on the
technology and skills to process them. What's more, globalization of
industries decouples the firm from the factor endowment of a single
nation, because a lot of factors are increasingly mobile or available
globally on comparable terms[3].
Before looking more closely at the specific national attributes of the
Dutch economy (sections 3 and 4) some critical remarks are made about
Porter's concept of national competitive advantage.

2. Some remarks about the 'diamond' concept

2.1 A break with the past

In some respects the 'Competitive Advantage of Nations' is quite a
turnaround compared to earlier work of Porter's about competitiveness. In
the first place, Porter switches over from a static (in 'Competitive Strategy' (1980) and 'Competitive Advantage' (1985)) to a dynamic view of
competition (Grant, 1991; De Man, 1994). In 1980 Porter is very negative
about domestic rivalry inside the industry, about competition between
buyers and suppliers, because it leads to lower profits. To the contrary, in
1990 he is much more positive about intense domestic rivalry - a central
element in his 'diamond' - being the basis for continuous and important
innovation in the industry (Porter, 1990a, 224). Porter's conception of
competitiveness seems to be influenced by developments in the Japanese
economy of the last decades. In its weakest aspects it is more or less a set
of generalisations derived from the these Japanese experiences (Auerbach
& Skott, 1995).

In the same way Porter's view of innovation has changed since the
eighties. Coming from a restrictive definition, Porter now defines innovation broadly in a more 'Schumpeterian' manner (Scherer, 1992; De Man,

1994). Porter comes very close to Schumpeter's 'creative destruction' concept, in the sense that industrial innovation leads to superior new goods and services, and simultaneously undermines the market positions of firms committed to old ways of doing business (Scherer, 1992). In Porter's own words:

> *Innovation* here is defined broadly, to include both improvements in technology and better methods or ways of doing things. It can be manifested in product changes, process changes, new approaches to marketing, new forms of distribution, and new conceptions of scope. (Porter, 1990a, 45)

De Man (1994), in his exegesis of the works of Porter, develops four propositions about Porter's latest work 'The Competitive Advantage of Nations':

1. Firms strive for competitive advantage
2. Innovation is the core of competitive advantage
3. Rivalry undermines competitive advantage
4. Firm and environment ought not to be separated
(source: De Man, 1994, 45)

The first proposition needs no further explanation. The second leads to the question: how do firms achieve innovation? This is a matter of firm strategies, underlying the national features promoting or inhibiting the competitive advantage of particular industries. Well known is that Porter distinguishes between two basic strategies: cost strategy and the strategy of differentiation. These strategies can both be followed in a 'broad' way or with more focus (ending up with four strategy types). The question is whether and how these four types of strategy determine competitive advantage of entire industries. If we look at the general treatment of these strategies in relation to competitive advantage of industries in a nation, the conclusion seems to be that they all may contribute. The emphasis throughout the book, however, is on 'long run dynamics', on innovation and adjustments of the 'diamond' factors to changing circumstances. Seen in this light, differentiation is clearly the superior strategy, as the following citation shows:

> There is a *hierarchy* of sources of competitive advantage in terms of sustainability. Lower-order advantages, such as low labor costs or cheap raw materials, are relatively easy to imitate (...) higher-order advantages usually depend on a history of *sustained and cumulative investment* in

physical facilities and specialized and often risky learning, research and development, or marketing (...) The third[4], and most important, reason competitive advantage is sustained is *constant improvement and upgrading*. (Porter 1990a, 49-51)

This relates closely to the strategy of differentiation. Differentiation in its turn is closely connected to technological change. The third proposition says nothing more than that firms have to provide for a continuing 'upgrading' of advantages, because in the long run intensive rivalry in the home market will undermine these advantages. Especially the last proposition, the relation between environment and firm, is pervasive in 'The Competitive Advantage of Nations'. Porter continually comes back to the subject of the significance of the firm's proximate environment (the effect of the national 'diamond' on the micro level), which promotes or impedes the innovation process of that firm[5]. Meeus and Oerlemans (chapter 7) carry the discussion of firm and environment further. They argue that not the environment determines a firm's competitiveness but the way in which the firm adjusts strategies, assets, etc. in the light of what occurs in that environment.

2.2 Standard of living - productivity - competitiveness

According to Porter there is no generally accepted theory that explains why some nations are competitive and others not; neither is it clear how 'competitive' is related to a nation. What is clear in Porter's book is that 'national' competitiveness is not a function of cheap and abundant labour, it does not depend on the availability of scarce natural resources, it is not very strongly influenced by government policy and finally has not much to do with differences in management practices (including labour-management relations)[6].
Porter argues that a nation's competitiveness is interrelated with its standard of living and its productivity, productivity being the prime determinant in the long run of a nation's standard of living, and therefore the only meaningful concept of competitiveness at the national level.

A rising standard of living depends on the capacity of a nation's firms to achieve high levels of productivity and to increase productivity over time. Our task is to understand why this occurs. Sustained productivity growth requires that an economy continually *upgrade* itself. (Porter, 1990a, 6)

Because of this, the focus of Porter's (longitudinal) study is on the process of gaining and sustaining competitive advantage in relatively sophisticated industries and industry segments, in short the key factors to high and rising (national) productivity[7].

Reich (1992) disagrees with Porter on this very subject. Instead of depending on the success of the nation's core corporations and industries, the standard of living is coming to depend more and more on the world-wide demand for their skills and insights. Even more the connection between corporate profitability and the standard of living is growing ever more attenuated. What in the world economy really counts and what makes it unique are the skills of a nation's work force and the quality of its infrastructure. These national features are what global webs of enterprise attract to a certain nation (Reich, 1992, 153).

In a review essay of Chandler's *'Scale and Scope'* (1990), Teece (1993) mentions that according to Chandler the competitiveness of nations is dependent in an important way upon the organizational and financial capabilities of firms and their supporting institutions. In other words the strategic and organizational choices made by managers shape or, what's more, determine both firm level and national economic performance (Teece, 1993, 199-200). It is the business enterprise, through the development of organizational capabilities, that played the central role in the industrial development of countries such as the United States, Britain, and Germany. To maintain the organizational capabilities once created the firms need to be in a process of constant organizational renewal (see further p. 211).

In Chandler's opinion the modern industrial enterprise played and *still* seems to play a central role in creating the most technologically advanced, fastest-growing industries. At the core of the dynamic of industrial capitalism are the organizational capabilities of the enterprise, such as the collective physical facilities and human skills, as they have been organized within the enterprise and created primarily in those capital-intensive industries where the interrelated investment in manufacturing, marketing, and management provided powerful competitive advantages. Once such organizational capabilities have been established, they have to be maintained in order to provide the specialized facilities and skills that give the enterprise an advantage in foreign markets or in related industries (Chandler, 1990, 594). Organizational capabilities provide the dynamic not only for the continuing growth of firms, but also for the industries which they have dominated, and for the national economies in which they have operated. Those core capabilities (knowledge and skills) are developed by learning through trial and error in a very specific organizational context. That's why they are company-specific and industry-specific and therefore are difficult to transfer from one industry to another (Chandler, 1992, 84).

Recently Hamel & Prahalad (1994) have pointed to the so-called 'core competencies' (resembling Chandler's 'organizational capabilities') as important tools for firms to maintain in the future. To sum up, in more 'Porterian' terms the competitive advantage of a nation is based on the organizational capabilities of its firms and respective industries.

2.3 Unit of analysis

Porter's model on the competitive advantage of nations is not about the overall strength of a national economy, which can be compared with other nations, although the title might suggest otherwise. Therefore it is unjustifiable, as some authors do (De Jong, 1990), to accuse Porter of taking the competitiveness of nations too literally. Notwithstanding the fact that firms, not nations, compete in international markets, Porter takes the narrowly defined industry or distinct segment within an industry as the basic unit of analysis[8]. Actually it is about the competitive advantage some industries in a specific country have, compared to the same industries in other countries. Porter defines an industry (whether product or service) as a group of competitors producing products or services that compete directly with each other. One of the explanations for Porter choosing the industry as unit of analysis is:

> (...) the influence of the nation seems to apply to industries and segments, rather than to firms *per se*. Most successful national industries comprise groups of firms, not isolated participants ... (Porter, 1990a, 10)

According to Auerbach & Skott (1995) Porter's truly distinctive unit of analysis is the cluster. Porter thereby offers a broad conceptualisation of the unit of analysis, which includes supplying firms and those making complementary products (Auerbach & Skott, 1995, 156). From this choice it does not follow that Porter pays little attention to the micro level of the firm. On the contrary, as we will see.

In order to determine the sources of competitive advantage, Porter starts at the micro level by explaining the way firms organize their entire value chain. The influence of the nation on the international competitive performance of firms occurs through the ways in which 'a firm's proximate environment shapes its competitive success over time'[9]. Furthermore, in order to explain what role the nation plays, we need to know how firms create and sustain competitive advantage[10].

Although Porter many times operates at the micro level, he still starts from the meso level as unit of analysis. One can argue if this unit of analysis is correct when determining the competitive advantage of a nation. For, however it may be, firms are the real competitors, not nations. Therefore to some authors (De Jong 1990, 1991; Chandler, 1992) it seems to be more correct to take the firm as the unit of analysis. However, by naming the three essential functions firms have to fulfil in a market economy, it is striking how much De Jong (1989) resembles the Porter of 1990. 'In the first place firms ought to organize production efficiently, secondly absorb and control rising uncertainty, and finally should innovate, perhaps not as first mover, but certainly in time with new market trends', and '(...) Competition is here rivalry among firms, that is to say dynamic' (De Jong, 1989, 1182-1183).

By questioning 'the determinants of competitive success in national industries and even national economies', Chandler is convinced that the unit of analysis must be the firm (Chandler, 1992, 99). The problem with Porter is that he jumps very easily from the macro (national) level to the meso (industry) and micro (firm) level and the other way around, when its suits him. We return to this subject in the subsection about clusters and networks.

2.4 Indicators and premises

Before we criticize Porter's framework some important indicators and underlying premises are discussed. The competitive advantage of nations means the search for the decisive characteristics of a nation that allow its firms to create and sustain competitive advantage in particular fields. As indicators of that competitive advantage Porter chooses: (a) the presence of substantial and sustained exports to a wide array of other nations; (b) and/or significant outbound foreign investment based on skills and assets created in the home country[11]. The restrictions of these indicators and possible alternatives will be the subject of chapter 2.

In the eyes of Porter a new theory of national competitive advantage must start from the following premises:

1. Competitive advantage is created and sustained through a highly localized process. Differences in national economic structures, values, cultures, institutions, and histories contribute profoundly to competitive

success. The role of the home nation seems to be as strong as or stronger than ever;

2. The home base is the nation in which the essential competitive advantages of the enterprise are created and sustained. It is where a firm's strategy is set and the core product and process technology are created and maintained. The home base will be the location of many of the most productive jobs, the core technologies, and the most advanced skills. Notably, the nationality of the shareholders is secondary, although the ownership of firms is often concentrated at the home base;

3. Competition is a constantly changing landscape in which new products, new ways of marketing, new production processes, and whole new market segments emerge. So we have to explain why some firms, based in some nations, innovate more than others;

4. A new theory must make improvement and innovation in methods and technology a central element. It must explain the role of the nation in the innovation process, especially how a nation provides an environment in which its firms are able to improve and innovate faster than foreign rivals in a particular industry;

5. Finally, since firms play a central role in the process of creating competitive advantage, the behavior of firms must become integral to a theory of national advantage. (Porter, 1990a, 19-21)

2.5 Porter's 'diamond' model

In trying to isolate the influence of the (home) nation we have to look for the determinants of national advantage. In short, Porter describes four broad attributes of a nation that shape the environment in which local firms compete that promote or impede the creation of competitive advantage:

1. *Factor conditions*: the nation's position in factors of production, such as skilled labour or infrastructure, necessary to compete in a given industry.
2. *Demand conditions*: the nature of home demand for the industry's product or service.
3. *Related and supporting industries*: the presence or absence in the nation of supplier industries and related industries that are internationally competitive.

4. *Firm strategy, structure and rivalry*: the conditions in the nation governing how companies are created, organized, and managed, and the nature of domestic rivalry. (Porter, 1990, 71)

To these four, two other variables are added:

5. *Chance*: developments outside the control of firms (and usually the nation's government), such as pure inventions, breakthroughs in basic technologies, wars, external political developments, and major shifts in foreign market demand.
6. *Government*: at all levels, can improve or detract from the national advantage. Antitrust policy affects domestic rivalry. Regulation can alter home demand conditions. Investments in education can change factor conditions. (Porter, 1990, 73)

Figure 1. The Determinants of National Advantage (Porter, 1990a, figure 3-1, 72)

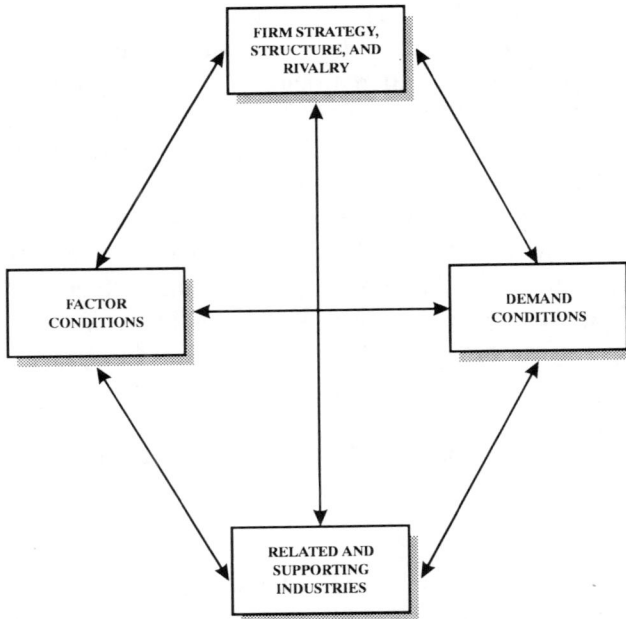

In Porter's view the 'diamond' is a mutually reinforcing system. In other words the effect of one determinant is contingent on the state of others. The most optimal situation is when the four 'corners of the diamond' are well developed and reinforcing each other to a considerable extent, in terms of creating advantages for achieving and sustaining competitive success in the knowledge-intensive industries[12]. On the basis of historical research Porter comes to the conclusion that there seems to be much more stability in these determinants of national competitive advantage, in spite of the speeding up of internationalisation. Below follows a critical analysis of some concepts/premises of Porter's framework.

2.6 The importance of home demand, home nation and domestic rivalry

According to Porter, having a large home market, which is missing in the Dutch case, offers little explanation why some industries are internationally successful and others not. So a lack of home demand is not the biggest problem firms have in contributing to the competitiveness of a small nation. The *quality* of home demand, including the nature of the home buyers (sophisticated, demanding and anticipatory of buyer needs), is more important than the *quantity* of home demand in determining competitive advantage[13]. Economies of scale are increasingly reached by selling abroad[14]. Although multinationals compete internationally by exporting and through foreign investment, producing and selling in many countries, the nation is still the home base for becoming a world leader in particular segments or industries. The nation was treated as the home base for a firm if it was either a locally owned, indigenous firm, or a firm that was managed autonomously though owned by a foreign company or investors. Therefore the central question to be answered is:

> Why do firms (including multinationals) based in particular nations achieve international success in distinct segments and industries? (Porter, 1990, 18)

Porter stresses the importance of the home base as being the place where strategy is set, core product and process development takes place, and the essential and proprietary (most advanced) skills reside[15]. In that sense Porter seems to go beyond Chandler (1992) in saying that those advanced skills are not only company- and industry-specific, but also nation-specific. With that he turns these specific core capabilities into 'national capabilities'. The home base is even more important because indigenous firms have the best information about buyer needs in their home market and are in open communication with their home buyers, due both to proximity and cultural similarity. This is a difficult thing to achieve with foreign buyers who are on a long distance from headquarters and when the firm is (culturally) an outsider (Porter, 1990a, 86-87). Porter doesn't overlook the fact that the home base of a firm or an industry can change over time. If the home nation is no longer the appropriate environment for the necessary innovations, 'a firm must shift its home base to a nation that better catalyzes and provides the needed tools for international success'[16]. Porter mentions several examples of firms which have created a new home base outside the home country of the parent company for some of their businesses (Sandvik (Sweden) in Germany; Siemens in the U.S.; Xerox in Japan).

Other authors (Chandler, 1990; De Jong, 1990; Reich, 1992), in contrast to Porter, more or less disconnect the success of firms or industries from the home base. The home base is no longer the place where the most complicated work - design and fabrication of the more intricate parts, and strategic planning, financing, and marketing - is done. A growing portion of American-owned corporations entails high-value problem-solving and -identifying outside the United States (Reich, 1992). To make his point Reich gives an example from General Motors (GM):

Italian stylists help GM produce a sleek-looking sports car, German design engineers ensure that its engine is dependable, and Japanese manufacturing engineers confirm that it can be reliably assembled at a low cost. (Reich, 1992, 123)

Although Porter agrees on one aspect with Reich, namely that advanced factors (human resources and knowledge) can be mobile among nations[17], he disagrees on the point that globalization eliminates the importance of the home base[18]. Porter doesn't stand alone by hammering on the importance of the home base. Harrison (1994) quotes Lazonick, who is criticizing Reich in this respect:

If the offshore divisions of American firms have recently been more profitable than their U.S.-located parents, as Reich correctly reports, then perhaps the explanation is that those overseas divisions are embedded within competitively efficient *foreign* diamonds. (Harrison, 1994, 227)

Or the other way around, the headquarters' operations of these successful 'foreign' divisions are confronted with a weak to nonexistent development of the clusters at their *home* base, the United States (Harrison, 1994).

Chandler has, according to Teece (1993), a slightly different opinion. The development of firms is not simply a microcosm of the development of the nation state, though Chandler seems to imply that the success of national enterprises and nation states are closely coupled. In Chandler's view the wealth of nations depends (in the first place) on the development of the above mentioned organizational capabilities To others, like Hamel & Prahalad (1990), 'the global economy is so intertwined today that in many cases it hardly makes sense to talk of a 'U.S.' company, a 'European' company, or a 'Japanese' company'. Most of the leading U.S. companies earn more than 50% of their revenues outside the United States, and the same holds true for many European companies (e.g. Unilever, Shell, Ericsson, Glaxo, Nokia and BMW). None of these companies view the U.S. or Europe as their home market. Each of them is 'local' wherever in the world it operates. But when it is a question of regaining competitiveness, Hamel & Prahalad do agree with Porter that the competitive enemies of U.S. companies are not 'the corporate warriors of Japan or Asia, but the unconventional tactics of *home-grown* rivals. IBM's problems weren't caused by Fujitsu, they were caused by Hewlett-Packard, EDS, and Compaq.' '(...) The real competitiveness problem is that too many large U.S., European and Japanese companies failed to anticipate, much less invent, the new rules of competition in their industries' (Hamel & Prahalad, 1994, 270).

De Jong (1990) makes an interesting remark in this regard about the existence of so many multinationals in the Netherlands (Shell, Unilever, Philips, etc.) in spite of such a small home market. He assumes that Porter's thesis about the central role of the home market should not be generalized. 'Maybe it is applicable to large countries (U.S., Japan), but the internationalization of the big companies from small countries (the Netherlands, Switzerland, Sweden, Belgium) has less to do with intensive rivalry on the home market (...) Rather it was and still is the limited size and the stagnation of the growth of the home market, or the only elsewhere obtainable raw materials' (De Jong, 1990, 1214, translated by the author).

2.7 Clusters and networks

To map the successful industries of the Dutch economy, as Jacobs et al. (1990) did, Porter designed a *cluster chart*, showing where the connections or relationships between the nation's competitive industries lie[19]. Jacobs et al. (1990) followed the clustering of industries in their study of the Dutch economy. To be selected, each industry must have a significant international market position at the time of the study. Porter defines (a) *cluster(s)* as 'a nation's successful industries, usually linked through vertical (buyer/supplier) or horizontal (common customers, technology, channels, etc.) relationships'[20]. This phenomenon of clustering is so pervasive that it appears to be a central feature of advanced national economies.

The reasons for clustering grow directly out of the determinants. Clustered competitive industries mutually support and reinforce each other in developing competitive advantage through continuous renewal and innovation. The more the industries are exposed to international competition the more pronounced the movement toward clustering will become[21]. So, for Porter, the amount of clustering becomes the ultimate yardstick to determine the competitiveness of 'our' national economy. The most fertile moment for competitive advantage is reached when interchange within clusters (e.g. the exchange and flow of information about needs, techniques, and technology among buyers, suppliers, and related industries) occurs at the same time with active domestic rivalry in each separate industry. A condition for this is the existence of enough mechanisms that facilitate the information flow between vertically or horizontally linked firms. Examples of such facilitators are of two kinds: (a) 'personal relationships due to schooling, military service; ties through the scientific community or professional associations; community ties due to geographic proximity; trade associations encompassing clusters; and norms of behavior such as belief in continuity and long-term relationships'; (b) sources of goal congruence because of e.g. (quasi-) family ties between firms, common ownership within an industrial group, interlocking directors, etc.

Clusters tend to widen horizontally (Japan) as established companies aggressively enter related industries and/or deepen vertically (Italy) as new companies spin off to serve ever more specialized niches and enter supplier industries[22]. The optimal situation is when both things happen at once.

Miles & Snow (1992) add to this the importance of suppliers working for different clients as a way to maintain and increase the supplier's technological expertise and flexibility. Over-specialization and limited learning easily occur when suppliers stick to one core firm. The athletic shoe producer Nike is very effective in this respect.

> Nike wants its suppliers to service other designers so that they can enhance their technical competence and so that they will be available when needed but not dependent on Nike's ability to forecast and schedule their services. (Miles & Snow, 1992, 63)

If the operating independence of the supplier is severely constrained, the core firm converts the network into a vertically integrated functional organization. Miles & Snow extend Porter's cluster concept by adding an important notion - which Porter fails to mention - namely if firms adopt network structures they will improve their self-renewal competence because of two unique characteristics of the network form: 'the essential relationships among components are *external* (and thus highly *visible* to all parties) and these relationships are *voluntary* (and thus must reflect *explicit* commitments)' (Miles & Snow, 1992).

Though Porter several times discusses the linkages between a firm and its suppliers, he never uses the concept of *networking*. When talking about the value of social networks within Japanese clusters, Porter did once use the concept:

> Interchange within clusters is also promoted by personal relationships. Japanese develop lifelong relationships with others in the same university class, and classmates often meet regularly for decades. This creates a network for interchange among related firms. (Porter, 1990, 154)

Porter does not provide further descriptions of networks in relation to his cluster concept. Therefore the whole concept of 'cluster' remains rather obscure (De Jong, 1990; Grant, 1991; Jacobs et al., 1994). In chapter 6 Boekema & van Houtum go deeper into Porter's cluster concept and its network aspects.

2.8 The importance of geographic concentration

The concepts and ideas of Porter's theory can be applied to political or geographic units smaller than a nation. Two chapters (6 and 7) of this book focus especially on this regional level. Internationally successful firms, and often entire clusters of industries, are frequently located in a particular city or region within a nation, because creating competitive advantage is a highly localized process.

That is why Porter, in his ten-country study, many times has explored in what way the firm's proximate 'environment' shapes its competitive success over time. In the vicinity of cities one finds not only concentrations of domestic rivals, but also concentrations of needed suppliers and the existence of sophisticated and significant customers. In Porter's opinion the city or region becomes a unique environment for competition in the industry[23]. For instance the majority of the Dutch cut flower producers are located in the western part of the Netherlands. The best environment, for heightening the influence of the individual ('diamond') determinants and their mutual reinforcement, is this close geographic proximity. In particular this close togetherness promotes improvement and innovation, since entrepreneurs tend to be very sensitive to the success of local rivals.

It seems that Porter wants to say that in all its aspects, as long as most local buyers, suppliers and rivals operate internationally, proximity is to be preferred above geographic decentralisation. Proximity makes a lot of things easier: it both increases the concentration and speed of information (flow), it raises the visibility of competitor behaviour and, in the case of the availability of local university activity, it promotes the exchange of know-how among researchers and competitors[24].

The problem with Porter is that he concentrates on national clusters thereby leaving out the possibility of 'border-crossing' regions, such as the Euro-regions, which often include more than two nations. What's more, suppliers in the automotive industry are not always found in the direct vicinity of the core-assembler. For example, the Dutch truck firm DAF cooperates with German suppliers without any big problems caused by long distances. Distance ought not to be a big problem in this era of information.

2.9 Strategic alliances

In the modern world economy it is not conceivable that the phenomenon of cooperation between firms soon will disappear. Therefore it is interesting to raise the question in what respect the so-called 'strategic alliances' contribute to the competitiveness of a nation's industries. Porter also looks at this aspect. He defines strategic alliances or 'coalitions' as long-term agreements between firms (mostly from different nations) that go beyond normal market transactions and encompass a whole variety of arrangements that include joint ventures, licenses, cross licenses, long-term supply agreements, and other kinds of interfirm relationships. Although cooperation between companies in the field of R&D becomes more and more important, Porter is not very enthusiastic about these alliances because today's partners become tomorrow's competitors. Moreover alliances are not stable, because they are in many respects costly arrangements (e.g. in terms of coordination). In the long run firms should incorporate important assets and skills themselves instead of relying on partners, otherwise the firm runs the risk of losing competitive advantage (65-66; 612-613). Considering this fact it is striking that the most successful alliances are highly specific in character, narrow in focus and oriented toward access to particular country markets or to particular technologies (67). In this case you may expect that firms try to integrate such new technologies as quickly as possible. So in Porter's terms alliances are rarely a sustainable means for creating competitive advantage. Some forms of interfirm cooperation are beneficial, many are not:

> Direct competitor to competitor cooperation usually undermines competitive advantage in the long run. It reduces incentives and saps rivalry, ultimately slowing progress. It limits the exploration of alternative approaches. (...) Joint production by leading competitors should be prohibited. (Porter, 1990a, 667)

In some circumstances *indirect* (horizontal) cooperation among competitors through independent entities can be beneficial according to Porter. For example, cooperative R&D through an independent entity is only appropriate when the majority of firms, including active rivals, also have access to it. It is only with the participation of active rivals that cooperative R&D stimulates private innovation in the national cluster[25]. In the same way this applies to cooperation through trade associations for the purpose of factor creation. Porter is more positive about *vertical* (buyer-supplier) cooperation, which is integral to the innovation process[26].

The economic historian Lazonick, quoted by Harrison (1994), argues that Porter 'has played up the relative importance of rivalry at the expense of drawing evidence from Porter's own case-studies on the relative importance of cooperation within the clusters'. Lazonick shows many examples of institutionalized cooperation in Porter's book, such as 'government supported technical institutes' and 'ties through the scientific community or professional associations' (Harrison, 1994, 227).

Porter doesn't stand alone in being negative about strategic cooperation. Commandeur & Den Hartog (1991) talk about advantages but also about some disadvantages inherent to alliances. In their interviews, managers considered cultural differences as the greatest disadvantage.

To sum up, Porter is generally 'negative' about cooperation. Only under certain conditions can cooperative R&D projects be beneficial. Such projects should be 'in areas of more basic product and process research, should include only a *modest portion* of firms' overall research in a field and, finally, should always be indirect'[27].

There are several arguments for cooperative research, of which Porter mentions three: (1) independent research by a number of firms is 'wasteful and duplicative'; (2) economies of scale in R&D are reaped through collaborative efforts; and (3) firms acting individually will underinvest in R&D because they cannot appropriate all the benefits[28]. Hagedoorn & Schakenraad (1989) add to these 'cost aspects' of R&D cooperation three other important factors that reveal the growth of strategic partnerships: (4) internationalization of markets, (5) the speed, complexity, cohesion and uncertainty of technological development, and (6) the necessity for large companies to control a spectrum of technologies (Hagedoorn & Schakenraad, 1989, 152). Hagedoorn & Schakenraad have access to a data bank of 2200 cases of cooperation agreements. On the basis of this data they have come to the conclusion that most agreements are between partners with equal levels of technological competence, with an emphasis on applied technology, and mostly on the basis of mutual and equivalent exchange. Still, for multinationals the primary choice is whether to develop important technological know-how or R&D potential by themselves, or to develop this potential by integrating. A recent example of this last strategy is IBM's hostile merger of software producer Lotus. This take over makes IBM at one go owner of the important software knowledge of the Lotus *whizzkids*.

Companies only decide to cooperate when it is necessary because of specific shortcomings in R&D potential or if the technology in question is of secondary importance. Hagedoorn & Schakenraad, like Porter, realize that in the long run many strategic partnerships are often not stable. One of the partners gets the upperhand and starts to compete against his former partner (Hagedoorn & Schakenraad, 1989).

A well known, though not very successful, European cooperative research project is ESPRIT, a cooperative R&D project among large European companies in the electronics industry. Although many promote the success of interfirm cooperation, because of reducing competitive duplication and facilitating information transfer in R&D projects, we must be careful not to exaggerate the significance of Japanese and European cooperative research. The goal of some government authorities (e.g. the

European Community) to push forward cooperative interfirm R&D efforts has also a cultural aspect. Comparable U.S. R&D joint ventures show that cooperation is not easily cultivated in that particular national environment (Scherer, 1992, 1429). Given the scope of this chapter it would carry us too far a field to go deeper into this subject here. Chapter 3 takes up the discussion of technological cooperation between rivals, while Kuijpers and Maltha (chapter 5) provide some detailed information about European R&D cooperation.

3. The Dutch 'diamond'

This review of the competitive advantage of nations, begins with a discussion of a Dutch study on the subject (Jacobs, Boekholt and Zegveld, 1990) which is quite similar to the 10-country study in the Porter book. Other Dutch studies are an analysis by the Ministry of Economic Affairs called 'Economy with Open Frontiers' (1990) and a long-term scenario CPB study of the Dutch economy for the period 1990 to 2015: 'The Netherlands in threefold' (1992). The CPB-study develops three possible scenarios for the Dutch economy: the Global Shift scenario, Balanced Growth and European Renaissance.
By beginning with the Dutch case, we can focus on specific themes relevant to small and open economies, and avoid lengthy discussions of the concept in general. It will turn out that important 'diamond' aspects such as domestic competition and national clusters are less relevant for the Dutch case. Rather, advanced factor conditions and technology prove to be far more important in the Netherlands[29].
In this context it is interesting to compare the characteristics of another small and open economy, Switzerland. Although Switzerland is, as far as factor conditions are concerned, comparable to the Netherlands (e.g. few natural resources, small home market, centrally located on major European trade routes, a well developed infrastructure), its economy better meets the requirements of Porter's 'diamond' model. The Swiss economy is even an outstanding example of it: sophisticated oriented industries which focus on narrow segments of the market, a demanding and critical home market, extensively clustered, active domestic rivalry, a tendency towards continuous improvement and therefore very R&D- and knowledge-intensive (Porter, 1990; Boks & Van Rietbergen, 1994). What is more remarkable is that the Swiss are among the best paid employees in the world! When we look more closely at the Dutch economy we see a different picture. An economy more oriented towards medium and low-

tech goods and compared to Switzerland a lower rate of R&D investment and 'upgrading'. Because of this situation Dutch employers' organisations and even unions are mainly worried about the height of labour costs (Boks & Van Rietbergen, 1994). For years now the Dutch trade unions' wage demand has been low to medium. Recently Kleinknecht (1995) caused a lot of commotion in the ranks of the Dutch trade union movement by advocating a high wage demand in order to stimulate employers to upgrade and innovate.

Though compared to the ranking of Switzerland the Dutch economy seems to be in a less favoured position, internationally the Netherlands does not score badly with respect to competitiveness. In 1991 the World Competitiveness Report put the Dutch economy in seventh place, behind such countries as Japan, Germany, the U.S. and Switzerland (Van Tulder, 1991). Two years later the Netherlands' star was rising and it claimed the third position on a competitive list of ten important industrial countries, behind Japan and Germany[30]. Zegveld (1994) compares nine OECD-countries to see to what extent they directed their strategy as a nation, during a one decade period (1979-1989), towards efficiency or differentiation. According to Zegveld this says something about the development of a nation's competitiveness[31]. The Netherlands and Belgium are the two countries with the highest degree of efficiency. On the basis of more recent data however the Dutch economy loses in both fields, in terms of efficiency and differentiation. Especially the loss of differentiation has led to a decrease in Dutch competitiveness (Zegveld, 1994).

It will be clear that these figures say something, but not all, about the competitiveness of Dutch industries. Moreover, this kind of research is always difficult to compare. As we shall see, also according to Jacobs et al. (1990, 1992), we must not be too optimistic about 'our' national competitiveness.

Before we undertake a review of the analyses of Jacobs et al. (1990, 1992 and 1995), we first sketch De Jong's (1987) colourful picture of the particular structure of the Dutch economy. De Jong sums up three determinants of the Dutch economic structure:

1. The Dutch economy is small and surrounded by relatively large markets in the neighbouring countries, from which follows its strong dependency on ascending and descending tendencies in the international economy;

2. This *delta-economy*, situated at the mouth of several big European rivers, has some remarkable characteristics: (a) a very developed infrastructure, needed to protect a relatively large population against flooding; (b) the development of a very strong food & beverages industry, based on indigenous as well as on imported raw materials. This processing industry is capital-intensive and therefore sensitive to cyclical fluctuations, but has multiplier-effects on supplier industries and is research-intensive in its use of relatively highly skilled workers. All these things considered it is no wonder that in this processing industry a lot of multinationals occur, including in the Netherlands; (c) the core of the industrial activity, the machine industry, is traditionally minor in the Netherlands. We are not very successful in industries like electric and nonelectric machines, car engines, computers, agricultural machines, printing presses. Driving industries in the Dutch economy have always been: agriculture (and fishery), water engineering, the processing industry, trade, services and international publishing activities;

3. The third determinant is the balance between freedom and solidarity in the Dutch society, which also has its effect on the economic field. For instance the delta-economic structure brings about cooperation and solidarity in such ways as a collective bargaining economy, business cooperation and the cooperation between companies and the Ministry of Economic Affairs. (De Jong, 1987, 23-24, translated by the author)

To this list of determinants we can add the previously mentioned relatively low wage costs. The wage costs per product-unit of the multinationals in the Netherlands are the lowest of Western Europe. Per hour the wage costs are broadly the same as in other European countries[32]. So one might come to the conclusion that this ought not to be of the greatest concern for Dutch (export) firms, but real life is different.

Table 1. The top 10 Dutch competitive industries according to their shares in world exports in 1986

SITC	rank	cluster		industry-%
29271	1	P	cut flowers	63,9
0251	2	F/B	bird's eggs in the shell	61,1
0013	3	F/B	porkers	56,6
2926	4	H/H	bulbous and living plants	56,4
02249	5	F/B	milk cream (no powder)	53,1
0722	6	F/B	cocoa, without sugar	48,6
0544	7	F/B	fresh tomatoes	43,4
3414	8	P/C	gaseous carbons	40,1
0541	9	F/B	fresh potatoes	35,5
07232	10	F/B	cocoa-butter	32,4

Source: Jacobs et al. (1990), p. 29
The clusters are: P = Personal; F/B = Food/Beverage; H/H = Housing/Household; and P/C = Petroleum/Chemicals
SITC= Standard International Trade Classification system

3.1 Competitiveness of Dutch Industries

When is a firm in a particular industry competitive? The major sign for the observer is a large market share under conditions of strong competition. What ultimately counts is the firm's ability to keep or enlarge this share under changing market conditions. Stable or growing shares in international markets over an extended period of time are thus a good indicator of competitiveness within an industry. In the Porter study, as well as in the Dutch study, the domestic industry's share in world exports of that industry is used as the measure of competitiveness. An industry is classified as competitive - although additional criteria also are used[33] - when its share is larger than the country's (average) share in world exports. For the Netherlands, the share in world exports in 1986 was 3.8%, so industries with a larger share in their world exports than this percentage were competitive in that year. Table 1 presents the 10 most competitive industries in the Netherlands in 1986 according to this criterion.

What makes these industries in the Dutch economy competitive? We first examine further the measurement of the industries' competitiveness and then discuss whether the 'diamond' can explain their strength.

Added to the industries' share in world exports can be a figure about the domestic industry's share in total Dutch exports[34]. This gives an impression of the significance of the industry's exports for the Dutch economy as a whole. While this looks like a useful extension of the analysis, at the same time it bears the danger of changing the model from an explanation of industry's competitiveness to one of national competitiveness. Let me explain both points briefly.

Since competitive advantage is restricted to a particular industry, no distinction can be made between a domestic industry which has gained a strong international position in a 'niche' market and one with a large share in a global market[35]. Examples are *cotton seed oil*, number one on the U.S. list in 1985 and had *commercial aircraft and helicopters* which was number four. The latter, however, had a share of 4.14% in U.S. exports, while the former only 0.06%[36]. Strictly speaking, Porter is only interested in why a country gained a strong position in a particular market, whether it is a small or a large world market. On the other hand, and related to the debate on national productivity in the U.S. in the 1980s, he states that the only meaningful concept of competitiveness at the national level is national productivity and that this is determined by improved efficiency in existing fields. National competitiveness is based on high productivity in 'old' industries which opens up the possibility to make investments in new fields:

> (national competitiveness is, ON) (...) the capability of competing success-fully in entirely new and sophisticated industries. Doing so absorbs human resources freed up in the process of improving productivity in existing fields. (Porter 1990a, 6-7)

This suggests that a country's firms should be strong enough in (old) sectors to finance investments in new sectors. The size of (old) industries does matter, therefore. At the same time, a country's relative strength in new fields is an indication of its firms' competitiveness too. We postpone the discussion of this last point and limit our analysis to the question of size. By taking the average share of a country in world exports as a benchmark, at least initially, the implication is that an industry with a certain volume of exports X in a country with, say, a 4% share in world exports is less competitive than the same industry in another country with exactly the same volume of exports, but with an average of 2% of world exports. As a country's world export share is an indication of the average competitiveness of its industries as well as the openness of its economy, some correction seems warranted. For a country like the Netherlands this is clear, as both exports and imports are approximately equal to domestic consumption. The industry's share in the country's export volume, however, is not such a correction. It only signifies the relative importance of a competitive industry for the Dutch economy as a whole. As suggested earlier, this bears the danger of 'translating' the competitive advantage of some national industries into a measure of overall national competitive advantage. This requires some ratio of the number and size of competitive industries (relative to the world market) and the size of the national economy. The Porter studies do not provide such a scale factor. In chapter 2, an alternative measure of industry's competitiveness is presented which reflects this problem. In chapter 5 a matrix of types of markets is presented which, indirectly, contains a measure of size.

The list of competitive sectors in Table 1, together with the other sectors with above average shares in world exports formed the basis of the Dutch study. Following Porter's approach closely, it was considered in which of the 16 standard clusters these competitive industries could be classified. Consequently, it could be established in which of the clusters the Netherlands was competitive or not. In order to examine whether the firms within a particular cluster really had interrelations and to understand whether and how the 'diamond' factors contributed to the firms' competitiveness, 11 industry studies were carried out. (Table 2 provides information about these industries).

Table 2. The 11 Industries in the Dutch Study

Name	Industry share in Dutch exports 1986	Cluster[a]
Road transport	4.14	T
Plastics and polymers	3.95	C
Dairy industry	2.50	A/F
Cut flowers	1.00	A/F
Trucks	0.87	T
Cacoa butter and powder	0.53	A/F
Copiers	0.37	E
Prerecorded sound carriers	0.30	E
Machines Food industry	0.24	A/F
Yacht building	0.11	T[b]
Industrial textiles	n.a.c	C
Total	14.01	

Source: based on Jacobs et al. (1990), especially p. 86/87
[a]The clusters are: T = Transportation; C = Petroleum/Chemicals; F/B = Agriculture/Food; E = Electronics.
[b]This sector is not really affiliated with the transport cluster in the Netherlands.
[c]This sector is so small that it does not show up in the trade statistics.

It is not our intention to discuss these 11 industry studies in depth. We concentrate on the question: 'Can their competitive strength be explained by the interplay of 'diamond' factors?' Generally, the conclusion is that several of the 'diamond' factors attribute to an explanation of the industries' competitive advantage[37]. A detailed analysis of the interplay of the four factors is missing, however. The general picture is that standard (and generalized) factor conditions, such as excellent grasslands, the country's central position in Northwestern Europe with regard to bulk products from outside the continent and transport to the rest of Europe, have played an important role in establishing such strong sectors as the dairy industry, road transport, bulk chemicals, cocoa. If we look at the more 'high-graded' factor conditions, like infrastructure and knowledge centres, then such sectors as cut flowers, the dairy industry, and machines for the food industry can be said to have profited from these conditions. Remarkable is that industries such as cocoa and yacht building seem to have been relying on expertise almost entirely built up within the sector (tacit knowledge). If we look at 'related industries', we see that the whole food/agriculture cluster in the Netherlands is well developed (i.e. interrelated), with the exception of the quite separate cocoa industry. The latter does have a small network of its own, but there are only two Dutch suppliers of machines, operating in segments of the market, while the connections with chocolate producers (the customers) have weakened lately. The Dutch truck producer DAF and the internationally operating 'transporters' will no doubt have been learning from each other, but real signs of a network of users, producers, and customers are missing. Yacht building has a small network of its own, but suppliers are mostly foreign. The copier industry and sound carriers seem to lack any significant domestic network of 'world class' suppliers and customers. The Dutch home market is relatively small and does not seem to have played a role, qualitatively or quantitatively, in any of the sectors. When we look at domestic rivalry, the general point can be made that strong competition does not exist in the agricultural sector in the Netherlands. Note that in Table 1 a large number of the most successful industries belong to this 'cluster'. If we look at the number of domestic firms in the industries mentioned in Table 2, the dairy industry has four internationally operating companies, road transport has many, cocoa has four which are regionally concentrated, and within plastics and polymers several Dutch players are present and many foreign companies have subsidiaries. In yacht building only the high quality segment is exporting, consisting of some fifteen firms. In machines for the food industry, copier machines, trucks, and prerecorded sound carriers there are one or two firms.

In a more recent study Jacobs et al. (1992) signal a general trend of decline in respect to Dutch export performance. In 1986 the Netherlands' share in world exports was 3.80% in 1988 3.66%. On the basis of this little shift in world export share, 39 Dutch industries disappeared from the cluster chart. The agriculture/food & beverage cluster relatively reinforces itself and nearly all the top-10 industries are characterized by relatively small scale firms. The high-tech component in the Dutch economy is still moderate. Jacobs et al. mention three large bottlenecks in the dynamic of the Dutch 'diamond', which all concern:

1. The application of the latest technologies (including environmental technology) in relatively traditional and small scale industries;
2. The application of technological advances to attractive products for clients, and;
3. The enlargement of the home market, because of Europe 1992.
   (Jacobs & De Vos, 1992, 150, translated by the author)

Our conclusion, based on the Dutch studies, is that home demand does not play any role; domestic rivalry and regional or national networks with related industries probably play a significant role in half of the cases; and that only factor conditions come about as an important item in most cases. The most successful Dutch exporting industries are still in agriculture. This field is characterised by a lack of domestic rivalry[38], a very well established public infrastructure (research, education, vocation), which strongly influences factor conditions, and a well established domestic network of suppliers, customers, services, etc. The food industry is closely related, but characterised by more rivalry among the domestic players.

The above conclusions may have drastic consequences. In Porter's analysis, the importance of domestic rivalry, home demand, and domestic related industries relies to a considerable extent on competition: competition between firms in the industry, which also stimulates suppliers, and competition in related industries which drives customers to be very demanding towards the industry in question. With a less dominant role for competition, the importance of national (advanced) factor conditions increases and the role of 'non-market driven' institutions[39] comes to the fore.

The above conclusion does not strongly support Porter's model. We want to pose two questions. The first is 'Are the Dutch industries examples of what Porter has in mind?', and the second is 'Has the model to be adjusted for small economies?' Both questions will be addressed in the subsequent chapters. With regard to Porter's world class industries/clusters, like the Swiss pharmaceutical industry, one cannot help wondering whether these are extreme cases. A subsequent question then arises about the extent to which the 'model' is based on the experience with 'extremes', and not on the analysis of, say, the best 20 industries in each country[40]. In chapter 5, Kuijper and Maltha give a matrix in which Porter's world class industries are only a fraction of the total set of competitive industries[41]. This matrix is also relevant for the question about a 'small-open economy's model' for competitive advantage. In chapters 6 and 7, regionally concentrated industries and clusters are discussed. On the one hand, this gives a better look at the regional aspects of national advantage[42], on the other hand it enables us to explore how competitive the more modest regional industries and clusters are and to what extent their success (or failure) can be explained in terms of the 'diamond' concept.

The authors of the Dutch study make the point that the service sector in the country is relatively large compared to manufacturing. As statistics of international trade in service industries differ from manufacturing, agriculture, and the like, a separate measure of competitiveness is developed and a list of competitive Dutch service sectors is provided[43]. A related, but more general point is to what extent industries with little or no international trade can contribute to the competitive advantage of a particular industry or cluster. For example, the construction of houses in the Netherlands is very efficient compared to other European countries[44]. The relevant market of this sector is mainly regional, not even national. Efficient regional or national industries, nevertheless, may contribute to a country's capacity to free money for new sectors and for research into the improvement of process technologies in existing exporting sectors. This aspect seems to fall outside the scope of Porter's 'diamond'; only exporting sectors are contemplated as parts of national clusters.

We come back to our earlier discussion about national advantage. If we take the Dutch study as an example, it is concluded that only the agriculture/food cluster is fully developed in the sense that competitive sectors exist in both width and depth. The chemical cluster is also quite broad, but lacks depth. For the remainder, competitiveness is confined to small industries, such as dredging, which will be discussed in chapter 5. What does this mean for the Dutch economy? Do we really lack competitive clusters, or are enough industries participating in international clusters? The 11 clusters studied for the Dutch case have a share of 15% in exports. As we have argued before, what counts is the size of the markets in which the Dutch firms have strong export performance. But we have also seen that efficiency in existing fields is not enough. New fields have to be entered. In addition to the size of existing markets, the capacity of Dutch firms to innovate in existing fields and to enter new fields is crucial. With regard to innovation in existing fields it is concluded that:

Dutch sectors which are top class internationally are: road transport, cocoa, the upper segment of yacht building, the cultivation of cut flowers, truck construction, the dairy industry and the upper segment of machines for the dairy industry ... (sectors) with less technological development are: the electricians for the dairy industry, the standard yacht building, industrial textiles and copiers. Finally, there are sectors which distinguish themselves least in terms of innovation and which are therefore threatened the most easily: plastics and polymers and prerecorded sound material. (Jacobs et al. 1990, 184, translated by the author)

We are not going to discuss these conclusions about innovativeness, but instead make a more general remark. If a Porter-like study is used as an indication for the competitive advantage of a nation, we need, in addition to an adequate export performance measure, a measure of the size and the growth rate of international markets. Similar to analyses of the competitiveness of firms, we can get an indication of a nation's competitive advantage by looking at the size and the growth rates of the markets in which its firms perform well. (Figure 2 gives a more refined classification of Dutch industries from this point of view).

Figure 2. The Dutch industries with some share in international markets

| | Markets with growth rates that are: | | |
	negative	modest	high
Small Markets	X	X	X
Medium-size	X	X	X
Large Markets	X	X	X

In this section we have tried to develop a 'strength-analysis' of the Dutch economy, or more specifically to determine the competitiveness of its industries and to determine to what extent Porter's 'diamond' therefore can be a practical tool. What we are not going to say is that this picture of the 'Dutch 'diamond'' is a suitable tool for predicting future industry evolution in the Netherlands. At this point we disagree with Porter. Porter not only claims that one could constitute the national economic agenda on the basis of the national 'diamond', but what's more, could, on the same basis, estimate 'the evolution of national competitive development'[45]. Kamann & Strijker (chapter 4) criticize Porter on this aspect. In the next section we turn to the role of a nation's historical, social and institutional factors to explain this competitiveness.

4. The role of historical, social and institutional factors

What we finally want to show in this section, when talking about the competitive advantage of nations, historical, social and institutional differences among countries really count and give more depth and colour to Porter's 'diamond'. In the beginning of his book Porter assumes that differences in management practices, including labour-management relations, are not fully satisfactory as an explanation for national competitiveness[46]. Outlining one of the determinants (*firm strategy, structure, and rivalry*) Porter only speaks of differences according to 'managerial approaches, attitudes of workers toward management and vice versa, social norms, goals of individuals and companies, all growing out of a nation's educational system, social and religious history'[47]. Even though Porter several times[48] mentions the important contribution of these differences in national economic structures, values, cultures, institutions, and histories to competitive success[49], he does not extensively analyzes these factors. The only time that he goes a little deeper into the subject of 'cultural factors', shaping the environment in which firms operate are the case-studies of countries in his book. Even then Porter is sparing of these factors, especially labour-management relations. This is strange, since Porter also establishes that the cultural factors of a nation, working through the determinants of the 'diamond', do count, because they change slowly and are difficult for outsiders to tap.

Other authors likewise point out, directly or indirectly, the influence of cultural differences on the development of managerial firms (Roobeek, 1988; Chandler, 1992; Van Gils & Van der Laan, 1993). Even Chandler concludes, after years of historical analysis, that the answer to why the development of industrial enterprise took such a different direction in Britain compared to Germany and the U.S. is still 'enormously complex, involving economic and noneconomic institutions, class and cultural considerations, and historical timing' (Chandler, 1992, 92).

In this section we explore the importance of the differences in social and political history, or more precisely the 'socio-institutional differences' among nations (Roobeek, 1988), for the role they play in the competitive advantage of their industries. Based on a comparative study of several European countries, Roobeek comes to the conclusion that there are 'still considerable differences among the industrialized countries in the areas of the organization of labour, style of management, education and training, labour relations and the extent to which governments intervene by means of R&D subsidy, the defense-sector or via the social system of the welfare state' (Roobeek, 1989, 255). These differences, extending over long periods of time and not easy to change or manipulate, influence the extent to which companies (within those countries) will innovate. Roobeek has developed a so-called national 'cloverleaf scheme of environment spheres', which is comparable to Porter's 'diamond'. She arrives at four broad determinants of national competitiveness: (1) the techno-scientific infrastructure / knowledge base, (2) the macro-economic environment, (3) the industrial structure and (4) the socio-institutional dimension (Roobeek, 1989). In this section we will concentrate on the fourth determinant, being a very heterogeneous combination of social and institutional aspects. It is a reservoir of concepts among which are:

(...) monetary and credit systems, patterns of government intervention, consultative structures between social partners, cooperation among firms and with universities, regional diffusion and labour mobility, education and training, promotion systems within firms, appreciation systems and forms of work structuring, internal labour relations within organizations, employment legislation and social stratification. (Roobeek, 1988, 212, translated by the author)

When we look at Porter's 'diamond' model we find some of these factors inside the 'diamond', among one of the determinants: *factor conditions* (e.g. public education), *firm strategy, structure and rivalry* (e.g. consultative structures between social partners) and outside the 'diamond', among *government*. It would be too much to pay attention to all these factors. Therefore we will focus on (1) patterns of government intervention and (2) consultative structures between social partners (neo-corporatism) including labour relations. The choice for the second has everything to do with the minor attention Porter pays in his book to this factor and because of the specific character of these consultative structures in the Netherlands. A point of special interest will be the way in which the Dutch neo-corporatist economy contributes to the competitiveness of Dutch industries.

4.1 The role of national, regional and local government

What are the possibilities and restrictions of the national, regional and local governments, according to Porter and others, for influencing the 'diamond' positively in order to reinforce the competitiveness of the Dutch industries? Porter insists very strongly, because of geographic concentration, that 'much more (government) attention is necessary at the regional and local level, in areas such as university education, infrastruc-

ture, local regulations, local research initiatives, and information'. At these levels such policies have more impact[50]. Boekema & Van Houtum (chapter 6 of this book) and Meeus & Oerlemans (chapter 7) will return to this subject.
Porter sums up some simple, basic principles that governments should embrace, which give a clear description of his opinion about the role of government. In general it should encourage change, promote domestic rivalry and stimulate innovation. More specific policy approaches of the government agenda are the following:

1. Focus on specialized factor creation
2. Avoid intervening in factor and currency markets
3. Enforce strict product, safety, and environmental standards
4. Sharply limit direct cooperation among industry rivals
5. Promote goals that lead to sustained investment
6. Deregulate competition
7. Enforce strong domestic antitrust policies
8. Reject managed trade
(Source: Porter, 1990b, 87-88)

All these government policies are a reflection of the four corners of Porter's 'diamond' and mostly speak for themselves. The overriding theme is: *always stimulate domestic rivalry in order to upgrade and innovate!* Some policies are more interesting. For example, there has always been a dispute (and still is) about whether or not economic growth goes together with environmental protection. In this context Porter makes an interesting point by saying that strict standards for environmental protection can be profitable for firms.

> When tough regulations anticipate standards that will spread international-ly, they give a nation's companies a head start in developing products and services that will be valuable elsewhere. (Porter, 1990b, 87)

In this way, what initially seems to be a disadvantage (tough environmental regulations) can turn into an advantage. So that is why Swedish firms, confronted with such measures in the home nation, became first movers internationally of providing safe and healthy prod-ucts. From this list of government policies it is once again apparent that Porter does not promote strategic alliances. Governments should not allow more cooperative R&D, with the exception of projects in areas of basic product and process research. In Porter's terms the policy of the Dutch

Ministry of Economic Affairs (1995) to provide for its industries 'organizational structures like university labs and centres of excellence, (to) reduce management problems' is counterproductive, because it minimizes the risk of rivalry. Further, government should direct its antitrust policy especially against 'horizontal mergers and alliances in the name of globalization and the creation of national champions that involve industry leaders'[51].

To Hamel & Prahalad (1994) a much more restrictive role is reserved for government: 'competitiveness is far more an issue of corporate policy than of industrial policy. Hundreds of millions Ecus and the brightest bureaucrats in Brussels couldn't save Europe's ill-conceived attempts to create a 'European' standard in high-definition television'. Protectionism or any kind of trade policy will not work in the long run. According to Hamel & Prahalad the role of institutional factors is often exaggerated, although there is no doubt that 'monetary and fiscal policy, trade and industrial policy, national levels of educational achievement, the structure of corporate ownership, and the social norms and values that predominate in a particular nation all have an impact on the competitiveness of firms therein domiciled. (...) But it is difficult to argue that a company is systematically disadvantaged by *every* aspect of its institutional environment' (Hamel & Prahalad, 1994, 270-279). Each company or business unit - U.S., European or Japanese - has to cope with the institutional factors of its home nation (be it the country of origin or a foreign country), whether they are in some respect more advantageous or disadvantageous in comparison with companies in other nations. Also Hamel & Prahalad seem to underestimate the significance of institutional factors for the competitiveness of a nation's industries. Therefore, let us look now more closely at two institutional factors that companies, in this case in the Netherlands, are confronted with.

4.2 Labour relations and the role of neo-corporatism

In this subsection labour relations in general, including (internal) labour-management relations at the firm level, and the role of neo-corporatism will be looked at. As we mentioned above, labour relations fall within one of the four determinants of Porter's 'diamond', namely *Firm strategy, structure and rivalry*. Though Porter pays attention to these relations in the country case-studies, in our opinion it is still minor. We hold different views in this respect. Therefore we want to show some positive effects labour relations and neo-corporatism can have on national competitiveness. For that purpose the situation in the Netherlands is illustrative. Before starting to depict the Dutch case, we shall quote some observations on countries extracted from Porter's case-studies.

In Porter's opinion it is not possible to generalize about labour-management relations. In some nations, (Germany and Sweden) unions are very strong and powerful, in others (the Netherlands and Japan) relatively weak. The strength of a nation's union(s) does not tell the whole story about the competitiveness of its industries, in the sense that powerful unions should undermine competitive advantage and weak unions do not. Germany and Sweden both have prospered and contain internationally recognised outstanding firms and industries[52].

It is interesting to see what Porter regards as a positive or negative contribution to competitiveness. According to Porter *positive* situations can be found in: Switzerland, where firms are subject to few labour conflicts and there is a pragmatism to labour-management negotiations[53]; Japan, where labour-management relations are respectful and strikes are rare[54]; and in the Germany of the past, where labour-management relations did not impede improvements or innovation and disputes were at a low[55]. Historically a more *negative* situation has existed in Britain. Porter speaks of 'an atmosphere (between labour and management) approaching class warfare' and of 'unions having great power to negotiate restrictive practices, which have inhibited innovation'. Partly due to the Thatcher government (e.g. legislation) a decline in union power occurred, which has improved labour-management relations and made restructuring more possible[56]. Nowadays German labour-management relations have been turned upside down in comparison to the past. Especially union leadership in Germany has become an increasingly conservative force because of its resistance to change[57].

Let us now focus on the special attributes of the Dutch economy. Van Hoof (1993) makes some interesting remarks about the benefits of neo-corporatist arrangements in the areas of labour market and educational policy. He comes to the conclusion that organizational renewal does not necessarily call for a breakdown of (neo-corporatist) labour relations institutions and the transformation towards a labour relations system which is completely oriented to the individual firm (level). Specifically a joint training and education policy at the industry level can prevent individual firms from under-investing in training. A second benefit of the neo-corporatist, collective labour relations system is that it sustains a climate of cooperation and trust. According to Van Hoof this mutual cooperation between trade unions, employers' organizations and government (at the industry level) has become more and more intensive (Van Hoof, 1993). Also other Dutch researchers (Van Hees, 1993;

Teulings, 1995) discuss in one way or another the benefits (e.g. efficiency) of neo-corporatist institutions in the Netherlands. Van Hees
(1993) deals extensively with the subject of the way firms can benefit
from unions, which are relatively strongly connected to works councils.
On the basis of a few Dutch case-studies, in situations of decline, Van
Hees suggests that unions can have a positive effect on the profitability of
firms, are helpful in supporting firms by reorganization and mostly join
with investment decisions of management. Theoretically unions can break
or even freeze planned investments. In the Netherlands these kinds of
union actions - blackmail, obstruction, resistance or non-constructive
behaviour - only occur on a very limited scale. There are also obstruc-
tions from within firms which are removed by unions. So the picture of
inflexible unions, that make transformation processes by firms more
expensive, seems to be wrong (Van Hees, 1993)[58].

The Netherlands belongs to the so-called 'German or Northern European model of labour relations' (Slomp, 1992). This model is characterized by consultation on government policy, coordination of bargaining
and some union-state conflicts at the national level, (extensive) collective
bargaining at the industry level and finally some collective bargaining and
worker participation at the firm level. The benefit of the German model
for Dutch employers is 'a low conflict level and a high predictability of
labour costs, thanks to the predominance of one- or two-year sectoral
bargaining, without interruption by strikes'. Furthermore the Dutch
national government takes a neutral position towards unions and
employers in collective bargaining situations and normally endorses
common employer-union proposals[59].
Teulings (1995) adds to this point that a system such as that in the
Netherlands, in which neo-corporatist organizations bargain for *initial*
wage-increase, and individual employers and workers for *incidental* wage-
increase, is more efficient than decentralized wage formation (as in the
U.S.). In the United States wage-contracts are based upon expected
inflation. Should the rate of inflation all of a sudden change, then there
are no neo-corporatist organizations to adjust these contracts to the altered
macro-economic circumstances. The result of this process is non-adjusted
contracts and uncertainty, both for the employer and employee. This will
hinder investments in human capital from either side (hold up-problem),
which can lead to under-investment in training. The Dutch neo-corporatist
organizations provide a kind of flexibility in this respect (Teulings, 1995).

A problem however is that these positive effects of the Dutch neo-
corporatist system seem to have become endangered. In the past few
years we have been confronted with an ongoing decentralization of labour

relations as a result of technological development, accompanied by individualization of management-labour relations, and a decline in unionization in the Netherlands (Albeda, 1993). In this context, according to Albeda, the backward growth of unionization in the growing service sector is alarming.

We hope that this brief sketch of the Dutch neo-corporatist economy illustrates the importance such an institutional factor can have. Within the scope of this chapter it would carry us too far a field to go much deeper into the pros and cons of a neo-corporatism for the competitiveness of national industries.

Notes

1. All short references relate to Porter (1990), unless it is otherwise mentioned.

2. Porter (1990a), p. 85.

3. Ibid., p. 14-15.

4. The first reason is the particular source of advantage and the second the number of distinct sources (Porter, 1990, 49-51).

5. In chapter 3 Beije goes deeper into the subject of technological change and innovation.

6. Ibid., p. 3-4.

7. Ibid., p. 22.

8. The arguments in this part of the text are based on Porter (1990), chapter 1.

9. For a detailed description of the meaning of industry structure and positioning within an industry, the reader is referred to Porter 1990, chapter 2, p. 34-44.

10. Ibid., p. 33.

11. Ibid., p. 25.

12. Ibid., p. 73.

13. Ibid., p. 86.

14. Ibid., p. 17.

15. Ibid., p. 69.

16. Ibid., p. 614.

17. Ibid., p. 76.

18. Ibid., p. 30.

19. Jacobs et al. (1990), p. 25.

20. Porter (1990a), p. 149.

21. Ibid., p. 149-152.

22. Ibid., p. 152-153.

23. Ibid., p. 156.

24. Ibid., p. 157.

25. Ibid., p. 637.

26. Ibid., p. 667.

27. Ibid., p. 636.

28. Ibid., p. 635.

29. For further explanation see chapter 3.

30. In Januari 1993 the German newspaper *Wirtschaftswoche* published a list of the nine most important industrial countries and Korea, as an example of an upcoming nation, based on a study by Empirica (Bonn). The country with the best score earned 100 points. In the field of labour the Netherlands scored internationally, except for wages, not badly: 100 for productivity, 80 for schooling and 74 for product quality! On the other hand weak points were the rate of R&D investment, a very moderate result concerning 'inventions' and a low score for education (48).

31. According to Zegveld countries with a high degree of differentiation (Japan, U.S.) control a considerable part of the world market of advanced and technologically complex products. In conformity with Porter (1990) Zegveld supposes that those countries usually upgrade and innovate more, thereby strengthening their competitiveness.

32. De Ven & De Kok (1994) mention this fact, based on the figures of *Basisstatistieken van de EG* (1992), in an ESB-article.

33. Other criteria are the imports of the country in the product groups belonging to the sector, and foreign direct investment as a substitute for international trade.

34. See Porter (1990) and Jacobs et al. (1990).

35. On the other hand, there are sectors which do not show up in trade statistics, because they are part of a larger product group. An example is the Dutch dredging industry which has a dominant position in the world market. This sector will be discussed in chapter 6.

36. See Porter 1990, 509.

37. See Jacobs et al. 1990, chapter 4.

38. See Kamann and Strijker's analysis of the dairy industry in chapter 4 of this book.

39. This perspective is discussed in section 4 of this chapter, under the heading of 'corporatism'.

40. This brings about a fundamental, methodological question concerning the model: Does it only explain (export) success at the top, or can it be seen as a model explaining success as well as failure? According to Porter, the latter vision is the right one. Success is explained by the existence and an effective use of the 'diamond' factors (including synergy between the factors and adjustments over time), and failure is due to a lack of good and interrelated factors.

41. This matrix is also presented in the Dutch study (Jacobs et al. 1990).

42. This point is recognized by Porter.

43. See Jacobs et al. 1990, 31.

44. See chapter 4? '...' in Admiraal, Beije and Groenewegen, *Verkenning van Technologie en Mededinging*, Beleidsstudies Technologie en Economie.., Ministerie van Economische Zaken, 1993.

45. Porter (1990a), p. 685.

46. Porter (1990a), p. 3-4

47. Ibid., p. 109.

48. See for instance p. 109, 115, 129 and 175.

49. Ibid., p. 19 and 129.

50. Ibid., p. 622.

51. Porter (1990b), p. 88.

52. Porter (1990a), p. 5.

53. Ibid., p. 325.

54. Ibid., p. 409.

55. Ibid., p. 375.

56. Ibid., p. 502; p. 506-507.

57. Ibid., p. 375.

58. Van Hees (1993), p. 171-172.

59. Slomp (1992), p. 16-18.

References

Albeda, W. - De toekomst van de overlegeconomie. - In: *Toekomst van de overlegeconomie* (Future of the corporative economy) / red.: N.A. Hofstra & P.W.M. Nobelen. - Assen/Maastricht: Van Gorcum, 1993

Auerbach, P. & P. Skott - Michael Porter's Inquiry into the Nature and Causes of the Wealth of Nations - a Challenge to Neoclassical Economics. - In: *On Economic Institutions; Theory and Applications* / J. Groenewegen, Ch. Pitelis & Sven-Erik Sjöstrand (eds.). - EE, Aldershot, England, 1995, 142-163

Boks, S. & T. van Rietbergen - Het succes van de Zwitserse industrie - In: *Economisch Statische Berichten (ESB)*, 24-8-1994, 742-745

Chandler, A.D. - *Scale and Scope: The Dynamics of Industrial Capitalism.* - Cambridge, Massachusetss: The Belknap Press of Harvard University Press, 1990

Chandler, A.D. - Organizational Capabilities and the Economic History of the Industrial Enterprise. - In: *Journal of Economic Perpectives*, volume 6, 1992, nr. 3, 79-100

Commandeur, H.R. & G.J. den Hartog - Voor- en nadelen van strategische samenwerking. - In: *Economische Statische Berichten (ESB)*, 31-7-1991, 773-775

Geest, L. van der - Bescherming en dynamiek. - In: *Economisch Statistische Berichten (ESB)*, 17-5-1995, 457

Gils, H.A.M. van & L. van der Laan - Cultuur en management binnen de Europese Gemeenschap. - In: *Economisch Statische Berichten (ESB)*, 5-5-1993, 405-410

Grant, R.M. - Porter's 'Competitive Advantage of Nations': an Assessment. - In: *Strategic Management Journal*, volume 12, 1991, 535-548

Hagedoorn, J. & J. Schakenraad - Strategisch deelgenootschap en technologische samenwerking (Strategic partnership and technological cooperation). - In: *Technologie en economie: licht op een black box?* / red.: W.C.L. Zegveld & J.W.A. van Dijk. - Assen/Maastricht: Van Gorcum, 1989, 128-155

Hamel, G. & C.K. Prahalad. - *Competing for the Future.* - Boston, Massachusetts: Harvard Business School Press, 1994

Harrison, B. - *Lean and Mean* (The Changing Landscape of Corporate Power in the Age of Flexibility). - New York: BasicBooks, A Division of HarperCollins Publishers, Inc., 1994

Hees, G.B. van - *Bedrijfsmatige effecten van vakbonden en ondernemingsraden* (Organizational effects of labour unions and work councils). - Leuven: Garant, 1993

Hoof, J.J. van - Organiseren in een veranderd arbeidsbestel. - In: *Organiseren op een breukvlak* / red.: W.J. van Noort, J.P. Laurier, M.C. Dozy. - SISWO: Amsterdam, 1993, 95-119

Jacobs, D., P. Boekholt, & W. Zegveld - *De economische kracht van Nederland.* - Utrecht: Stichting Maatschappij en Onderneming (SMO), 1990

Jacobs, D. & A. de Vos - Nederlands meest concurrerende sectoren. - In: *Economisch Statische Berichten (ESB)*, 12-2-1992, 148-151

Jong, H.W. de - Externe organisatie en industriepolitiek. - In: *Industrie- en technologiebeleid* / red.: H. Schenk. - Wolters-Noordhoff, 1987

Jong, H.W. de - Concurrentie, concentratie en het Europese mededingingsbeleid. - In: *Economisch Statistische Berichten (ESB)*, 29-11-1989, 1183-1187

Jong, H.W. de - Frau Antje en de diamant. - In: *Economisch Statistische Berichten (ESB)*, 19/26-12-1990, 1213-1216

Jong, H.W. de - Beide! - In: *Economisch Statistische Berichten (ESB)*, 23-1-1991, 107-108

Kleinknecht, A. - Wat moeten we aan de poort met innovatie. - article in *NRC*, 16-6-1995

Man, A.P. de - 1980, 1985, 1990: Een Porter Exegese. - *Tijdschrift voor Politieke Economie*, 17e jaargang, nr. 3, 1994, 32-54

Miles, R.E & C.C. Snow - Cause of ·Falure in Network Organizations. - In: *California Management Review*, Summer 1992, 53-72

Porter, M.E. - *The Competitive Advantage of Nations.* - New York: The Free Press, 1990a

Porter, M.E. - The Competitive Advantage of Nations. - In: *Harvard Business Review*, March-April 1990b

Reich, R.B. - *The Work of Nations: Preparing Ourselves for 21st-Century Capitalism.* - New York: Vintage Books, A Division of Random House, Inc., 1992

Roobeek, A.J.M. - *Een race zonder finish. De rol van de overheid in de technologiewedloop.* - Amsterdam: VU-uitgeverij, 1988

Roobeek, A.J.M. - De vergeten dimensie in de technologiewedloop. De socio-institutionele omgevingssfeer als voorwaarde en als draagvlak voor de diffusie van nieuwe technologieën. - In: *Technologie en economie: licht op een blackbox* / red.: W.C.L. Zegveld & J.W.A. van Dijk. - Assen: Van Gorcum & Comp. B.V., 1989

Scherer, F.M. - Schumpeter and Plausible Capitalism. - *Journal of Economic Literature*, volume XXX, september 1992, 1416-1433

Slomp, H. - Westbound, the Northern or the Southern trail? Western Europe as a Model for Central and Eastern European Labour Relations. - In: *Westbound?*, eds. / J.J. van Hoof, H. Slomp & K. Verrips. - SISWO: Amsterdam, 1992, 9-31

Teece, D.J. - The Dynamics of Industrial Capitalism: Perspectives on Alfred Chandler's *'Scale and Scope'*. - *Journal of Economic Literature*, March 1993, 199-225

Teulings, C.N. - Efficiënte loonvorming door sociale partners - In: *Economisch Statistische Berichten (ESB)*, 17 mei 1995, 460-464

Tulder, R. van - Dat verdraaide concurrentievermogen. - In: *Economisch Statistische Berichten (ESB)*, 13-11-1991, 1141-1144

Ven, A.D.M. de & A.G. de Kok - De toekomst van de industrie. - In: *Economisch Statistische Berichten (ESB)*, 23-3-1994, 264-268

Zegveld, M.A. - Nederland efficiencyland. - In: *Economisch Statische Berichten (ESB)*, 11-5-1994, 432-435

Chapter 2

M. KOUTSTAAL, P.J. LOUTER

MEASURING ECONOMIC PERFORMANCE

1. Introduction

This chapter focuses on Porter's approach to revealing the 'competitive advantage of nations'. It offers two alternatives to his export performance criterion for identifying a nation's 'competitive industries'. The first alternative, total value added per inhabitant, is discussed most extensively (in sections 4 to 7). The second, a 'multi-dimensional' approach, is the subject of section 8. Discussing these alternatives makes clear that the competitiveness of industries depends on the criteria used.

First of all, however, we need to clarify what we mean by 'economic performance' and how that concept relates to 'competitiveness'. The difference between both concepts relates to the confusion over the title of Porter's book which has already been discussed in chapter 1. The title suggests that competitive advantage is merely explained at the national level, but competitive advantage is also created by one firm against another at the micro level (De Jong, 1990; Van Houtum, 1991) or at the meso level (i.e. market competition). In this chapter, we focus on the 'outcome' of this process, which we denote 'economic performance'[1]. Implicitly, Porter walks the same path, as he distinguishes the elements which determine competitiveness (his 'diamond') from the selection of competitive industries on the basis of their economic performance. We subscribe to his analysis of how 'competitiveness' is created. However, we do not agree with his selection procedure for identifying industries with a favourable economic performance. This is reflected in our use of the terms 'economic performance' and 'competitive advantage'. In contrast to Porter we prefer the term 'economic performance' to indicate that performance by industries (and by firms within an industry) determines the competitive advantage of nations, while the 'diamond' factors at the national (regional) level explain performance.

In our argumentation we first briefly discuss the general outline of Porter's approach (section 2). Then attention is focussed on Porter's criteria for determining the economic performance of industrial sectors (section 3) and disadvantages of this approach. In section 4, the first alternative measure for revealing economic performance of a nation and its industries is introduced, that is: value added per inhabitant.

The empirical application of this measure consists of three sections. First, some general characteristics of manufacturing industries are compared (section 5). Second, the relative performance of fourteen OECD countries is highlighted (section 6). Third, the relative performance of the Netherlands with respect to a number of manufacturing industries is reviewed (section 7).

A second alternative ('multi-dimensional') approach to measure economic performance is suggested in section 8. Much statistical information is needed for an empirical application of this approach. As an example we compare the economic performance of Dutch regions. However, if data were available, this approach could also be applied at the level of countries instead of (Dutch) regions.

Results are summarized and conclusions drawn in section 9.

Before continuing our argument, some of the choices made in this chapter should be pointed out.

- Attention mainly will be focussed on description and empirical analysis, not on explanations and theoretical considerations. Tettero (1987) distinguishes two types of approach to measure the competitive strength of nations. First there is the 'theoretical approach', based on theories of international trade. Second is the 'Revealed Comparative Advantage' (RCA) approach (Balassa, 1965). Our approach is consistent with the Revealed Comparative Advantage approach.
- It should be stressed that our calculations are based on figures for 1981 and 1988. Thus, results are rather out-dated. The analyses can of course be repeated for more recent years.
- Economic performance of nations has only been measured with respect to manufacturing industries. Due to lack of data, some of the important 'economic bases' of the Dutch economy (agriculture and horticulture; transport and distribution) have not been taken into consideration.

2. Setting the stage: a short note on Porter's approach

Porter's framework to explain the competitive advantage of nations consists of three main steps:
1. the selection of 'competitive industries' by use of an export criterion;
2. the explanation of the rise of competitive industries (by means of the 'diamond');
3. the explanation of the competitive advantage of nations by means of a development concept in which countries may follow four 'stages' (factor-driven, investment-driven, innovation-driven and wealth-driven).

In this section we make a few remarks about steps 2 and 3. Disussion of step 1 begins in section 3.

The first remark is about the concept of development. The successive stages of a nation's development path reflect different 'factors of production': land and labour (factor-driven stage), capital (investment-driven stage) and knowledge (innovation-driven stage). In the wealth-driven stage investment in capital and knowledge is insufficient to sustain competitive advantage in the long run. According to Porter the development concept does not imply complete determinism; a nation may skip a stage or may return to a former stage and even more generally he states that the ...'trajectory by which the economy passes (or does not pass) through the stages is a reflection of each nation's unique circumstances with respect to the diamond' (Porter, 1990, 562). One point of critique here is that the model is too general and that it might therefore explain any development path. Another point is whether a country, once it is in the innovation-driven stage, cannot compete anymore in industries characterized by factor conditions related to land, labour and capital. Put otherwise: can a country like the Netherlands only compete through innovation-driven industries? In chapter 5 it will be argued that Porter's internationally competitive industries form only a part of the total group of manufacturing industries in a country.

A second remark is about the 'diamond' concept and its four determinants: 'The determinants, individually and as a system, create the context in which a nation's firms are born and compete' (Porter, 1990, 71). These determinants and a large part of the system are not entirely new ideas. Some of them stem from regional economics and economic geography. For example, in elaborations of the well-known life cycle theory concerning international trade (Vernon 1966) and economic geography (Thompson 1968) the importance of national - or even regional - concentration of home demand, human resources, knowledge resources and networks of supplier industries and related industries have been emphasized. These attributes of countries or regions create an innovative 'milieu' in which new industries can develop and flourish and/or established industries can maintain competitive advantage[2].

Also, emphasizing the impact of geographical concentration of (similar) economic activities on development potential is not Porter's innovation - and he does not claim so either. (See for example Porter, 1990, 791: 'While economic geography has not been seen as a core discipline in economics, my research suggests that it should be'.) However, it is rather unfortunate that Porter almost exclusively refers to the work of his protégé Michael Enright in this respect (Enright, 1990). In economic geography spatial 'clustering' of the four elements of Porter's 'diamond' has been denoted as 'agglomeration advantages' or 'agglomeration economies'. The historical development (sometimes due to 'coincidental circumstances') of agglomeration economies gives rise to spatial concentration of innovative, competitive firms. As a consequence of, among others, the work of Scott (1988) and Storper and Walker (1989), a revival of the recognition of the impact of agglomeration economies (in the tradition of Alfred Marshall's 'industrial districts') has occurred. Various examples of clustering of similar economic activities due to agglomeration economies (or - in Porter's terms - due to advantages throughout the 'diamond') can be given. Clustering both occurs in 'knowledge-intensive industries' (' .. that form the backbone of advanced economies' - see Porter, 1990, 73) like the semiconductor industry in Silicon Valley and consultancy firms in large metropolitan centres and in 'traditional industries' like wearing apparel, footwear and leather products (for example in the 'Third Italy'). Though the knowledge-intensity in those industries is low compared to high-tech industries, specific countries or regions can achieve and sustain competitive success in traditional industries. That success is attained because of the relatively (compared to firms in the same industries in other countries or regions) high knowledge-intensity of firms operating in traditional industries and the embeddedness of those firms in an innovative 'milieu'. (See Louter, 1993 for elaborations on the theme of knowledge-intensity.) Insights from regional studies will be more fully compared with Porter's work in chapter 4.

3. Porter's approach to identifying competitive industries

Descriptions of the competitive development of nations and the explanation of the rise of 'competitive industries' are only possible if those competitive industries can be identified. Porter states: 'The presence of competitive advantage in international terms is measured here by a significant and sustained share of world exports to a wide array of nations and/or foreign direct investment reflecting skills and strengths created in the home nation' (Porter, 1990, 283). Thus, the starting point for preparing 'cluster charts', in which the competitive industries of a nation are included, were the UN trade statistics. First of all, Porter used an indicator, developed by Balassa (1965), to identify nominees for a list of competitive industries: industries in which the nation's share of the world market exports in the industry equalled or exceeded the nation's average share of world trade (referred to as the nation's cut off).

Then a number of conditions were added. Eliminated from the list were industries:
- with a negative balance of trade, unless the nation's share of world exports in the industry was two or more times its average share, or
- where the nation's exports were believed to be dominated by foreign companies who produced in the nation as part of global manufacturing startegies, or
- where trade was almost exclusively with neighbouring countries.

    Added to the list were industries:
- where the nation's firms had made substantial foreign direct investments (if those investments were based on skills and strengths developed in the nation), or
- whose export value was in the the top fifty in the nation and whose trade balance was positive to modestly negative, even if the nation's share of world exports fell below the cut off.

At first glance, Porter's approach to identifying 'competitive industries' appears to be straightforward. However, some of its implications should be considered further. First there is the fact that - as Porter admits - some of the 'added conditions' are rather arbitrary. Others are theoretically interesting, but hardly measurable in practice (especially the domination by foreign companies of the nation's exports and the size of the nation's firms' direct foreign investments per industry).

Second, and even more importantly, Porter's main criterion for identifying competitive industries ('industries in which the nation's share of the world market exports in the industry equalled or exceeded the nation's average share of world trade - the nation's cut off') is not a very good indicator of economic performance. Suppose a country shows very poor export performance in general. Then for a specific industry even rather poor export performance (compared to export performance of that industry in other countries) might suffice to be denoted 'competitive'. Also, if an industry supplies large amounts of intermediate goods on its domestic market to important export industries, the supplying industry's export might not exceed the cut off. Thus, ironically, Porter's criterion sometimes works to the detriment of supplier industries which flourish due to home demand for their products or services. An example of a domestically oriented industry is Dutch telecom which will be discussed in chapter 5. While the importance of home demand is stressed by Porter in his 'diamond', home demand does not contribute to the value of his (export-) criterion to measure economic performance of an industry.

4. An alternative approach to measure economic performance

Instead of Porter's criterion to measure economic performance of a nation's industries, we suggest an alternative, that is: 'an industry's total value added per inhabitant in a country, compared to other countries'. Three remarks are in order here.

First, we prefer comparison of the economic performance of an industry with the performance of that industry in other countries to comparison with other industries within its own country. The reasons for this have been given in section 3: By comparing industries with the average export performance of a country, you may, end up along the lines of the adage 'in the country of the blind the one-eyed man is king'.

Second, we prefer total demand (both foreign and domestic) for an industry's product or service to foreign demand solely. Porter uses export value to select industries with a high economic performance, while in his 'diamond' he stresses the importance of home demand. As indicated in section 3, by using Porter's cut off criterion some supplier industries will be treated unfairly, while other industries quite easily exceed the cut off because the over-all export performance of their country is rather poor. Comparing an industry's export value per inhabitant (a slight modification to Porter's export-share criterion) between countries is not a very good indicator either. Because in many industries economies of scale are of importance, small countries can only specialize in a limited number of industries. In those industries a large share of production will be exported, while goods of industries in which the small countries are not specialized will be imported. Thus, in small countries both exports and imports per inhabitant tend to be high. For example, in the Netherlands both exports and imports per inhabitant are much higher than in the United States. However, approximately eighty percent of Dutch trade is with other countries of the European Community. Actually, Dutch export performance should rather be compared with Ohio or Illinois than the United States, a country which due to its size might be self-sufficient with respect to almost any industry[3]. In order to avoid the unjustifiable influence of spatial scale on 'performance' of industries, home demand per inhabitant should be added to foreign demand per inhabitant.

Third, we prefer value added to production. It is not production that counts, but value added. If large amounts of money earned by selling products or services are spent to buy inputs from abroad, an industry does not create much prosperity for the inhabitants of its country. Value added of the production of goods (or of delivering services) is the source of wages of employees, dividends of shareholders and investments (promoting industrial growth) of firms[4].

Apart from the choice of an alternative indicator for Porter's export measure there is the more fundamental question whether measuring performance of an industry in this way is sufficient. Should one not look at the change of performance over time and at the size and growth rate of the markets for which performance is measured?[5] We discuss these points briefly here.

First one could say that for an evaluation of performance of an industry two 'general conditions' are of importance, that is: the size of an industry (the size of the market) and its growth performance (expansion of the market). Performing well in a large (and/or fastly growing) world market is more favourable than performing well in a small (and/or slowly growing) one. This point has been touched upon in chapter 1 and is also discussed by Kuijpers and Maltha in this book.

Second, the (relative) economic performance of a nation's industries can be measured in two ways: static and dynamic. 'Static economic performance' is calculated by dividing value added per inhabitant of a country by the average value added per inhabitant in a group of countries. This indicator will be denoted PVA (economic Performance, measured by Value Added). 'Dynamic economic performance' is calculated as the percentage change of PVA over two points in time.

5. A quick scan of manufacturing industries

First, some data are given of the size and growth of industrial sectors in the group of countries we investigated. Details about the data we used can be found in Koutstaal (1993). In order to be able to measure total value added instead of exports we applied OECD data instead of UN statistics. OECD data on value added are less detailed than UN data on exports. Thus, we make use of four- or even three-digit SITC codes instead of five-digit SITC codes. Also, our 'group of countries' does not consist of all the countries of the world, but of fourteen OECD countries[6].

Table 1. A quick scan of manufacturing industries for fourteen OECD countries

Industry	Size 1988	Growth 81-88	Industry	Size 1988	Growth 81-88
High-tech			*Low-tech*		
Radio, TV, comm. equipm.	6.2	6 %	Food	8.3	4 %
Professional goods	3.0	7 %	Metal products	6.3	3 %
Comp. machinery	2.5	8 %	Printing and publis-		
Drugs and medicines	2.4	8 %	hing	5.6	6 %
Aircraft	2.4	1 %	Iron and steel	4.1	2 %
Electr. industrial machinery	2.4	4 %	Paper, paper pro-		
Electrical apparatus	1.7	7 %	ducts	3.6	5 %
Electr. appl., housewares	.8	7 %	Textiles	3.2	3 %
			Other non-metal.		
Total high-tech	**21.4**	**6.1 %**	prod.	2.8	4 %
			Beverages	1.9	3 %
Medium-tech			Wearing apparel	1.9	1 %
Motor vehicles	8.0	7 %	Petroleum refineries	1.9	-2 %
Industrial chemicals	5.7	6 %	Wood products	1.7	4 %
Other machinery, equipment	5.1	4 %	Non-ferrous metals	1.5	3 %
Plastic products	2.9	9 %	Metal machinery	1.4	2 %
Special industrial machinery	2.6	2 %	Furniture, fixtures	1.4	3 %
Soap, clearing preparations	1.3	4 %	Rubber products	1.2	4 %
Other chemical products	1.2	8 %	Tobacco	1.1	6 %
Paints, varnishes, lacquers	.5	3 %	Glass, glass pro-		
			ducts	1.0	4 %
Total medium-tech	**27.3**	**6.0 %**	Shipbuilding, repai-		
			ring	.6	-5 %
			Agricultural ma-		
			chinery	.5	-1 %
			Petroleum, coal		
			prod.	.4	4 %
			Footwear	.3	-2 %
			Pottery, china, etc.	.3	4 %
			Leather, leather		
			prod.	.2	1 %
			Total low-tech	**51.3**	**3.3 %**
			TOTAL	**100.0**	**4.6 %**

Explanation: 'Size' is the share (in percentages) of value added of an industry in total value added in manufacturing industries in the fourteen OECD countries. 'Growth' is the yearly average growth in terms of percentages of value added in an industry.

In Table 1 a 'quick scan' of manufacturing industries is given. The 'size' is calculated as the share of an industry's value added of total value added in 1988. The 'growth' is calcalated as the average yearly growth between 1981 and 1988.

Three groups of industries have been distinguished, namely high-tech, medium-tech and low-tech. This grouping has been based upon the potential for technological innovation of industries (more or less consistent with the position in the life cycle). In order to do this, various researchers' lists using different criteria (such as, for example, number of patents, share of scientific professions, average level of education) have been compared and merged (see Louter, 1991)[7].

About half of value added of manufacturing industries is created by low-tech industries (51.3%; in 1981: 55.9%), and the other half by medium-tech industries (27.3%; in 1981: 24.8%) and high-tech industries (21.4%; in 1981: 19.3%). However, in both high-tech and medium-tech, growth of value added exceeded growth in low-tech. Of all industrial sectors in high-tech and medium-tech only value added in the aircraft industry and special industrial machinery showed slower growth than the 3% rate of total low-tech industry. None of the 23 low-tech industries obtained a higher growth rate than the 6% average growth of high- and medium-tech. Thus, there appears to exist a correlation between growth of value added and the technological potential of an industry.

Table 2. Export and import orientation of manufacturing industries

Industry	Export share (% of production)	Import share (% of consumption)
Industrial chemicals	36.5	28.7
Non-electrical machinery	35.8	31.7
Transport equipment	29.9	23.2
Electrical machinery	27.9	30.4
Basic metal industries	26.2	27.3
Other chemicals	24.3	17.6
Textiles	22.4	27.8
Professional goods	21.6	21.5
Apparel, leather and footwear	16.8	42.3
Rubber and plastics products	16.2	16.8
Paper and paper products	16.1	19.5
Tobacco	13.2	7.3
Non-metallic mineral products	13.0	14.1
Metal products	12.3	11.6
Beverages	10.9	11.9
Food	10.8	10.2
Wood products	10.1	16.2
Furnitures and fixtures	8.8	16.7
Petroleum refineries	8.8	12.4
Printing and publishing	4.1	3.3
TOTAL	**21.5**	**21.2**

Note: Figures based on seven OECD countries (United States, Germany, United Kingdom, France, the Netherlands, Belgium and Sweden).

In order to assess the relative importance of international trade, in Table 2 two indicators of the orientation of industrial sectors on foreign markets have been given: exports as a percentage of total production and imports as a percentage of total consumption. In industries like chemicals, machinery, electronics, transport equipment and basic metal, international trade is relatively important. On the other hand, some industries mainly are dependent on home demand, for example printing and publishing, petroleum refineries and food and beverages.

In general, it can be concluded that the home market of domestic industries is larger than the markets abroad. Thus, Porter's export-based criterion to select industries with a high economic performance (while in his 'diamond' he stresses the importance of home demand) can be critized from this respect[8].

6. A comparison of OECD countries

In Table 3 fourteen OECD countries have been ranked according to the value of their PVA (value added per inhabitant of a country divided by average value added per inhabitant in the fourteen OECD countries) in 1988: an indicator of 'static economic performance'. Apart from that, the value of PVA in 1981, the change of PVA in terms of percentages (an indicator of 'dynamic economic performance') and the share of a country's value added (in manufacturing industries) in total OECD value added has been given.

Table 3. Static and dynamic economic performance of manufacturing in fourteen OECD countries

OECD country	Share 1988	PVA 1981	PVA 1988	Growth PVA
Japan	25.8	1.04	1.46	41 %
Germany	12.7	1.37	1.44	5 %
Sweden	1.3	1.12	1.08	-4 %
United States	37.1	1.23	1.05	-15 %
Finland	.7	.97	.95	-2 %
United Kingdom	6.7	.88	.81	-8 %
Denmark	.6	.67	.78	16 %
France	6.2	.85	.77	-10 %
Belgium	1.0	.71	.70	-2 %
Austria	.7	.62	.68	10 %
Norway	.4	.66	.63	-4 %
the Netherlands	1.2	.54	.57	7 %
Italy	3.7	.50	.45	-10 %
Spain	2.0	.39	.35	-9 %
TOTAL	**100.0**	**1.00**	**1.00**	**0 %**

Explanation: 'Share 1988' is the share of value added of a country (in percentages) in the total value added of the fourteen OECD countries. 'Growth PVA' is the growth of PVA (in terms of percentages) in the period 1981-1988.

Considering static economic performance Japan and Germany appear to be the most competitive manufacturing countries[9], quite far ahead of the United States. In the Netherlands relatively little value added per inhabitant is created in manufacturing industries.

Considering dynamic economic performance, the most important 'winner' during the eighties was Japan. The Netherlands seized fourth position, behind Japan, Denmark and Austria. A decrease in economic performance especially can be noted for the United States and for the large European countries (except for Germany).

Table 4. The technology-mix of fourteen OECD countries

OECD country	PVA HT	PVA MT	PVA LT	Share HT	Share MT	Share LT
Japan	1.52	1.46	1.44	22.4 %	27.1 %	50.5 %
Germany	1.34	1.91	1.23	20.0 %	36.1 %	43.9 %
Sweden	.76	1.17	1.17	15.0 %	29.6 %	55.4 %
United States	1.19	.97	1.03	24.4 %	25.2 %	50.4 %
Finland	.45	.68	1.30	10.1 %	19.6 %	70.3 %
United Kingdom	.75	.75	.87	19.7 %	25.1 %	55.2 %
Denmark	.54	.58	.99	11.9 %	20.3 %	64.8 %
France	.57	.68	.90	15.7 %	24.2 %	60.1 %
Belgium	.35	.66	.87	10.9 %	25.6 %	63.5 %
Austria	.44	.51	.87	13.9 %	20.2 %	65.9 %
Norway	.29	.49	.85	9.8 %	21.1 %	69.1 %
the Netherlands	.43	.59	.62	16.0 %	28.1 %	55.9 %
Italy	.27	.51	.49	12.7 %	30.9 %	56.4 %
Spain	.16	.34	.43	9.9 %	26.5 %	63.6 %
TOTAL	**1.00**	**1.00**	**1.00**	**21.5 %**	**27.2 %**	**51.3 %**

Explanation: HT = high-tech; MT = medium-tech; LT = low-tech; Share = share of value added in total value added of manufacturing industries in a country.

In Table 4 an impression of the 'technology mix' of the fourteen OECD countries has been given, that is: their relative orientation towards technologically advanced manufacturing industries. The PVA's for high-tech, medium-tech and low-tech industries (see Table 1 for this typology), and their shares in the country's total value added are shown.

The variations between countries in the values of their PVA's are highest for high-tech and lowest for low-tech. Thus, exclusivity is especially evident for technologically advanced industries. Low-tech industries have been dispersed across most OECD countries. Only three countries show a PVA below .80 for low-tech, while eleven countries show a PVA below .80 for high-tech (and ten for medium-tech). Japan, Germany and the United States (in that order) are the best performing high-tech countries, far ahead of all the others. Germany is the medium-tech champion (machines, chemicals, cars), followed by Japan, Sweden and the United States. Strikingly enough, Japan is number one with respect to low-tech as well[10]. However, Scandinavian countries like Sweden and Finland are also important low-tech countries (especially with respect to paper and wood products).

Compared to other 'small' countries, the Netherlands' share of high-tech industries in total value added is relatively high (though much lower than in Japan, Germany and the United States). The share of medium-tech industries in total value added even surpasses the over-all average. Thus, the technology mix of Dutch manufacturing industries is not as unfavourable as the results of the Dutch 'Porter' study suggest (see chapter 1). However, total Dutch volume of value added in manufacturing industries is moderate (see Table 3).

7. 'Strong' sectors in the Dutch economy

In Table 5 a ranking of 31 broad industrial sectors in the Netherlands has been made. Apart from the value of PVA (the static economic performance) the growth in terms of percentages of PVA (the dynamic economic performance) in the period 1981-1988 and the size of an industry and its growth of value added in the fourteen OECD countries are shown[11]. Also, as a mark of their 'technological potential', high-tech and medium-tech industries have been indicated.

Table 5. Static and dynamic economic performance of manufacturing industries in the Netherlands

Industry	Size OECD	Growth OECD	PVA 1988	Growth PVA
Tobacco	1.1	6 %	1.75	-21 %
Industrial chemicals **(M)**	5.7	6 %	1.56	53 %
Shipbuilding and repairing	.6	-5 %	1.23	-8 %
Paints, varnishes and lacquers **(M)**	.5	3 %	1.06	23 %
Beverages	1.9	3 %	.93	-10 %
Food	8.3	4 %	.91	-7 %
Electronic equipment **(H)**	8.7	7 %	.74	-2 %
Printing and publishing	5.6	6 %	.74	-4 %
Agricultural machinery	.5	-1 %	.60	49 %
Metal products	6.3	3 %	.59	9 %
Petroleum refineries	1.9	-2 %	.58	125 %
Other chemical products **(M)** ·	1.2	8 %	.56	-3 %
Non-metallic mineral products	4.1	4 %	.55	13 %
Paper and paper products	3.6	5 %	.54	14 %
Basic metal industries	5.6	3 %	.50	20 %
Other plastic products	2.9	9 %	.49	9 %
Wood products	1.7	4 %	.43	-9 %
Other machinery equipment **(M)**	5.1	4 %	.41	4 %
Petroleum and coal products	.4	4 %	.41	42 %
Drugs and medicines **(H)**	2.4	8 %	.40	-13 %
special ind. mach. **(M)** and metal and woodw. mach.	4.0	2 %	.40	37 %
Textiles	3.2	3 %	.39	-2 %
Furnitures and fixtures	1.4	3 %	.38	-3 %
Footwear	.3	-2 %	.35	-7 %
Rubber products	1.2	4 %	.29	-13 %
Soap and clearing preparations **(M)**	1.3	4 %	.27	3 %
Motor vehicles and aircraft industries **(M/H)**	10.4	6 %	.24	-4 %
Wearing apparel and leather	1.9	1 %	.20	-13 %
Electrical industrial machinery **(H)**	2.4	4 %	.18	-17 %
Computing machinery **(H)**	2.5	8 %	.13	-58 %
Professional goods **(H)**	3.0	7 %	.12	-38 %
TOTAL	**5 %**	**4.5 %**	**.57**	**7 %**

Explanation: 'Size OECD' = Share of an industry (in percentages) in total OECD value added; 'Growth OECD' = Average yearly growth (in terms of percentages) of value added in fourteen OECD countries; 'PVA 1988' = Value added per inhabitant in the Netherlands as an index of the average OECD value added per inhabitant; 'Growth PVA' = Growth of PVA (in terms of percentages) in the period 1981-1988; '(H)' = High-tech; '(M)' = Medium-tech.

Although the industrial sectors which are at the top of the list are familiar (see also Tettero, 1987 and Jacobs et al., 1990), in general their 'static economic performance' as measured here (value added per inhabitant divided by the OECD average) is rather low. With respect to dynamic economic performance development during the eighties was more favourable: In various industries the growth of value added per inhabitant was higher than the OECD-average (especially in parts of the chemical industry and some other capital intensive industries, and machinery industries).

How can the results of Table 5 be interpreted in greater detail? As an example, we shall focus our attention on four industries[12] with significant 'size' in the OECD, that is: industrial chemicals, food, electronic equipment and motor vehicles and aircraft industries[13].

Industrial chemicals had been the star of the Dutch economy in the eighties. This industry with quite high technological potential and an above-average growth rate in the OECD, shows a high value as well as a high growth of PVA (that is: high static and dynamic economic performances). The food industries and the (technologically very advanced) electronic equipment industry show PVA values below the OECD average (but above the Dutch average). The growth of PVA is below the OECD average, indicating a relatively slow growth of value added per inhabitant for these industries, compared to the average OECD growth rate. However, that average OECD growth rate is much higher for electronic equipment than for food[14]. The value of PVA is very low for motor vehicles and aircraft industries. Especially with respect to motor vehicles this concerns a sizable industry which has experienced quite a high growth rate in the OECD (see Table 1).

How can the low values of the PVA's be explained, considering the fact that the Netherlands is supposed to be an important exporting country? First, various important export products are of agricultural or horticultural origin (see Jacobs et al 1990, 29). In this chapter only manufacturing industries are taken into consideration. Second, in export statistics production figures are used instead of figures for value added. Using production in manufacturing industries per inhabitant divided by the OECD average would result in a score of .79 (instead of .57 for value added) for the Netherlands. Apparently, on average relatively little value is added to inputs in Dutch manufacturing. This can probably be explained by the country's large share of bulk production (especially in food and chemicals) in total manufacturing.

Third, although many products are exported, imports are relatively high in the Netherlands as well (see section 3)[15]. Thus, the position of Dutch industries in their home market is relatively unfavourable. As an illustration of this, in Table 6 value added of exports per inhabitant (EVA

divided by the average of seven OECD countries[16]) and total value
added per inhabitant (PVA) have been compared among four countries for
twelve industrial sectors.

**Table 6. Economic performance for exports and total value added in four
countries**

Industry (broad sectors)	PVA (based on total value added)				EVA (based on exports)			
	USA	Ger	Swe	Neth	USA	Ger	Swe	Neth
Food, beverages, tobacco	1.04	1.16	.87	.95	.48	1.50	.51	3.86
Textiles, apparel, leather	1.05	1.11	.44	.34	.20	2.43	1.32	1.26
Wood products, furniture	1.03	1.20	2.15	.40	.45	2.18	8.52	1.39
Paper (-products), printing	1.22	.63	1.83	.62	.44	1.62	9.68	1.75
Chemical products	.97	1.64	.76	.78	.37	2.38	1.61	2.37
Non-metallic mineral prod.	.87	1.45	.91	.63	.26	2.76	1.64	1.26
Basic metal products	.91	1.62	1.36	.59	.28	2.59	2.53	1.22
Metal products	.96	1.61	1.47	.60	.24	3.38	3.83	1.05
Non-electrical machinery	1.00	1.78	1.02	.36	.60	2.53	2.45	.86
Electrical machinery	.90	2.00	.84	.68	.54	2.68	2.03	.89
Transport equipment	1.06	1.51	1.34	.22	.50	2.67	2.72	.38
Professional goods	1.53	.57	.42	.09	.95	1.32	2.19	.54
TOTAL	**1.03**	**1.42**	**1.06**	**.57**	**.47**	**2.41**	**2.40**	**1.35**

While the value of the American PVA (1.03) is much higher than
the Dutch PVA (.57), the export performance of Dutch manufacturing
industries (EVA is 1.35) is better than the American export performance
(EVA is .47). This can be explained by the better position of American
firms in their home market. However, the export performance of Dutch
manufacturing industries should not be exaggerated either. The export
performance of the German and Swedish manufacturing sectors is better
than the Dutch performance[17].
While in none of the twelve broad industrial sectors an above-average
value of PVA is attained, in eight out of twelve sectors export performance of Dutch manufacturing industries is better than the average of the
seven OECD countries.
Measured in this way, sectors like chemicals; food, beverages and tobacco; and paper and paper products make their appearance as 'strong,
competitive' industries in the Dutch economy (see also Tettero 1987 and
Jacobs et al 1990). Modern, technologically advanced industries (machi-

nery, electronics, transport equipment and professional goods) show moderate export performance.

As can be deduced from Table 2, in the OECD on average only a minor portion of the products of the tobacco, food and beverages sector is exported. In the Netherlands, various segments of that broad industrial sector export a large share of their production. However, in comparison with other countries, home demand is relatively small.

If Porter's export-criterion to select 'competitive industries' is used (at the 3-digit SITC level, for the seven OECD countries - see note 16), food, beverages, tobacco, paper (-products), printing and all segments of 'chemical products' (industrial chemicals, other chemicals, petroleum refineries and rubber and plastic products) come to the fore[18]. However, only for tobacco and industrial chemicals is the value of PVA higher than 1.0.

8. A multi-dimensional approach: the example of Dutch regions

In the previous sections an alternative approach to indicating strong industries in a country has been discussed. In our view, a country will gain competitive advantage if it succeeds in sustaining the propensity to create value added in a wide range of industries. Although we believe that our approach to selecting strong sectors has some advantages in comparison to Porter's (export) criterion, it also suffers from problems which are unavoidable when trying to reveal complex phenomena (like 'competitiveness') by using just one indicator. In this section a 'multi-dimensional' approach is suggested to measure economic performance. As an example we will apply this to a regional division of the Netherlands. By comparing regions rather than countries the practical problems of comparability of data are greatly reduced. Of course, if data of sufficient quality were available, this approach might also be used to compare various countries[19].

Four indicators have been used to display the competitive strength of regions with respect to manufacturing[20]:
1. Value added in manufacturing industries per inhabitant.
2. Value added in manufacturing industries per employee.
3. Technological potential.
4. Knowledge-intensity of manufacturing industries.

All indicators have been calculated for the year 1990. Value added per inhabitant has been calculated as in sections 6 and 7 and needs no further comment. Value added per employee gives an indication of the labour productivity of manufacturing plants located in the region[21]. Technological potential has been indicated by the presence of technologically advanced manufacturing industries and the scale of Research and Development activities[22]. Knowledge-intensity gives an impression of the average knowledge level of the employees in the manufacturing firms[23].

As far as Porter's model of four stages (see section 2) is concerned, one might hypothesize:

- that a high value added per inhabitant (much industrial activity per inhabitant) might be attained in all stages;
- that a high value added per employee (high labour productivity) may be characteristic of both the investment-driven stage (capital-intensive industries) and the innovation-driven stage (products with high value added), and
- that the technological potential and the knowledge-intensity of industries is a feature of the innovation-driven stage[24].

    In Figure 1 the regional variations of the four indicators have been shown. In order to enhance comparability, all variables have been transformed into standardized values. Also, the legends of the maps are identical. Some striking differences between the maps come to the fore. For example, value added per inhabitant gives markedly different results from technological potential and knowledge-intensity. As can be deduced from Figure 1a, value added per inhabitant is very high in the southwest of the Netherlands (chemical industries, among others) and in some areas in other parts of the Netherlands (chemicals in Delfzijl; steel in IJmond; electronics in the Eindhoven region). Value added per inhabitant is also high in Limburg and parts of the eastern Netherlands (for example Twente).

    Value added per employee (Figure 1b) is very high as well in the southwest, Delfzijl and IJmond, but not in the southeastern and eastern parts of the Netherlands. Differences between regions with respect to the capital intensity of their most important industries offer part of the explanation for this.

Figure 1. Regional variations in economic performance, 1990: manufacturing industries (a and b)

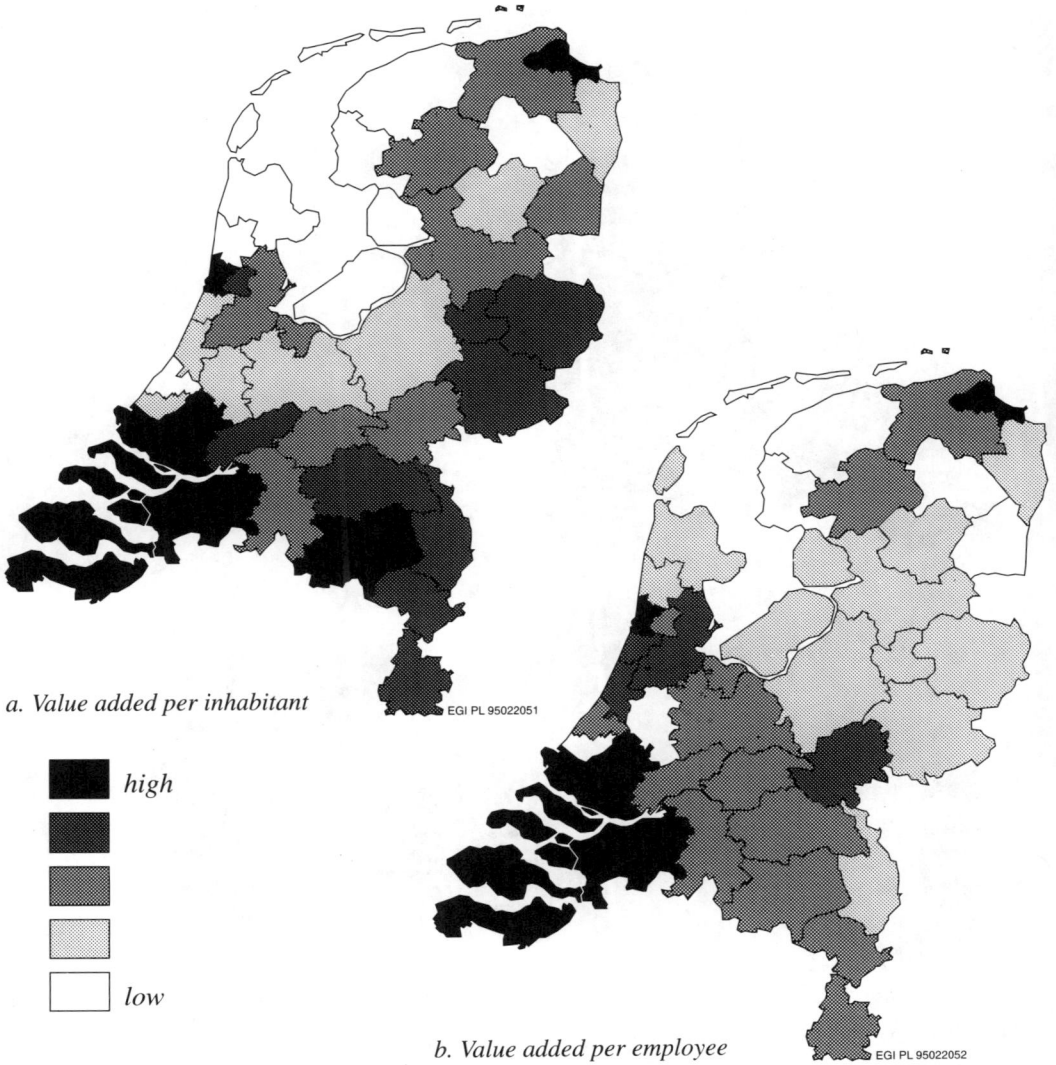

a. Value added per inhabitant

EGI PL 95022051

high

low

b. Value added per employee

EGI PL 95022052

Technological potential (Figure 1c) is high in regions like Twente, Gooi and Vechtstreek, Delft and environment, Eindhoven and environment and the northern part of Limburg. Each one of those regions is characterized by the presence of a number of large technologically advanced firms (in electronics, pharmaceutics, office machinery) with large R&D-departments, and networks of small high-tech firms.

Figure 1. Continuation (c and d)

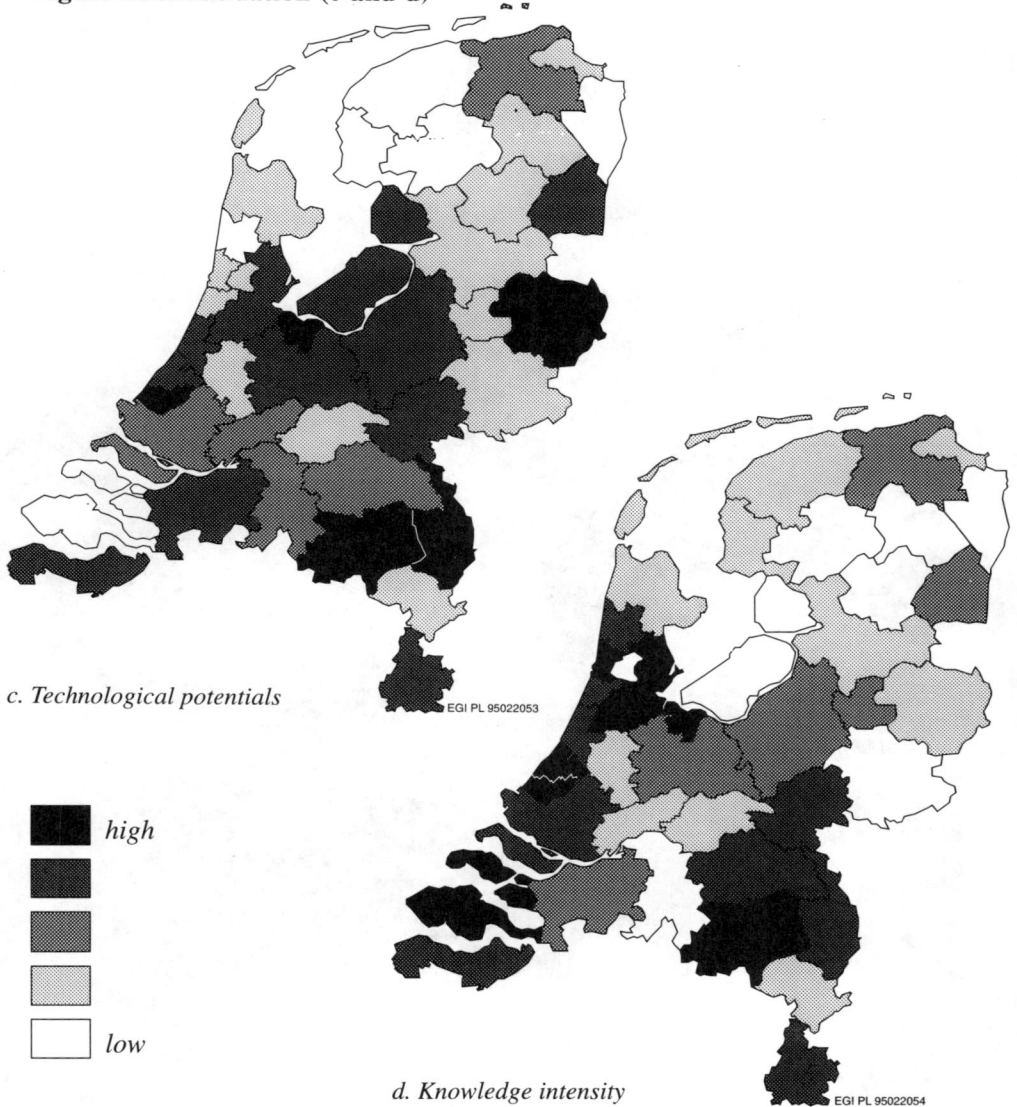

c. Technological potentials

EGI PL 95022053

■ *high*

■

▨

░

□ *low*

d. Knowledge intensity

EGI PL 95022054

The knowledge-intensity of manufacturing (Figure 1d) is high in parts of the Randstad region and in parts of the southeast. In many parts of the Randstad value added per inhabitant appeared to be moderate. However, the average knowledge-intensity of its manufacturing firms is quite high.

The overriding conclusion is that the selection of a specific performance indicator seems to influence the ranking of regions considerably.

In order to investigate if, on the basis of their scores on the four indicators, a typology of regions with respect to the economic performance of their manufacturing industries can be made, we have used a cluster approach[25]. Six groups of regions have been distinguished. They are shown in Figure 2. The average scores on the four indicators are shown in Table 7.

Figure 2. A typology of regions and the economic performance of their manufacturing industries

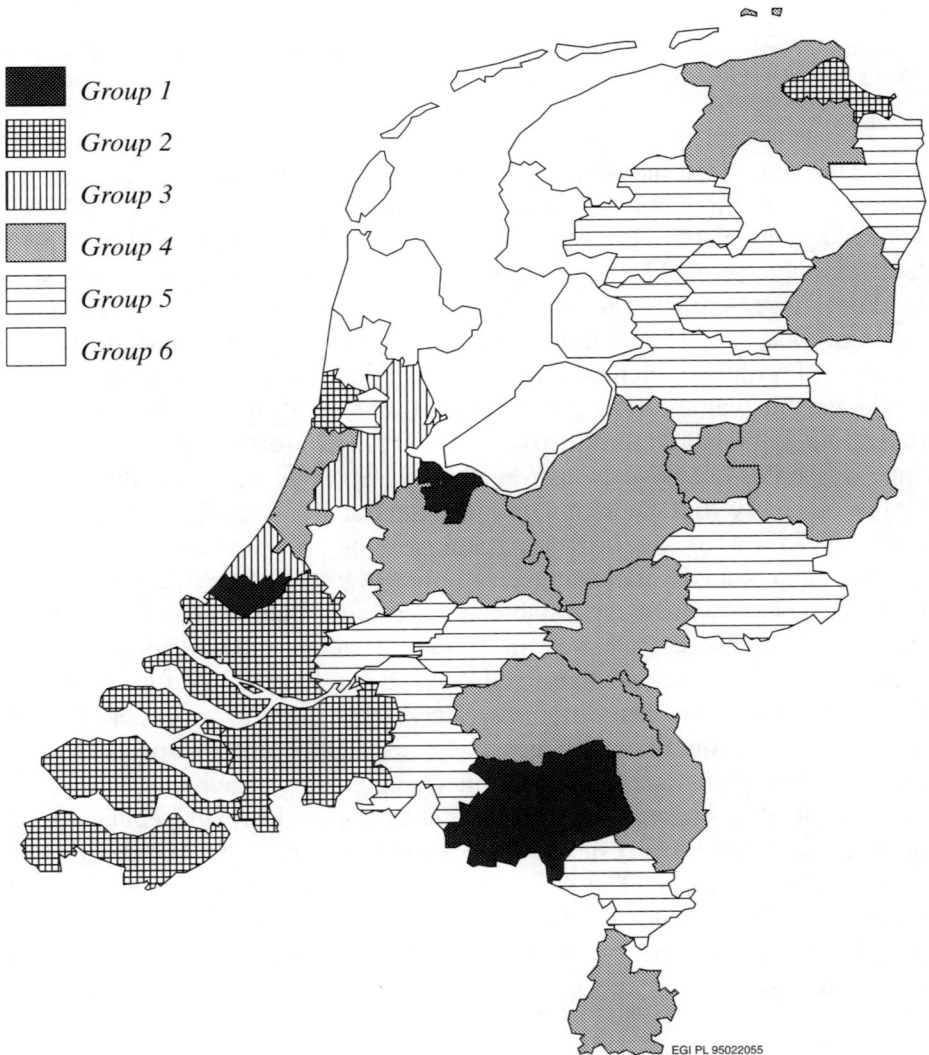

Group 1
Group 2
Group 3
Group 4
Group 5
Group 6

EGI PL 95022055

Table 7. Profiles of performance of manufacturing industries in six groups of regions in the Netherlands, 1990

Group (see Figure 2)	Value added per inhabitant	Value added per employee	Technological potential	Knowledge-intensity
Group 1	.63	-.24	1.93	2.28
Group 2	1.26	2.15	.01	.32
Group 3	-.60	.47	.53	1.56
Group 4	-.03	-.04	.52	.20
Group 5	.18	-.21	-.39	-.88
Group 6	-1.36	-.97	-.80	-.64
Weighted average	**.00**	**.00**	**.00**	**.00**

Note: Because the scores of the various regions on the indicators have been standardized (with an average of 0.00 and a standard deviation of 1.00) the figures in the table are mutually comparable.

One may examine which type of region is performing 'best'. Group 1 consists of three regions with very high technological potential and knowledge-intensity. However the value added per employee is lower than average (probably because much knowledge and labour intensive work - like research - is done here). These regions can be considered breeding places of technological innovation. On the other hand, in the six regions of group 2 technological potential and knowledge-intensity are moderate, but value added per inhabitant and per employee is very high, indicating high labour productivity. They are characterized by the presence of capital intensive industries and appear to be the cash cows of the Dutch economy, but their innovation potential is rather low. In group 3, consisting only of the urban agglomerations of Amsterdam and The Hague, value added per inhabitant is rather low. However, these manufacturing industries which are established there are characterized by a high knowledge-intensity. Probably, in former decades, manufacturing industries with a low knowledge-intensity left the expensive urban areas. Group 4 consists of twelve regions. They show quite a favourable profile (though less favourable than group 1), especially with respect to their technological potential. In regions in group 5 (ten regions) value added per inhabitant is higher than the national average. However, technological potential and (above all) the average knowledge-intensity of the firms in those regions are low. The seven regions of group 6 show unfavourable scores on all indicators. The group consists of some regions in the peripheral northern part of the Netherlands and some suburban regions in the western part.

We will not dwell extensively on the consequences for employment in manufacturing industries here[26]. Of interest here is the money-earning power of industries (the creation of sufficient value added) for the inhabitants of their region. Various types of regions appear to show different characteristics in this respect. For example, regions with mature, capital intensive industries (group 2) could be distinguished from regions with technologically more advanced industries, like group 1 and (to a minor degree) group 3 and group 4. In a similar way the economic performance of countries might be classified with respect to various 'dimensions'.

9. Summary and conclusions

Discussions about the competitiveness of industries or countries are not new. For example, in the beginning of the eighties the competitiveness of the Dutch economy was already under discussion. At the end of the 80s and beginning of the 90s, due to a slow-down of economic growth, this debate has gained momentum again (see for example 'Economy with open frontiers' Ministry of Economic Affairs, 1990). Michael Porter's boók and its application to the Dutch situation by TNO (Jacobs et al., 1990) have been of major importance in this respect. In Porter's approach, to reveal the competitive industries of a country, a 'selection part' (based on export performance) and an 'explanatory part' (based on the 'diamond') should be distinguished. In this chapter we have focussed attention on the selection part. We have suggested the use of value added per inhabitant to judge the economic performance of a country and its industries as an alternative to Porter's export criterion. In order to further the discussion even more, in section 8 we showed the implications of using various criteria for assessing the 'economic performance' with respect to manufacturing industries. A 'multi-dimensional' approach, based on value added figures, technological potential and knowledge-intensity of manufacturing industries has been applied to forty regions in the Netherlands. The results show that competitiveness in terms of economic performance is sensitive to the choice of criteria for competitiveness. Consequently, if sufficient data were available it would be useful to apply our approach to countries as well.

Our main issue is that Porter's selection criterion (comparing an industry's export share on the world market to the national export share for all industries) is unfortunate (and peculiar, as in Porter's 'diamond' the importance of home demand is stressed).

For example, we pointed to the phenomenon that in countries with a very moderate export performance, some industries may appear to be performing well, while actually they are only 'the one-eyed king in the country of the blind'. We emphasized the importance of an industry's performance in the foreign as well as in the home market.

Using our alternative indicator of economic performance, the economic performance of Dutch manufacturing has been compared to the average of fourteen OECD countries. Although in various industries the Netherlands shows above-average performance with respect to exports, total value added per inhabitant in manufacturing industries is rather low. Exceptions to the rule are industries like tobacco; industrial chemicals; shipbuilding and repairing; paints, varnishes and lacquers. Industries like beverages; food; other electronic equipment; printing and publishing; agricultural machinery; metal products and petroleum refineries perform better than the Dutch average as well. During the eighties, relatively high growth of value added per inhabitant (compared to the other OECD countries) occurred in capital intensive industries like chemicals, basic metal industries and paper and paper products and in parts of the machinery industry.

Of course, to judge the importance of an industry for the welfare of a country measuring static and dynamic economic performance (which have been determined in comparison with the performance of that industry in other countries) is not sufficient. 'General conditions' like size of an industry's world market and its growth are important as well. For example, in the Netherlands value added per inhabitant is high for both 'industrial chemicals' and 'shipbuilding and repairing'. However, both the size of the market and its growth are substantially higher for industrial chemicals (see Table 1).

Distinguishing industries (or 'clusters') with a favourable economic performance (in comparison with the economic performance of those industries in other countries) is one thing. However, in order to judge long term economic prospects, assessing opportunities for growth is important as well.

We think judging economic opportunities on the basis of current exportshares of industries is not enough. Judgements based on an industry's value added and its growth in a country, combined with the opportunities on the world market (size of the industry and its growth), offers an alternative.

Even more interesting (though far more difficult to measure) would be a comparison of industries between countries with respect to the relative size of that industry (value added per inhabitant), the labour productivity of the industry (value added per employee), the technological potential (for example R&D-intensity and number of patents) and knowledge-intensity (average education of workers and the extent of scientific occupations in the workforce). In this way, apart from identifying the current important industries (or clusters) on the basis of their value added per inhabitant in a country, 'potential' growth industries might be identified as well, that is: those industries which at the moment do not show high value added per inhabitant, but which show a favourable profile in comparison with other countries with respect to other indicators of economic performance, like labour productivity, technological potential and knowledge-intensity. These differences between 'static' and 'dynamic' competitiveness may have policy implications. Mainly supporting the industries and clusters which are strong at the moment and not developing new ones will be insufficient for long term growth. Can the Porter concept also explain 'dynamic' competitiveness? It will be argued in the next chapter that creating new technologies and new industries can not be explained properly with the 'diamond'.

Notes

1. Economic performance can be measured for industries. It can also be measured for countries or regions, as the combined performance of their industries.

2. In some instances, causality can be reversed. In the opinion of Storper and Walker (1989) new industries, which more or less by coincidence concentrate in some regions, in due course create their own innovative 'milieu'.

3. Exports to countries outside the European Community amount to 12.7% of Dutch gross domestic product, while 11.0% of US gross domestic product is exported (OECD figures of 1992). In general, the share of exports in the gross domestic product tends to decrease with increasing spatial scale.

4. There is another reason why value added per inhabitant should be preferred to production per inhabitant. Even if we compare two countries with a closed economy (no exports and imports) and the same value added per inhabitant, their production per inhabitant is not by definition the same because of differences in the degree of vertical integration of production: In the country with a high degree of vertical integration production per inhabitant is lower than in the country with a high degree of vertical disintegration.

5. Of course, apart from applying these yardsticks with respect to total value added per inhabitant, they might also be applied to export per inhabitant.

6. Ten of the 24 OECD countries were not included in our analysis, because the sectoral disaggregation of data was not sufficient. In the fourteen countries 95% of total OECD value added is created.

7. The division of manufacturing industries in high-tech, medium-tech and low-tech has been based on their ability to generate product innovations. Industries characterized by many product innovations generate more growth than industries characterized by many process innovations (Katsoulacos, 1986; Reijnen and Kleinknecht, 1992). Of course, at the level of individual firms, process innovations can create important competitive advantage and growth rates above the industry-average.

8. Although Porter does not mention it explicitly, availability of export figures (and lack of value added figures) for 5-digit industrial sectors probably is an important reason for his choice of an export-based (instead of a value added-based) performance indicator.

9. Due to the fact that a sufficient degree of sectoral disaggregation was not possible, some OECD countries have not been included in the table. However, calculating the PVA for total manufacturing industries was possible. Of the other OECD countries, Switzerland shows a very high PVA of 1.40. The value of PVA is lower for Iceland (0.66), Canada (0.64), New Zealand (0.46), Australia (0.45), Greece (0.16), Portugal (0.15) and Turkey (0.06).

10. Part of this may be explained by the fact that many of the suppliers of high- and medium-tech industries on the domestic market are low-tech. Also, low-tech industries probably benefit from the expanding Japanese domestic consumer markets.

11. Due to data limitations some of the industries in Table 1 have been aggregated in Table 5.

12. Those industries more or less are similar to the four broad clusters identified in Jacobs et al (1990): agriculture/food, chemicals, electronics and transportation. A direct comparison with their approach is not our intention here, because in their analysis Jacobs and co-workers focus attention on specific segments within those broad sectors.

13. Unfortunately, the OECD data on motor vehicles and aircraft industries could not be seperated out for the Netherlands.

14. In the Netherlands, value added for food has grown by 3% a year in the period 1981-1988, while value added in electronic equipment has grown by 6.5% a year.

15. For example, a very large share of Dutch investment goods (machinery, among others) is imported from Germany.

16. Due to insufficient data on the other countries of the OECD, the EVA- and PVA-indicators in Table 6 are based on seven countries (United States, Germany, United Kingdom, France, the Netherlands, Belgium and Sweden). Accordingly, the values of PVA in Table 3 and Table 6 are not completely identical.

17. For a further comparison it is useful to mention that the value of EVA is 1.05 for France and .89 for the United Kingdom.

18. The share of Dutch exports for total exports of the seven OECD countries is 6.4%.

19. Actually, as has been indicated in section 2 already, Porter's approach might be applied to comparing the economic performance of regions (instead of countries) for its own sake (see Van Houtum, 1991). However, our intention is to use the Dutch regions as an example to elucidate differences between various indicators of economic performance.

20. Each one of these indicators highlights characteristics of the manufacturing industries, located in a region. In order to measure the economic strength of regions it is also possible to use indicators of the 'production environment' like characteristics of the labour market, knowledge infrastructure and physical infrastructure, which are supposed to increase competitive advantage. Actually, this implies operationalizing Porter's 'diamond'. Both approaches can be combined of course, by trying to explain regional (or national) variations in economic performance using elements of the production environment (Van der Knaap and Louter, 1988; Louter, 1991).

21. Both value added per inhabitant and value added per employee have been log-transformated.

22. Manufacturing industries have been divided into three groups: high-tech, medium-tech and low-tech. Then employment and the number of establishments in high-tech and medium-tech (with a weight of two for high-tech) per inhabitant have been calculated. Also, the number of employees in Research and Development per inhabitant has been determined. After log-transformation and standardization of the three indicators, they have been added to a total score per region. For further details: see Louter, 1991.

23. The share of scientific occupations in total employment and a weighted average of the education level have been used as indicators of the knowledge-intensity of the manufacturing firms in a region. Those two indicators have been added. For further details: see Louter 1993.

24. For example (when applied to countries), while Finlands score is quite favourable with respect to value added per inhabitant (see Table 3), its 'technology mix' (see Table 4) is not very favourable. This might impede the long-term growth potentials of the Finnish economy, because (as Table 1 indicates) technological potential and growth potential are related.

25. Ward's method was used for this. In that method regions are merged according to their degree of resemblance with respect to their scores on the four indicators.

26. For example, even if value added growth were huge, employment growth in manufacturing in the 'high productivity regions' of group 2 probably would be moderate due to labour-saving capital investments. However, their money-earning capacity for the Dutch economy and indirect employment effects are large. Supplier and related industries in their own, but also in other regions might benefit from spin-offs in terms of employment.

References

Balassa, B. - Trade liberalization and 'Revealed' Comparative Advantage. - In: *Manchester School of Economics and Social Studies* 33 (1965) 1

Enright, M.J. - *Geographical Concentration and Industrial Organization.* - Harvard University, 1990

Houtum, H. van. - *The competitive advantage of regions.* - Tilburg: Katholieke Universiteit Brabant, 1991

Jacobs, D., P. Boekholt and W. Zegveld. - *De economische kracht van Nederland.* - The Hague: SMO, 1990

Jong, H.W. de. - Frau Antje en de diamant. - In: *Economische Statistische Berichten* (1990), p. 1213-1216

Katsoulacos, Y. - *The employment effects of technical change.* - Brighton: Wheatsheaf Books, 1986

Knaap, G.A. van der and P.J. Louter. - *Regionale variaties in economische gezondheid* (REVAREG). - Rotterdam: Erasmus Universiteit, 1988

Koutstaal, M. - *De concurrentiekracht van de Nederlandse industrie.* - Rotterdam: Erasmus Universiteit, 1993

Louter, P.J. - Zuid-Limburg in beeld. - Rotterdam: Erasmus Universiteit, 1991

Louter, P.J. - Kijk op kennis. - Rotterdam: Erasmus Universiteit, 1993

Ministry of Economic Affairs (Ministerie van Economische Zaken) - *Economie met open grenzen (Economy with open frontiers).* - The Hague; SDU, 1990

Porter, M.E. - *The competitive advantage of nations.* - New York: Free Press, 1990

Reijnen, J.O.N. and A.H. Kleinknecht. - *Technologie en de vraag naar arbeid.* - The Hague: OSA, 1992

Scott, A.J. - New industrial spaces. - London: Pion, 1988

Storper, M and R. Walker. - *The capitalist imperative.* - New York: Basil Blackwell, 1989

Tettero, J.H.J.P. - *Het concurrentieprofiel van Nederland.* - Alblasserdam: Kanters, 1987

Thompson, W.R. - Internal and external factors in the development of urban economies. - In: Issues in urban economics / Red.: H.S. Perloff and L. Wingo Jr. - Baltimore, John Hopkins Press, 1968

Vernon, R. - International investment and international trade in the product cycle. - In: *Quarterly Journal of Economics* 80 (1966) - p. 190-207

Chapter 3

P.R. BEIJE

COMPETITIVENESS OF INDUSTRIES AND THE ECONOMICS OF INNOVATION

1. Introduction

There is no doubt that Porter sees the creation and use of new technology as the major source of sustained competitive advantage. The use of new technology at as many places in the 'value chain' as possible is inherent to both differentiation and cost strategies (Porter, 1985). In the 'diamond' concept (Porter, 1990), technology plays an equally important role. Firms and industries can only stay competitive when they innovate more or less continuously. Remarkably Porter (1990) is not very explicit about his innovation theory. He emphasizes that technological and organizational change are the main elements of sustained competitive advantage, but processes of innovation are not made explicit in the 'diamond' concept. Consequently the relation between innovation and export performance, the main indicator of competitiveness, remains implicit too. Nevertheless, Jacobs et al. (1990) conclude in their assessment of the competitiveness of the Dutch economy that the main problem is a lack of innovation, especially radical innovation (see chapter 1 of this book).

In this chapter we first discuss the main aspects of the creation and use of new technology in the 'diamond'. Thereafter the relation between innovation and export performance is examined. A separate section is devoted to the issue of technological cooperation, about which Porter is rather negative. An alternative theory in which technological cooperation is an element is discussed. As already suggested above, 'a continuous stream of innovations' means that Porter largely focuses on incremental innovations. The final section is devoted to incremental versus radical innovation. In our opinion, the 'diamond' is better able to explain incremental than radical innovation.

2. Innovation and the 'diamond'

Porter has a broad view on innovation; not only technological innovations, but also new forms of organization and management, marketing, etc. are included. He mentions several causes for innovation creating competitive advantage: New technologies, new or shifting buyer needs, the emergence of a new industry segment, shifting input costs or availability, and changes in government regulations (Porter, 1990, 45-47). The question is how some firms in particular industries in a country create advantage through innovation, while other firms in the same industry in another country do not.

Seen from an innovation perspective, the most important aspect of the 'diamond' concept is its continuous 'upgrading of factor endowments' and how the four sets of factors interact in this process. Upgrading is closely related to what in the innovation literature is called 'incremental innovations'. And indeed Porter states that innovation efforts of firms are largely directed at small, but continuously created innovations (Porter, 1985 and Porter, 1990, 49). The 'diamond' can be said to create a more or less continuous stream of incremental innovations. The question is: how? Elsewhere he argues that competitiveness in some industries strongly depends on high productivity (process innovations) which, at the national level, makes resources free for investment in entirely new technologies and industries (ibid., 7). The results of the latter investment are called 'radical innovations' in economic theory. The question is if and how the 'diamond' factors are stimulating such radical innovations too.

The role of the 'diamond' in stimulating incremental innovations is quite clear in Porter's thinking, although a detailed theory of how innovation processes are undertaken is lacking. In ascertaining the whole concept from this incremental innovation perspective we see two main forces: domestic competition and close relationships between domestic firms. Competition between domestic firms is a stimulus for incremental innovations: 'Domestic rivalry not only creates pressures to innovate but to innovate in ways that *upgrade* the competitive advantage of a nation's firms.' (119) Close relationships between domestic firms are implicit in the cluster chart concept. For example, 'Perhaps the most important benefit of home-based suppliers... is in the *process of innovation and upgrading.*' (103) Demanding customers and internationally competitive suppliers within the country not only stimulate innovation by the 'producers' (our first argument), but they facilitate information exchange for and coordination of innovation activities. According to Porter this is done through 'facilitators of information flow', such as personal or professional relationships and belief in long-term relationships and 'sources of goal congruence or compatibility within clusters', such as minority stakes and interlocking directors (153), as has been already mentioned in chapter 1.[1] This can be related to two main arguments in the innovation literature. First, coordination among innovation efforts from various firms is needed. This is because of increasing complexity and speed of innovation processes. Coordination ex ante clearly saves time and at the same time facilitates 'learning from the complex technologies of other firms'. Because of the tendency of firms to concentrate on so-called core technology and because products are increasingly made from various technologies, innovations of one firm depend more and more on innovations of other firms. Second, this coordination is facilitated by common language, culture, attitudes, beliefs, etc. of the persons involved.[2]

'Upgrading' has been related to the acquisition and use of available new technology as frequently as it has been to incremental innovations. But the two are closely related, we argue. The processes of creation and use of many innovations cannot be sharply separated. Many customers cooperate, formally or informally, with the creators of new products. According to Von Hippel (1988) customers may even take the initiative for the development of machines or parts ultimately produced by 'supply industries'. Furthermore, customers may acquire innovative suppliers. In terms of Porter's 'diamond' the geographical proximity of producers in a sector and their customers and suppliers can be expected to enhance the mutual stimulus of creation and use of new technology. The interplay of the 'diamond' factors clearly stimulates the creation of incremental innovations and their use simultaneously.

Does the 'diamond' also promote radical innovation? Porter states that radical change often comes from outsiders to the industry (ibid., 48). This statement is supported by empirical findings from other studies (see, especially Jewkes et al., 1961). Since outsiders are not yet confronted with competitors, rivalry does not provide the conditions for radical change. According to the innovation literature vertical and diagonal relationships between firms do not necessarily provide such conditions either, as within these networks rigidities occur (Håkansson, 1987) and a common perception of the world is stimulated by close ties (Henderson and Clarke, 1991). Porter, however, does argue that clusters of 'related industries' bring about radical change:

> The cluster becomes a vehicle for maintaining diversity and overcoming the inward focus, inertia, inflexibility, and accommodation among rivals that slows or blocks competitive upgrading and new entry. The presence of the cluster helps increase information flow, the likelihood of new approaches, and new entry from spin-offs, downstream, upstream, and related industries. It plays, in a sense, the role of creating outsiders from within the nation that will compete in new ways. (151)

It is consistent with the literature that these clusters promote a continuous stream of incremental innovations. It is not made clear by Porter how they, at the same time, overcome an inward focus, inertia, etc.[3] It can merely be assumed that a combination of 'cluster' and 'rivalry' will do the job. Isolated clusters may be susceptive to the earlier mentioned rigidities, but firms in each cluster also belong to specific industries and rivalry between firms in different clusters may avoid looking inward and the like.

At several places in this book it is argued that Porter's cluster concept is not clearly defined and distinguished from interorganizational networks. Here we state that it is unclear if a cluster is made up of the networks each competitor has with domestic customers and suppliers.[4] As a consequence, it remains unclear whether the combination of rivalry between firms and the presence of clusters is a sufficient condition for radical innovation.

Information flows and goal congruence in the cluster point at some form of cooperation. It is remarkable that Porter is quite negative about cooperation between private firms. He states that 'Direct cooperation among competitors, an approach advocated as a means of avoiding duplication and reaping economies of scale, undermines competitive advantage unless it takes some limited and specific forms. It eliminates diversity, saps incentives, and slows the rate of industry improvement.' (122) Admittedly, this quote relates to horizontal cooperation whereas within a cluster vertical and diagonal forms of cooperation dominate. Our critique is that Porter does not sufficiently explain how cooperation within a cluster can bring about radical innovations. From empirical studies it has become clear that cooperation among firms in the same industry is quite common[5], and that in industries with rapid technological change cooperation is directed at radical innovations and new generic technologies. Examples are the MCC joint venture in the U.S.A and private joint ventures 'around' ESPRIT.[6] This underscores the point that incremental innovations and radical innovations are quite different and that perhaps the 'diamond' concept cannot explain both.

After having shown the implicit innovation theory of Porter and its similarity and difference with respect to received innovation theory, the question is how innovation relates to the core variable of the 'diamond': export performance.

3. Innovation and export performance

There is little doubt that innovation will enhance a firm's competitive position compared to the situation in which the firm does not innovate.[7] New products and advanced production processes give a firm the opportunity to compete on international markets. To a considerable extent, product innovations support a differentiation strategy while process innovations reinforce a cost strategy. Related to Porter's concept, the creation and use of new technology in an industry will be positively related to its productivity (process) and export performance (product or process). According to many, Porter's 'diamond' concept is 'inspired' by the success of the Japanese economy. It is therefore worthwhile to mention some empirical studies of the above relations for Japan. Odagiri and Iwata (1986) found that over the period 1966-1982 R&D expenditure as a ratio to value added positively influenced total factor productivity of the 135 to 168 Japanese manufacturing companies studied. Interindustry differences do occur however. Ito and Pucik (1993) studied three factors influencing the export performance of Japanese manufacturing firms: R&D spending, domestic competitive position, and firm size. They conclude that a firm's export ratio is related to the size of the firm, but not to the firm's and the industry's R&D intensities. We come back to this point when discussing a Dutch study on this topic. A further conclusion is that follower-firms are characterized by higher export ratios than market leaders. This suggests that a relationship exists between the pattern of domestic competition and the international competitiveness of Japanese firms. Technology may be important to explain exports, but the kind of technology strategy matters.

Innovation, therefore, is no guarantee of success. Innovation capabilities must be accompanied by so-called complementary assets (Teece, 1986), such as efficient production and distribution facilities, which enable firms to appropriate innovation profits. At the industry level, innovation will only affect export performance positively when the firms in country A have a better innovation performance (including 'complementary' performances) than the firms in country B which compete in the same foreign markets. This dependence on 'foreign technological performance' may disturb a positive relationship between R&D in an industry and its export at the national level. An alternative is to compare industry X in various countries.

The comparison of innovation performance in an industry in two countries is difficult for at least two reasons. First, innovation performance as such is difficult to measure. Second, each industry usually consists of firms that do and firms that do not innovate and the countries may differ in this respect. The industry in country A may perform better than in B simply because in A relatively more firms undertake R&D.

In the economics literature a series of empirical studies have been undertaken in the last twenty years in which trade performance is related to technology. In a review of this literature Soete (1987, 103) states: 'Technology has undoubtedly emerged as one of the most important factors in explaining international trade flows.' His own empirical tests relate a country's share in total export of a product among OECD countries, expressed in the country's total share of OECD exports (the so-called revealed comparative advantage index), to a number of explanatory variables, including the country's share of total patents granted in the U.S. for each product.[8] It is interesting to note that Soete uses the revealed comparative advantage index in combination with a measure of relative net exports in the same way as Porter does. There is no reference by Porter to this study or to most other empirical studies on this topic. In comparison to most studies in this field, Soete uses an innovation output indicator instead of the input indicator of R&D (intensity). The limitations of patents given[9] - an output indicator - is a better approximation of innovation performance than R&D. R&D intensity of industry X in countries A, B, C, etc. might reflect as much 'imitative behaviour' on the part of firms with respect to R&D budgets of competitors as efficiency in carrying out innovative activity.[10] The main conclusion of Soete's research is that technological performance related to the international market (indicated by patents granted for the U.S. market) gives a forceful explanation of relative export performance within the OECD. More specifically, the greatest influence of the technology factor was found in industries with a high patent intensity and non-significant results or, on the negative side, where industries are bound to be strongly dependent on the availability of natural resources or 'homogenous' labour and capital. Or, as Soete formulates:

> One might indeed expect that any increase in a country's relative (i.e. as compared to its competitors) technological performance will be more rewarding in terms of relative export performance, in technology-intensive industries than in non-technology-intensive industries. (Soete, 1987, 124)

One important factor, according to Soete, not included in the empirical tests is the availability of science and technology personnel as an innovation input indicator.[11] This relates to Porter's study and especially to the role of human capital in the advanced factor supplies.

Interesting therefore is the study by Daniels (1993) which concentrates on trade performance in technology-intensive industries in relation to R&D and human capital. The main disadvantage of this study is that 49 three-digit SITC product groups representing 'technology-intensive' manufacturing products were aggregated into one broad category. Compared to Soete's study many more countries were included (i.e. about 50) and indicators for 'direct' innovative activity were supplemented with measurement of the available supply of human skills or capital. The empirical results show that various measures of export performance correlate significantly with the technology indicators in almost all of the countries[12] and with the national availability of human capital in 37 countries. Space limitations prevent us from presenting recollecting Daniels' conclusions extensively, but after having concluded that direct measurements of innovative activity have a stronger link with trade performance than with the 'national pool' of human capital he states:

> However, the results do support the contention that high levels of invest-
> ment in general education may well be a necessary, but not sufficient,
> condition for attaining national technological superiority as demonstrated
> by TI (technology-intensive, PB) trade success. (Daniels, 1993, 226)

Empirically the study cannot give an answer to the question why certain industries in certain countries (within the broad category of technology-intensive products) are world-class performers and others not. What remains is a confirmation 'at the national level' of Soete's results that patents positively influence trade performance in 'high-tech' sectors. In addition, it is worthwhile to mention that Daniels included the availability of science and technology personnel in the direct measurement of innovative activity. At the theoretical level the study is interesting because it follows closely the concept of Dosi et al. (1990) in which innovation, trade performance, features of the national economy, macroeconomic investments, the industrial structure and other characteristics of the production system are explicitly linked to each other. Moreover, existing theoretical building blocks are used to explain these linkages. An example is the innovation theory, based on Schumpeter, in which learning and path dependency are crucial, enabling innovators to appropriate profits for a certain period of time and explaining that in the production system success tends to breed success. This is an important element in the more 'intuitive' approach of Porter. He could have easily linked his work to the above kind of studies. In this respect it is interesting to present the conclusions of Dollar (1993) in relating technology and trade theory with new approaches like Porter's. After the statement that new technology in the long run is a public good and therefore cannot account for comparative advantage of one country above the other he concludes:

> How then can one reconcile the importance of technology in the short term with its long-term character as a public good? A possible answer lies in the special nature of knowledge as a productive factor. Knowledge is unique in that it can be employed *simultaneously* in different uses. It contributes to production of goods and services; it is an input into the next generation of R&D; and it is an input into training specialized labour. Often these three activities occur in the same location. Apparently there is some efficiency in producing the current state-of-the-art output, developing the next generation of technology, and training technical labour all in the same location. (Dollar, 1993, 423)

Brouwer and Kleinknecht (1993)[13] have undertaken a similar study to the one mentioned above by Soete for the Netherlands. An important difference is that in addition to an analysis of factors determining export performance at the industry level, the Dutch study offers an empirical test of factors explaining export performance at the firm level. In terms of Porter, this is interesting because they show that not necessarily all firms in a particular 'world-class' industry have a high export performance. The question becomes 'why are some firms in sector X of country A more competitive than other domestic firms in X?'

The main results of the Dutch study can be summarized as follows. At the micro level the factors which explain export's share of total sales of 2,165 firms for 1988 are analysed. The effects of R&D have been controlled by a number of variables of which scale effects, sector-specific features, regional location, R&D cooperation with foreign partners and the purchasing of advanced machinery and equipment had a systematic influence.[14] R&D itself kept its significance, though only for product-related R&D activity. Process-related R&D activity did not have a significant positive influence on export intensity. At the meso level, 41 Dutch industries are compared with similar sectors of the main trading partner of the Netherlands: Germany. For the years 1983 and 1988 the relation between R&D intensity and export performance has been estimated[15], again controlling for the effects of some other variables. The main result is that a positive correlation can be found between the development of the R&D intensity of 41 Dutch industries in 1983-88 and their exports. This significant influence disappears however when exports of Dutch industries are corrected for import penetration. Instead, 'investment per employee' becomes significant. This can be interpreted as the adoption of capital-embodied technological change. Apparently, Dutch industries improve their export performance by increasing R&D intensity, whereas positions against import penetration are defended by purchasing technologically advanced machines and equipment.[16] Worth mentioning is that growth of domestic sales leads to less exports (and more import penetration), but also to an increase of R&D intensity in the sector. This translates into an improved export intensity later on. This finding gives some indication of the complexity of exports and total demand variables, discussed in chapter 2.

To sum up, a positive correlation exists between a sector's R&D efforts and exports. This supports the general idea of the importance of innovation in the 'diamond' concept. At this level of analysis the question remains whether firms with R&D do indeed perform better than firms without R&D in the same sector. More interesting therefore is perhaps the second finding of the study of Brouwer and Kleinknecht concerning the firm level. Here it appears that R&D focused on product innovation leads to improved export performance, while the purchasing of new or advanced technology provides a defence against import penetration. The question which remains is whether this technology is purchased from domestic or foreign firms. Only the first case is consistent with the 'diamond' concept.

4. Technological cooperation

In this section we begin with a brief analysis of a firm's limitations in R&D and innovation. Then we discuss cooperation as a way to overcome these limitations. The first point is an attempt to 'enrich' Porter's analysis with insights from innovation theory in economics. The second is related to a specific element in the 'diamond', namely the cluster in relation to innovation.

At the micro level several limitations for innovation may exist. For example, the well-known SAPPHO study concludes that whether an innovation project is a success or a failure depends on the 'value' of the following five factors: the inclusion of buyer needs in the product development process, the public relations and marketing of the innovative concept itself, seniority and authority of the innovator, the use of specialized outside information and advice, and the efficiency of the development process (Rothwell et al., 1974).

Such limitations on innovation at the firm level may differ in importance depending on the kinds of innovations one looks at. Freeman (1982) classifies a number of innovation types according to their degree of uncertainty. This uncertainty variable is constructed on the basis of two subvariables: technological uncertainty and market uncertainty. Technological uncertainty results from the fact that an innovating firm does not know ex ante the results of an innovation project. Market uncertainty reflects the situation that, even when the firm successfully concludes its innovation project, it does not know the innovation benefits, because rivals in the market may do better or buyer needs differ from those anticipated. Radical product innovations have the highest degree of uncertainty.

The more theoretically oriented innovation literature recognizes the importance of market and technological uncertainty.[17] This uncertainty is one of the arguments for market failure with respect to innovation. Given the competition among firms, a reduction of this uncertainty is then a strategic issue. Uncertainty reduction can be established by firms themselves or by government. Government can reduce uncertainty by providing R&D subsidies or tax facilities, or more generally, by setting up a technology policy programme. Private firms reduce uncertainty in several ways. Market uncertainty is reduced when patents are obtained or new standards are set by an innovating firm. Technological uncertainty is reduced when innovations are delayed[18] or when firms cooperate. Several forms of so-called technological cooperation exist. Some reduce the costs of innovation of the individual firm, others 'combine' diverse competencies. Many forms of technological cooperation reduce not only technological uncertainty but, at the same time, market uncertainty; within a cooperation 'externalities are internalized' thus making 'what other firms do more transparent'.

Technological cooperation may be looked at as a sign of weakness of the firm willing to cooperate. An innovating firm cooperates with another firm when it cannot accomplish the number and quality of innovations needed for 'international competitiveness' on its own. There is also the danger that one party profits much more from the cooperation than the other. One problem is that a firm engaging in cooperation does not know the 'real intention' of the other party; another is that unequal results from cooperation shift an originally balanced distribution of power into the direction of dominance by one firm (Hamel, 1991). Such a shift will usually terminate the cooperation. Cooperation must therefore be assessed in a careful and strategic manner. Teece (1986) provides a useful framework in this respect.

The core of his argument is that whether an innovator appropriates the benefits from his innovation depends on three (sets of) variables: the appropriability regime, the life-cycle of technology and the complementary assets in the industry in which the firm operates. The 'appropriability regime' determines the degree of protection of the innovation against imitation by other firms. It depends on the legal protection by patents and the like and on the nature of the technology involved in the innovation. For example, the more tacit the knowledge inherent to the innovation the more difficult is imitation. In the life-cycle of technology two stages are distinguished. In the first stage, firms in the industry have different product designs and the market has not yet decided which 'product-design-technology' is the best. In the second stage, such a so-called 'dominant design' is chosen. In that stage firms accept the basic product design and they compete with prices. The established design allows for process innovations which make large-scale production possible. Then the third variable comes in: 'complementary assets'. The question is which assets - alongside the product innovation - the innovator needs to become commercially successful. Two main types are distinguished: 1. complementary production and distribution facilities; 2. complementary technology, such as components. We limit our analysis to an examination of the viability of cooperation under different circumstances defined by the three variables.

According to Teece the appropriability regime is usually weak. If so, cooperation bears the danger of leakage of strategic information about the new product to the partner. In the first stage of the industry's technology life-cycle nobody knows which firm, if any at all, will develop the dominant design. This makes the consequences of imitation in terms of a loss of potential innovation profits less severe. At the same time, however, this uncertainty about the future design makes long-term investment risky and it must therefore be kept to modest proportions, including investment in cooperation. Minority stakes or loose cooperative agreements seem viable. In the second stage of the life-cycle the consequences of cooperation might be much bigger. When the innovating firm does not possess or control specific complementary assets[19] cooperation might be required, but the danger of imitation and a loss of innovation profits is clearly present under such circumstances. How does this theory relate to Porter's assessment of cooperation?

One remark to begin with. Teece's theory relates to industries in which a single dominant design occurs and mass-scale production techniques for this design can be developed (Teece, 1986, is not very clear about this assumption). In a later study Teece (1992) recognizes that in industries with a regime of 'rapid technological change' and increasing internationalization of competition, specific technological competencies are dispersed among different firms and technological cooperation might be needed to 'combine' these competencies into new products. Related to Porter the question becomes: Are competitive industries of the 'mass-scale' type or the 'rapid technological change' type? And, is Porter's 'prescription' for cooperation relevant for only one of these types? Such questions cannot be answered because, as stated earlier, Porter's innovation theory remains implicit. Nevertheless, his arguments can be interpreted in the following way. Developed countries must increasingly focus on industries with a high innovation and knowledge content, because labour costs are too high to follow a strategy of low-cost and mass-scale production in 'low-tech' industries. To the extent that mass-scale production is indeed becoming less important in high-tech industries, the most advanced countries should specialize in markets with a 'regime of rapid technological change'. And, although a delicate balance between competition and cooperation may exist, many studies point to an increasing number of cooperations between firms in such industries (see for example Hagedoorn, 1994).

Earlier in this chapter we pointed at the relation between current production and next-generation technology at a single location, which is clearly related to Porter's emphasis on the role of a nation (or region) in explaining the competitive advantage of domestic firms in a specific industry. There may be a difference between radical and incremental innovation in this respect. We turn to this difference now.

5. Radical and incremental innovations

The main question related to Porter's concept is whether radical and incremental innovations can result from a cluster at the same time. Let us first be more precize about both types of innovation. To simplify the discussion, the complete set of innovations is divided into incremental and radical innovations.[20] Radical innovations are defined here as innovations which shape a new technological trajectory in which firms are operating (Nelson and Winter, 1982; Dosi et al., 1988). Incremental innovations are all innovations which take place within such a trajectory.

From the innovation literature it follows that innovation networks may differ substantially, depending on whether they focus on radical or incremental change. 'Radical innovation networks' usually involve a combination of private firms and (public) research institutes and the private firms are quite often potential rivals. 'Incremental innovation networks' consist mainly of private firms and their relations are predominantly vertical (and diagonal). With an eye on our earlier discussion of Porter's implicit innovation theory our conclusion here is that, apparently, the 'diamond' stimulates incremental innovation, that cooperation between rivals for such innovations is dangerous and that indeed clusters mainly consist of vertical relations between private firms. Radical innovations, according to Porter, usually occur outside industries. The question arises how can these radical innovations be stimulated? As argued before, cooperation between rivals and of private firms with public research units is quite common here. Related to this all is the question whether government 'intervention' with regard to innovation and the use of new technology is required.

6. Technology policy

In most of the OECD countries technology policy by national government remains an important issue despite the tendency to deregulate and to 'let the market work'. In the Netherlands the recently published 'Technology Report' of the government (Ministry of Economic Affairs, 1995) makes clear that budgets to stimulate private R&D and to stimulate a better adjustment of 'demand' and 'supply' in the knowledge market will be increased in order to reduce the 'technology gap' with the leading OECD countries. Apart from the budget the report makes clear that the Dutch government - although emphasizing repeatedly the major role of private initiatives - sees as one of its major tasks the stimulation of private investment in R&D and a high-quality public infrastructure. Does this view differ substantially from Michael Porter's?

In Porter's analysis, as we have argued, a well-developed 'diamond' seems to be the sufficient if not major condition for incremental innovations. The question of radical innovations is not properly addressed in his analysis. While accumulation of technological expertise implicitly plays a major role in the 'diamond' we propose the following stages in the development of the firm's knowledge base: 1. establishment of the base which leads to world-class performance; 2. protection and adjustment of the base, driven by competition. 3. radical change of the base (i.e., again stage 1 followed by stage 2). The point is that the establishment of the base does not necessarily require strong competition, or better, the creation of technology which ultimately establishes new trajectories often takes place outside domains of strong competition. Let us briefly assess the merits of technology policy on the basis of the above distinction. According to Porter there is obviously a role for government to play in the creation and development of a new technological base of industries and clusters. His view on this part of technology policy is not worked out well. In the Dutch technology report the promotion of start-up firms in new technological areas, a more favourable tax regime for new technologies coming from abroad and research from the public infrastructure which is more focused on the needs of domestic firms indicates clearly the importance government attaches to policy with regard to radical innovations and the establishment of new trajectories.

With respect to incremental innovations within an established trajectory Porter sees a very limited role for government. Although the use of R&D subsidies and tax facilities are not excluded completely, the 'diamond' analysis mainly focuses on the rivalry between private firms and the importance of geographical proximity to establish strong vertical relations within clusters. In the Dutch technology report much more emphasis is put on 'getting R&D expenditure on the level of the OECD average' and if possible in the range of the top countries such as Japan, USA, Sweden, Germany. This brings about a fundamental question: Is the Dutch R&D intensity too low because incremental innovations are not stimulated as much as in other countries or because the economy lacks the conditions prescribed by the 'diamond' concept? It is beyond the scope of this chapter to give a clear answer. It suffices to state two different answers to demonstrate the question's complexity. On the one hand, almost all of the top OECD technology performers are countries with a relatively low public expenditure on R&D compared to the R&D expenditure of their private firms. On the other hand, empirical studies based on the 'technology gap theory' (Fagerstrand, 1986) suggest that an explanation of differences in technological performance in relation to economic growth among OECD countries requires a careful and detailed institutional analysis of technology transfer mechanisms. Consequently, Porter's 'diamond' concept must be reviewed carefully on the basis of what actually has happened in terms of how the successful firms in a country's industry were able to create or use a specific technological base, whether his 'diamond' factors can explain the sustained success once the base has been established, and what the role of government has been in both stages. For the time being we support the conclusion of Auerbach and Skott (1995, 159) that Porter's analysis lacks a true historical perspective and that the current success of firms in relation to their home base is wrongly 'projected back onto the past' as a prescription for how to improve a country's competitiveness.

Notes

1. Both factors largely overlap in our opinion.

2. See, among others, Von Hippel (1988), and some specific literature on networks, for example Håkansson (1986).

3. Porter mentions Silicon Valley as an example of long-term competitiveness. It remains to be seen whether the 'networks' in that region are similar to the clusters of competitive industries discussed elsewhere in his book.

4. A question is whether Porter thinks that these networks within the cluster should have an overlap or not to be able to sustain diversity and the like.

5. See, for example Hagedoorn (1994) and Mowery (1989).

6. For a description of the MCC joint-venture, see Peck (1986) and for ESPRIT and private initiatives in the IT sector, see for example Mytelka and Delapierre (1987) and Peterson (1993).

7. Of course the firm could realize innovations at such great (R&D) costs that on balance a negative performance results.

8. This revealed technology advantage index is calculated in the same way as the relative export performance measure. Note that export performance of country A in industry 1 is not a matter of technological sophistication of the country but of the technological performance of country A's industry 1 compared to the other industries in the country.

9. See, for instance, Pavitt (1982).

10. A remaining problem is the existence of innovative and non-innovative firms in the same industry. Porter argues that not all the firms in a country's exporting industry are necessarily innovative and 'world-class' exporters, but the tendency exists that one successful firm stimulates the other and the 'diamond' factors that favour one can favour the others.

11. R&D intensity was included originally, but this variable and some other explanatory variables were highly correlated, causing multicollinearity.

12. Interestingly, Japan is one of the exceptions. Its exports of technology-intensive products are much more pronounced than can be expected on the basis of its R&D as a percentage of GDP (in the study for the year 1983).

13. This report is partly reflected in Brouwer, Kleinknecht and Reijnen (1993) and Brouwer en Kleinknecht (1993).

14. Factors such as patents applied for, purchase of licenses, investments in software, and office automation did not have a significant influence.

15. In fact a simultaneous equation model has been estimated in which both the influence of R&D intensity on exports and the influence of exports on R&D intensity have been determined.

16. Interesting is whether Dutch firms purchase these machines and equipment from abroad or from domestic firms. In the first case the export performance of the Dutch 'machine and equipment' sectors would deteriorate.

17. See, for example, Kamien and Schwartz (1981) who distinguish a third type: profit uncertainty.

18. By delaying innovation a firm may make fewer mistakes and it may learn from the 'general' development of ideas in relevant fields of technology. See the explanation of the time-cost tradeoff curve (Scherer, 1984?).

19. Specific complementary assets are assets which are only used for the new product.

20. For a more detailed classification of innovations, see, for example, Freeman (1982).

References

Auerbach, P. and P. Skott Michael - Porter's Inquiry into the Nature and Causes of the Wealth of Nations : a Challenge to Neoclassical Economics. - In: J. Groenewegen, Ch. Pitelis and S.-E. Sjöstrand / *On Economics Institution; theory and applications*. - Edward Elgar: Aldershot, 1995

Brouwer, E. and A. Kleinknecht - Technologie en de Nederlandse Concurrentie positie; een onderzoek op micro- en meso-niveau. - In: *Beleidsstudies Technologie Economie* 23, Ministry of Economic Affairs, The Hague, 1993

Brouwer, E., A. Kleinknecht and J.O.N. Reijnen - Employment Growth and Innovation at the Firm level. - In: *Journal of Evolutionary Economics* 3 (1993) 153-59

Brouwer,E. and A. Kleinknecht - Technology and a Firm's Export Intensity: The Need for Adequate Innovation Measurement. - In: *Konjunktur Politik*, vol. 39 (1993) 315-325

Daniels, P. - Research and Development, Human Capital and Trade Perform ance in Technology-intensive Manufacturers: A Cross-country Analysis. - In: *Research Policy* 22 (1993) 207-41

Dollar, D. - Technological Differences as a Source of Comparative Advantage, AEA session on 'What do we know about the long-term sources of comparative advantage?' - AEA Papers and Proceedings, May - In: *American Economic Review* 83, no. 2 (1993) 431-435

Dosi, G. et al. - *Technical Change and Economic Theory*. - Pinter: London, 1988

Dosi, G. et al. - *The Economics of Technical Change and International Trade*. - Hemel Hempstaed: Harvester/Wheatsheaf, 1990

Freeman, Ch. - *The Economics of Industrial Innovation*. - Pinter, London, 1982

Håkansson, H. - *Industrial Technological Development: a network approach*. - Croom Helm: London, 1986

Hamel, G. - Competition for Competence and Interpartner Learning within International Strategic Alliances. - In: *Strategic Management Journal* 12 (1991) 83-103

Hagedoorn, J. - Understanding the Rationale of Strategic Partnering: Inter organizational Modes of Cooperation and Sectoral Differences. - In: *Strategic Management Journal*, 14 (1994) 371-385

Henderson, R. and K. Clarke - Architectural Innovation: The Reconfiguration of Existing Product Technologies and the Failure of Established Firms. - In: *Administrative Science Quarterly*, 35 (1991) 9-30

Hippel, E. von - *The Sources of Innovation*. - Oxford University Press, Oxford, 1988

Ito, K. and V. Pucik - R&D Spending, Domestic Competition, and Export Performance of Japanese Manufacturing Firms. - In: Strategic Management Journal 14 (1993) 61-75

Jacobs, D., P. Boekholt, W. Zegveld - *De Economische Kracht van Nederland.* - SMO: Den Haag, 1990

Kamien, M.I. and N.L. Schwartz - *Market Structure and Innovation.* - Cambridge University Press: Cambridge, 1981

Ministries of Economic Affairs, Science and Education, and Agriculture - Kennis in Beweging. - *Technology Report of the Dutch Government.* - The Hague, 1995

Nelson, R.R. and S.D. - *Winter An Evolutionary Theory of Economic Change.* - Belnap Press: Cambridge (MA), 1982

Odagiri, H. and H. Iwata - The Impact of R&D on Productivity Increase in Japanese Manufacturing Companies. In: *Research Policy* 15 (1986) 13-19

Pavitt, K. R&D - Patenting and Innovative Activities. - *Research Policy* 11 (1982) 33-51

Porter, M. *Competitive Advantage: Creating and Sustaining Superior Performance.* - New York: the Free Press, 1985

Porter, M.E. - *The Competitive Advantage of Nations.* - New York: The Free Press, 1990

Scherer, F.M. - *Innovation and Growth; Schumpeterian Perspectives.* - MIT Press: Cambridge (MA), 1984

Soete, L. - The Impact of Technological Innovation on International Trade Patterns: The Evidence Reconsidered. - In: *Research Policy* 16 (1987) 101-30

Rothwell, R. et al. - SAPPHO updated-project. - In: *Research Policy* 3 (1974) 285-291

Teece, D.J. - Profiting from Technological Innovation. - In: *Research Policy* 15 (1986) 286-305

Teece, D.J. - Competition, Cooperation, and Innovation: Organizational Arrangements for regimes of Rapid Technological Progress. - In: *Journal of Economic Behavior and Organization* 18 (1992) 1-25

Chapter 4

D.J.F. KAMANN. D. STRIJKER

THE DUTCH DAIRY SECTOR IN A EUROPEAN PERSPECTIVE

1. Introduction

1.1 The sector components

In this chapter we analyse the competitiveness of the Dutch dairy sector, using the concept developed by Porter (1990). As presented in chapter 1, this sector emerged as one of the 11 successful export sectors in the TNO study *The economic clout of the Netherlands* ('De econo- mische kracht van Nederland'; Jacobs, Boekholt and Zegveld, 1990) in which the Porter concept was used. The findings of that study already indicated the important role of the world market, the impact of the Common Agricultural Policies (CAP), the competition from large Euro- pean food industries and the need to change the strategies of the dairy processing firms, both on the supply side - facing the farmers - and on the demand side - facing large private European players (p. 95, 96). Since the TNO study, especially in the critical factors mentioned, quite dramatic changes have occurred: the changes in the CAP, the GATT negotiations, the restructuring of formerly centrally planned economies and further concentration in the European diary industry. A good reason to have a new look at the industry.

The TNO study mainly focused on the processing industry of the dairy sector and their industrial suppliers like the machine industries and engineering. However, on page 69, the study points at the close relation- ship between the processing industry and dairy farming. This supports our approach of analysing both the *farms* where the raw material milk is pro- duced and the *processing* industry that collects the milk from the farms, processes it into products like butter(oil), cheese, fresh products (milk, yoghurts, desserts), or powder, either for direct consumption (baby food, creamers) or further industrial use. Both parts of the total dairy sector and their *filières* (Kamann & Boekema, 1989) will in turn be analysed using Porter's 'diamond' concept. Figure 1 summarises the filière of the total dairy industry.

Figure 1. The filière of the Dutch dairy industry

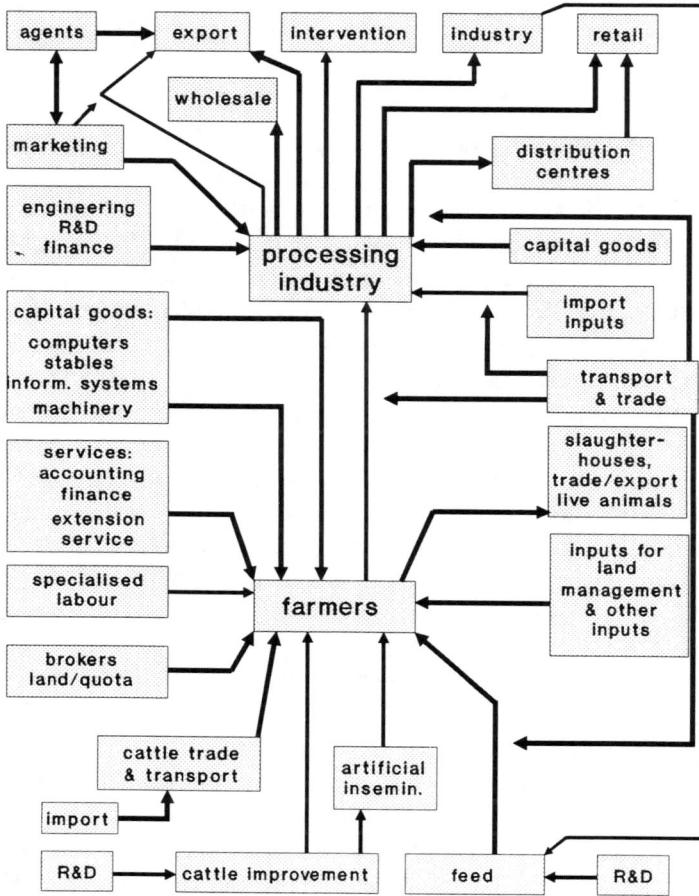

All larger companies perform their own marketing and distribution, some smaller ones do not. Given the fact that a large share of the sector - in some countries 70 to 80 percent - is organised in cooperatives, the policy decisions of industry and farms are in many cases rather 'interwoven'. This means that the well-being of the industrial processing part of the sector may be sacrificed to attain higher incomes on the farms and - in theory - vice versa.

1.2 Dairy: a regulated market

According to Porter, a regulated market 'usually works against the upgrading of competitive advantage in an economy. It has double negative consequences. The first is in stifling rivalry and innovation. Without competition, firms lose dynamism and become preoccupied with dealing with regulators and protecting what they have. (...) The nation in which competition was least regulated was often the international leader in the industries we studied.' (Porter, 1990, 664). In the case of dairy, we first of all find that the *entire* EU market is regulated by the same 'regime' - the EU Common Agricultural Policy. Also under this single set of rules, there are winners and losers: those who are able to use the regime to their advantage and those who are not. We will find that in spite of a lack of rivalry, neither the farming nor processing industry in the Netherlands initially suffered from this but built up leading positions in the world.

Porter does point at regulated markets *and* situations of deregulation. The transition itself is - as is the origin of it - treated as a *black box*. It is not a part or subject of the strategies studied. That seems to suggest that the regulatory system or regime is something autonomous; something given. It is our view that the outcome and nature of the regulatory regime in any market is politically determined and therefore is subject to influence from lobbies by interested parties. When lobbies of particular parties lose their effectiveness, the regulatory regime becomes less favourable for those parties. Then, it is important to see whether those parties that directed the - failing - lobbies realise the changing tide and adjust their company strategies to suit the new regime.

Therefore, as we noted in section 1.1, the regulatory system that favoured or enabled the success of the dairy industry (Jacobs, Boekholt & Zegveld, 1990, 98) changed and became more deregulated in certain aspects. The way the various actors in both parts of the sector responded - in terms of effective strategies and behaviour - to this challenge of a changing regulatory regime *together* with other changes in the external environment determines the performance and success for the future. Or, when missed, may shed some light on the processes and dimensions that prevent such adequate actions being taken.

As we will see, the *farming* part of the sector does not seem to suffer in its ability to meet challenges by having been in a regulated market in the past. It still is able to adjust to changes in the regulatory regime. The *processing part* however seems to be unable to cope adequately with the transition towards a more deregulated regime.

1.3 The structure of this chapter

The structure of this chapter is the following. First, we discuss the competitiveness of Dutch dairy *farming* in a European context, using Porter's concept (section 2). Then, we describe the situation of the European dairy *industry* in general terms, presently in a state of turmoil (section 3). Section 4 focuses on the Dutch dairy processing industry and discusses its competitiveness, using Porter's concept. In section 5, we will give a possible explanation for the findings of the earlier sections. Section 6 draws conclusions about the sector and the usefulness of Porter's model in providing explanations and assisting in finding remedies.

2. Dutch dairy farming in a European[1] perspective

2.1 General introduction

Dairy farming is one of the leading activities in Dutch agriculture. It generates about one-third of gross agricultural production. With less than 2% of the agricultural area of the EC-12 it produces roughly 10% of EC dairy production. About 55% of the 2 mln hectares of agricultural land is grassland. Including green maize, 65% of the total agricultural area can be used for the dairy herd.

Gross production value in dairy is 3.7 bln ECU (1991). Total Dutch imports of dairy products is 1.9 bln ECU and export of dairy products amounts to 3.1 bln ECU, of which two-thirds goes to EC-12 countries. The share of the Netherlands in EC dairy exports to non-EC countries is about one quarter.

From these figures it is clear that Dutch agriculture[2] is specialised in dairy production. Relative to its volume of production Dutch dairy farming is strongly dependent on its exports to the EU and elsewhere, compared to other member-states. This makes the Dutch sector vulnerable to changes in world market conditions and EU export regulations. In the following section this particular Dutch position is explained in terms of Porter's 'diamond' factors, given some current developments and threats.

2.2 Dutch dairy farming in the light of Porter's 'diamond'

In this section, we discuss dairy farming using Porter's 'diamond' factors. We will start with *factor conditions* including *(i)* human resources, *(ii)* physical resources, *(iii)* knowledge resources, *(iv)* capital resources, *(v)* infrastructure and *(vi)* factor creation. Then, (2) *demand conditions* is discussed, followed by (3) *foreign influence*, (4) *related and supporting industries*, (5) *farm strategy, structure and rivalry*, (6) *government* and, finally (7) *chance*.

Porter's 'cluster chart' (Porter, 1990, 288; incorporating the changes proposed by Jacobs et. al, p. 34 e.f.), would be the following for dairy farming. The final product 'raw milk' is one of the major specialty inputs for the processing industry, to be discussed in section 3.

Final products	Raw milk, cattle
Machinery	Stable equipment, stables, mowing and sowing machines, computers, milking machines and robots, milk storage systems
Specialty inputs	Feed, seeds for grass and green maize, fertilizers, breeding
Services	Software, R&D, advisory and extension services, trade, transport, printed information, feed management systems, artificial insemination services

2.2.1 Factor conditions[3]

(i): human resources

In 1992, 5% of the total Dutch work-force was working in agriculture and horticulture (250,000 annual working units, a.w.u.). The amount of a.w.u. in dairy farming is estimated at 80,000. Another 70-80,000 a.w.u. is employed in the specialised supply and processing industries.

Compared to other EC countries the level of education of Dutch farmers is high. In 1985 about two-thirds of the farmers had an agricultural education (two-thirds at *agricultural* vocational school level; one-third at more advanced levels such as agricultural polytechnic or agricultural university). Among younger farmers (< 40 years) 78% had an agricultural education.

(ii): physical resources

Land quality and climate are quite favourable for dairy farming. Originally large parts of the country were not suitable (too wet) for arable crops. After forty years of rural restructuring most of the land can be used (in principle) for all activities, but the basis for specialisation has been set. This specialisation based on land quality was fostered by the small farm size. Animal production - also intensive dairy production -

offers better opportunities for intensification than arable production. These opportunities have been grasped from the beginning but were even more exploited in the 1970s with the introduction of tank-milking, requiring quite high investments. This proved detrimental for mixed farms.

We find that farms in the Netherlands are highly specialised. Half of all farms are classified as land-based animal husbandry farms. There are in total 40,000 (1993) dairy farms, mostly fully specialised. The average number of dairy cows per dairy farm is 36 (1990), compared to 17 in the EC. The herd-size is comparable to Denmark, and only the UK has a markedly greater size (65).

The number of dairy farms has decreased sharply, from 116,000 in 1970, to 92,000 in 1975, 67,000 in 1980 and 40,000 in 1993. The rapid reduction in the last decade was caused by the introduction of the EC milk quota in 1984. The market value of the production rights was such that smaller farmers were unable to expand their farms, and often decided to terminate.

The milk quota-system also caused a rapid decrease in the number of dairy cows, from 2.4 mln in 1980 to 1.7 mln in 1993. This was not only due to the need to reduce the volume of milk production but also in that period an increase in the yield per cow was (again) realized. As a consequence, dairy farm buildings and equipment became underutilised. For buildings this underutilisation has been estimated at 25-40% (Kamann Consultancy, 1993).

Average farm size is 16 ha, just above the EC average. This figure is misleading because 24,000 horticultural farms have an average size of just 4 hectares. The average size of a dairy farm is estimated at 24 hectares.

Average yield per cow is high compared to other EC countries (1,200 kg above the EC average). On the more specialised dairy farms the yield was 4,900 kg in 1975, 6,900 kg in 1990 and 7,100 kg in 1992. Milk has become richer in its useful components of protein and fat in recent years. Protein content increased from 3.35% in 1975 to 3.49% in 1992, fat increased from 3.98% to 4.46%. This development is quite contrary to the development in consumer demand, where 'light' is ruling. Domestic demand for full-fat consumer milk sank from 38.8 kg in 1980 to 16.7 (!) kg in 1992, for low-fat milk it increased from 27.5 kg to 41.7 kg.

Of the 11 mln tons of milk produced, 0.5 mln is used on the farm, either for direct consumption or for home-production. Nearly all milk that leaves the farm is transported with bulk-carriers. Although this makes it very difficult to separate different qualities from different farms, it still enables companies to send milk from a particular area that tends to be more suitable for, for example, cheese production to a cheese factory.

(iii): knowledge resources

Dutch agriculture is science-based. A key element in the restructuring of agriculture after the second world war was the development of extension services, paid for by the government. The basic structure today is that fundamental research in agriculture is done at Wageningen Agricultural University. Applied scientific research takes place in a number of institutes, coordinated by a branch of the Ministry of Agriculture (DLO). The next layer is formed by the research centers where applied research at the farm level is performed (IKC's). A further development towards meeting farmers' needs is carried out by a fourth layer: the extension farms. As in many countries, public research for primary production is much more developed than research for the agricultural products processing stage. Of course the universities, especially the Agricultural University, execute fundamental research. Applied research for the agricultural products processing stage traditionally takes place in institutes, which are financed by the processing industry. This was the case when the individual firms were small. Increasingly this type of research tends to be performed by individual firms themselves, for the claimed reasons of strategy and competition. This trend stems from the fact that *some* companies grow and do not want to share R&D results, while other large companies try to reduce costs and do not value innovativeness very highly. Hence, they try to reduce the compulsory contributions to the common - research - institutions.

(iv): capital resources

Specialised dairy farms are capital-intensive. The value of assets per farm on the larger dairy farms in the Netherlands was in 1992/93 slightly over 2 mln guilders, of which three-quarters is in farmers' hands. The EC average is 0.6 million guilders. The 2 mln is even an underestimation, because the value of the milk quota, unless bought from other farmers, is not incorporated. Including this brings the capital to 3 mln guilders. The main other elements on the farm balance sheet are land and buildings (1.2 mln) and equipment and animals (0.5 mln guilders).

(v): infrastructure

Infrastructure is a key factor for large-scale dairy production. Traditionally the existence of waterways was important for the collection of milk and for exports of dairy products to other regions or abroad. After the war many land consolidation projects were executed, changing water into roads. Individual farms became accessible for large trucks. This facilitated cheap bulk-transport of feed, upgrading the quality of the diet of dairy cows. It also stimulated the introduction of tank-milking, which caused the specialisation mentioned earlier. It enabled the introduction of new, large-scale production technologies, and reduced transport costs of milk considerably.

(vi): factor creation

The Dutch agricultural business complex in the dairy industry functions as a well-coordinated network (Boekema & Kamann, 1989). The various activity cycles of the actors are interwoven, enabling mutual specialisation (Kamann & Strijker, 1992; Axelsson & Easton, 1992). This state of interwoven activity cycles takes a long time to grow. Paradigms - both technical and social - have to be adapted and sets of shared beliefs have to be developed. Standards, recipes, and practices that suit all participants have to be agreed upon. This all creates a synergetic surplus (Kamann, 1989) that comes out of properly linking up complementarity, supplementarity and similarity in the resources and activities of actors. It capitalises on a well-organised value system of individual value chains (Porter, 1985).

When this advanced state of *interconnectivity* (Capineri & Kamann, 1995) occurs, the network becomes sustainable[4]. This means that external shortcomings can be eliminated by the network and endogenous growth and strength take place (Kamann & Strijker, 1994a).

2.2.2 Demand conditions

Demand comes from the cooperatives owned by the farmers (around 80% of all milk processed), from private processors like Nestlé (after taking over four 'indigenous' companies in the past decades of which three production sites are left), Nutricia, Menken & van Grieken, de Kievit and from a small number of traders. Members of a cooperative are obliged to sell their milk to the cooperative and the cooperative has to accept and buy the milk supplied by its members. Leaving the cooperative because of more attractive prices elsewhere leads to stiff penalties[5]. Cooperatives tended to stimulate a high fat-content milk by taking this as a basis for the price system. More recently, the protein percentage proved more valuable than the fat[6]. Because of this, demand shifted towards less fat containing but more protein-containing milk. This in its turn results in a demand for cows that produce protein rich milk. Breeders, farmers and the feed industry are trying to meet this by new hybrids and different diets.

The non-cooperatives follow the cooperatives in prices of the raw material milk[7].

2.2.3 Foreign influence

Demand from foreign firms comes only from Belgium. One of the firms involved has been taken over by the Dutch Campina-Melkunie to stop or at least reduce this 'leak'.

2.2.4 Related and Supporting Industries

A couple of industries are supplying and supporting primary dairy production. Partly they belong to other types of primary agriculture: breeding activities, etc. In the international context these activities are well-known and rewarded. Dutch bulls have international ranking. Breeding of cows in the Netherlands is scientifically based. For many years there has been a significant export of dairy cows (presently to the Baltics, Ukraine, Middle East, Nigeria).

The supplying and supporting industries which do not belong to primary agriculture are, for instance, the producers and suppliers of all kinds of equipment for milking and for the management of grasslands (sowing machines, mowing machines etc.) and for feed-management. There are a number of well-known Dutch firms in these areas also internationally operating. Still, the share of Dutch firms in the home-market is not overwhelming.

For milking machines, the Dutch product share is less than 10%. For other equipment used in cow barns, the share is higher. In many cases of this type of equipment, it comes close to 100%. In this segment, Dutch firms are also important in neighbouring countries. For equipment for grass- and feed production, the share of Dutch produced machines runs from less than 10% for complicated equipment to 15-20% for more simple machines.

In production of seeds for grass and green maize, the Netherlands is one of the world leaders.

2.2.5 Farm strategy, Structure and Rivalry

Farmers do not directly compete, since most of them are member of the same cooperative in the area to increase the countervailing power of the farmers vis-à-vis the processing industry and traders. As such, Porter's main argument that favours a strong industry fails here. However, professional pride is rewarded by awards for efficient production, subsidies for proper mix of fat and protein, and volume of milk per cow. When farmers in an area belong to different cooperatives, price differences between the cooperatives cause social discomfort. Farmers do not savour being supplier to a cooperative that pays less than the cooperative the neighbour is supplying to. Not only because of the financial consequences, but also because of the perceived lower status it carries. Because of this, the basic aim of dairy farmers in relation to the dairy industry is to strive for the highest price for milk[8]. Since most dairy firms are cooperatives, farmers have a quite direct influence on the price of milk. There is however tension between the long-term viability of the cooperative and the short-term maximilisation of the price of milk. It appears that the time-horizon of the farmers/members is shorter than that of the dairy industry, with very negative consequences for the industry as a whole (see below). The central role of the price of milk even seems to be an element of prestige. Being a member of a cooperative with a relatively low milk price seems to have negative psychological effects. The annually published lists of prices paid by dairy firms stresses this element.

For many years there has been a close relationship between farmer and cooperative. More and more this ideological connection is overruled by short-term interests like the price of milk. Cooperatives increasingly find themselves competitors for milk, a competition which only takes into account the price of milk and not the long-term viability of the cooperative.

There is a tendency that leading Dutch dairy farmers (innovators) sell their activities because of all kinds of institutional restrictions, combined with high prices for production-rights (quota). They move either to Denmark, where quota are cheap, to Canada, where (environmental) restrictions are less severe, or to the former GDR, where land is inexpensive, subsidies are high and pioneers are welcomed.

2.2.6 Government

The first important role of government in the 19th century was the regulation of the quality of dairy products for export purposes. After World War II export subsidies became an important instrument to foster the development of the dairy sector (Strijker, 1986).

In the mid-fifties this policy became extremely expensive, because of the rapid growth of production and exports. But before the support was cut the Netherlands became an EC member. The policy of export support could be continued because the EC was only a marginal net exporter (Meester en Strijker, 1985). Although EC production soon started to grow, it took two decades to change the policy. In 1984 a quota-system for milk was introduced (the super levy), which did cut the production of milk and made increase of production impossible (see above). From the mid-eighties on, dairy farming also came under the pressure of (national) environmental regulations. These regulations made it more difficult to enlarge farms. It is to be expected that this type of government policy will function increasingly as a bottleneck for further development of the dairy sector.

From the fifties onwards, rural restructuring, research and extension services became key-instruments for the development of a modern dairy sector. More recently these instruments have become less important, because of budget problems and nature conservation discussions.

2.2.7 Chance

Since 1984, some major decisions have been taken on dairy policy in the EC: the quota-system and the GATT agreement. The quota-system terminated the continuous growth of production, urged the firms to take more care of the market, and made exports to the world market less attractive. Especially the Dutch dairy sector was sensitive to these changes (rapid growth, bulk producer and with an important share in EC world exports). Because of the presence of a fully developed quota system, the effects of the GATT agreement do not seem to be very large.

Both the quota-system and the GATT agreement can be seen as shocks to the system. For the future, several changes are foreseeable. In the *first* place, the EC agricultural policy is under continuous pressure. It is difficult to say what the consequences will be for the dairy sector for the coming years. A *second* development is the introduction of *BST* (a 10-12% milk production boosting hormone). Its use is not yet accepted by the public. Dairy farmers all over the world have no clear cut opinion, but the producer of BST - Monsanto - is putting on heavy pressure on all parties involved. Acceptance by certain countries could lead to a rearrangement of markets. BST-users coulde lose sensitive consumer markets - depending of course on the ability to discriminate BST products from non-BST products in labelling. BST-users could on the other hand get stronger positions in bulk markets.

Finally, as a future development we mention the general introduction of *milking robots,* already sparsely in use. This type of technology only is possible on larger farms. Within the EC, this could favour countries like the Netherlands, Denmark, Great Britain and the former GDR and make their positions stronger.

2.2.8 Conclusions: dairy farming

Since the final product of dairy farming as such is *not* exported directly but only as a processed product, dairy farming can hardly classify for Porter's 'diamond' approach. However, dairy farming *is* highly dependent on what happens abroad (CAP, GATT, export of processing industries) as we saw above. Furthermore, it is rather successful in terms of income generated for the entrepreneurs involved: the farmers. And they managed to promote their interests best by *exporting* their produce through the cooperative dairy processors they controlled and by *lobbying* the national and EU capitals to keep subsidies on those products high. However, as we will see in the next section, what was the basis for success has been slowly eroded. Its 'success' even proved to be a trap which the processing industry fell into.
Another criterium used by Porter - strong domestic competition - is also not fulfilled. Still, Dutch dairy farming is at the leading edge world-wide.
     Apparently, even when neither two criteria are fullfilled, an industry - in this case dairy farming - can be successful.

3. The European dairy industry: a general overview

3.1 Introduction

The European dairy[9] industry is in a state of turmoil. Reduction of subsidies by the CAP -Common Agricultural Policy - and the impact of the GATT agreement is forcing many dairy companies to reassess their strategies. Sometimes, this reassessment even leads to a 'cold' elimination of those firms that were for too long in subsidized production (see further Kamann Consultancy, 1993).
     In some areas the wave of reorganisations seems to be over - e.g. Denmark, now has two cooperatives totalling 80% of the market and the Netherlands has three closely cooperating cooperatives totalling 70% of the market. In other areas like Germany, the industry is still going through a thorough shake-up and shake-out while in Southern Europe the

air remains calm. The aim of this section is to see whether we are able to find distinctly different *strategic groups* in Europe. A strategic group can be characterized as clusters of companies having similar characteristics (Porter, 1980; Johnson & Scholes, 1989, McGee & Thomas, 1986). The point of this exercise is to come to a better understanding of the performance - both domestic and in export - of the companies included.

The analysis is performed on a set of the 25 largest European dairy companies in a cross-country comparison (Kamann Consultancy, 1993; Kamann & Strijker, 1994b).

A wave of reorganisations

As stated, we find a wave of reorganisations spreading through Europe. Scandinavia and the Netherlands seem to be in an 'after-wave'-state. In Germany, many cooperative companies are in a very weak financial and marketing position. France already had some major reshuffles in ownership of the large cooperatives. Also, the U.K. and to a lesser extent Ireland are regrouping and reorganising activities. Further south, we find a relatively quiet situation. Portugal and Spain seem to be the playground for foreign companies-investing, taking minority shares, sometimes pulling out after heavy losses, sometimes staying. Italy and Greece show a very fragmented industry with some large players, and still are far from a concentration in the style of Denmark or the Netherlands.

Table 1. Overview of the European dairy industry

Country	Concentration	Role private firms	Exporting	Foreign ownership
Denmark	2 cooperatives process 80% of the milk	present	yes 50%	Nestlé Kraft
the Netherlands	3 cooperatives process 70% of the milk	present	yes 50%	Nestlé Unigate Bongrain
Belgium	3 largest = 60%	present	yes 45%	Campina-Melkunie Besnier ULN Avonmore
Germany	in turmoil; many small local cooperatives	present	yes <20%	Nestlé Campina-Melkunie BSN Parmalat Unigate
U.K.	5 largest= 66%	increasingly becoming dominant	minimal	Nestlé, Bongrain MD Foods Avonmore
Ireland	5 largest= 80%	cooperatives turned into PLC's	yes 50%	
France	fragmented with some large firms	70% of all firms	yes large firms: 50-60%	Kraft Unigate
Italy	very fragmented 24% remains farm 67 largest= 42%	strong		BSN, Besnier Nestlé, Kraft Bongrain
Spain	fragmented	strong		important
Portugal	concentrated	strong		dominant
Greece	very fragmented	strong	yes; net importer	Nestlé, BSN FFD[10] (Noynoy)

Source: derived from Kamann Consultancy, 1993.

We can summarize the situation in the various EU member states in Table 1. From that table, we can conclude that *countries* differ in the institutional structure of their industry in terms of concentration the role of cooperatives and private firms, and of foreign investors.

In some countries - especially in Greece and Italy and to a lesser extent also in Germany and France - many small-scale firms operate next to a few very large companies. Furthermore, we see that some names of companies are mentioned as foreign owners or important shareholders in a number of countries. They seem to go for an all-European playground. Therefore, let us take a closer look at the *larger dairy companies* in Europe and their strategy.

3.2 Possible strategies

In theory, companies in the food industry may opt for any of the following five strategies (Kamann Consultancy B.V., 1993)[11]:

1 *producer of A-brands*: products for which the consumer is willing to pay more and which are preferred to private label products; this implies high costs for R&D, promotion, sales and therefore usually a large volume/area (Europe) to recoup these costs, or rather high margins provoking new entrants.
2 *low cost producer*: this requires low costs for inputs like milk and/or labour, capital, efficient production, low over-heads, efficient marketing. Companies that follow this strategy are likely suppliers of products under private labels.
3 *niche-producer*: specialising in a particular segment of the market; requires specialised knowledge of products, demand, customers and R&D with focused promotion efforts. Usually requires international approach to obtain scale effects to recoup R&D.
4 *regional/local producer*: usually small companies, catering to local suppliers and local buyers; adapted to local taste and levels of hygiene; low volume prevents high costs for R&D; therefore usually followers, not introducers/leaders.
5 *subcontractors*: producing products for other companies; either under private label or clients' labels; implies no ownership of brand names or labels; low over-head, cheap facilities; requires efficient production under set standards of hygiene.

Small companies are likely to choose for strategies 2 (low cost), 4 (local producer) or 5 (subcontractor). In Greece for instance, these are the predominant strategies among the numerous small firms (Feka & Kamann, 1994). Strategy 1 (A-brand producer) normally requires volume to offset the investments and high costs that go with this strategy or a very high margin. In (geographically) isolated areas - like Norway, parts of Switzerland and France etc. - we find the latter case quite often occurring. In other areas, with easy access, high margins will lead to new entrants, putting the margins under pressure and making scale effects more relevant. Strategy 3 (niche-producer) may also be possible, although when high costs of R&D, investments in specialised machinery and intensive marketing/distribution are required, small firms may lack enough volume to support these costs.

Large companies also have a limited choice. For them, the role of local/regional producer is only possible for a business unit of the company, not for the entire company. The size of the company prevents it being only 'local'. Size also plays a role in negotiating contracts as sub-contractor. While (mutual) outsourcing between 'symmetric' - equal - companies is quite common in the sector, small companies that operate in commodity markets are rather reluctant to outsource part of their production to a large and powerful competitor because of fear that it will take over their market. Niche-players and A-brand producers are less restricted here because of their competitive advantage in brand-name, distribution and client relationships.

That leaves for large companies the A-brand strategy (costly), low-cost producer strategy (requiring low over-head and efficient production that very few large companies are able to effectuate) or the role of niche-producer. The last strategy again is usually not enough to be the sole activity. Some - French and Italian - cheese producers however seem to be successful here. Other companies usually have one or more business units that operate under the niche-strategy.

From the previous statements, we may conclude that while it may be possible to classify the strategy of a firm as *one* of the above strategies for small firms, large firms are expected to show multiple strategies. One business unit may operate as a niche-firm - industrial products, baby food, specialised type of cheese - another one as local producer of fresh milk, another owner as A-brand producer. Having multiple strategies may require multiple organisational cultures to suit the different strategies and types of activities. This demands clever organisational skills of the corporate management.

When only a single business unit of a large company carries an A-brand, it usually operates on a specific segment of the market. In this case, we classify such a *unit* as niche-producer rather than the entire company. Examples are Mona-desserts (Campina-Melkunie; predominantly having a low-cost producer strategy), Friesche Vlag coffee creamer

(FFD with a similar low-cost strategy as Campina), Dana blue (MD Foods), Riedel (fruit juices; subsidiary of bulk producer Coberco).

We collected information on the major European dairy companies, ranked in size of turnover in Dutch guilders (Kamann Consultancy, 1993). Data was collected on turnover, quantity of milk processed, ownership structure and the ratio turnover/kilogram milk. A *high* score on this ratio indicated that *more* costs were being added per kilogram milk before it was sold than a low score on this ratio[12]. More *costs* added runs parallel to more value added. Estimated R&D figures for some companies were included (Table 2).

Ranking the companies according to the ratio of turnover/kilogram milk - an indicator for value added - showed a rather distinct difference between the private firms at the top and the cooperatives following. In general, the private firms showed a higher added value per kilogram milk. Cooperatives scored lower. Although all major firms exported and had interests in companies abroad, apparently the private firms managed to score higher. This characteristic turned out to be independent of size; both small and large private companies fulfilled the rule.

The role of 'mission'

A possible cause for this difference in performance could well be the difference in *mission*. All cooperatives historically have the mission to *sell the milk, supplied by the farmers/owners.* Therefore, their first question always is how much milk is involved in producing a product. Then questions follow like how much risk is involved and how much marketing effort it requires. Producing something with a lot of additives, extra processing and a small proportion of milk is against the 'nature' of the cooperative. Cheese for instance is a popular product, since 1 kilogram of cheese takes 10 kilograms of milk. Cooperatives are *supply driven.* Private companies, on the contrary, have a rather different mission. They have to provide a certain minimum rate of return on invested capital - usually between 12 and 15% - and new projects have to break even within 3 to 5 years in cash flow. Therefore, they only undertake activities when these criteria - ex-ante - are met. Private companies do not *have* to process milk; only when they need it for certain selected products. Private firms are therefore *demand driven.* Cooperatives simply *have* to process the milk supplied to them by the farmers.

Table 2. Ranking of dairy companies in Europe

COMPANY	Turnover/kg	Turnover	Kg Milk	Nature	R&D[13]
	(hfl/kg)	(Milj HFL)	(000 ton)		Hfl/per ton
Nutricia	16.27	1,253	77	private	n.a.
BSN	5.56	8,620	1,550	private	38.19
Bongrain	2.93	2,200	750	private	27.26
Parmalat	2.61	1,095	420	private	n.a.
Nestlé NL[14]	2.36	1,300	551	private	n.a.
Menken	2.32	529	228	p/40%c	n.a.
Unigate	2.17	3,900	1,800	private	n.a.
Sodiaal	2.08	5,680	2,730	cooperative	11.79
FFD[15]	1.89	4,041	2,136	cooperative	7.53
ULN[16]	1.74	3,767	2,160	cooperative	6.58
Arla (est.)[17]	1.70	3,340	1,970	cooperative	5.09
Besnier[18]	1.64	6,250	3,800	private	6.89
Campina Melkunie **	1.60	7,966	4,983	cooperative	5.13
Valio (est.)	1.57	3,550	2,264	cooperative	10.98
Coberco	1.45	3,697	2,548	cooperative	4.70
Klover	1.34	860	640	cooperative	n.a.
Nordmilch	1.29	1,037	807	cooperative	2.50
Belgomelk	1.19	894	750	cooperative	n.a.
MD Foods[19]	1.11	3,300	2,980	cooperative	4.80
GI Recolte	1.00	500	500	cooperative	n.a.
Dairy Crest	0.98	3,900	4,000	cooperative	4.80
MGN	0.96	1,008	1,050	cooperative	n.a.
MZO	0.95	1,893	2,000	cooperative	n.a.
Dairy Gold	0.94	850	901	cooperative	n.a.
Golden Vale	0.87	570	655	cooperative	n.a.
Avonmore	0.75	970	1,300	cooperative	2.60
Waterford	0.63	630	1000	cooperative	n.a.
Camp Melkunie includes German Südmilch and Belgium Comelco; 40% Menken not included; R&D Südmilch=5.83					

Sources: Kamann Consultancy, 1993; R&D: NIZO (for some recent figures: see end notes).

3.3 Clustering European dairy companies

Based on a limited number of variables - turnover in Hfl and kg, employees, and the ratio turnover Hfl/kg milk - we used SPSS to cluster the 25 largest dairy firms in the EU (see further: Kamann & Strijker, 1994b) to find common characteristics among the largest dairy companies.

The following clusters were found[20]:

1. *smaller,* lower and medium yielding *cooperatives.*
a. Nordmilch,, Belgomilk, Klover, Golden Vale, GI Recolte [small, medium yield]
b. MGN, Dairy Gold, Waterford, Avonmore (medium size, low yield0

2. *larger,* medium yielding *cooperatives*
ULN, Friesland, Coberco, MD Foods, MZO[21], Sodiaal[22], Dairy Crest[23]

3. *small/medium* sized high yield *private* firms
Unigate, Bongrain, Nestlé Netherlands, Parmalat, Menken

4. *very large,* high yield *private* firms
Besnier and BSN

Further, two firms have not been added to any cluster yet because of their large Euclidean distance. This implies that their characteristics on one or more variables differs significantly from the other firms, already included. These two firms are:

5. Campina Melkunie (very large, medium yield cooperative)
6. Nutricia (very small, extremely high yield private company)

When we compare these results with the last column of Table 1 (Foreign Ownership), we find in particular cluster 3, 4 and 5 firms active in foreign ownership. This enables multinational *production* of their products. By doing this, they can allocate and switch production for certain markets depending on market characteristics and local factor costs among production sites in Europe. Cooperatives are handicapped in switching sources of their inputs, since they are obliged to accept and buy the milk from their member/suppliers. These members would not accept[24] their milk being refused if *their* company wanted to use cheaper milk produced elsewhere, from non-members.

3.4 Conclusions for the European industry

It follows from section 3 that *private* firms tend to have a higher turnover or value added per kilogram milk. This indicates that they add more additional costs to the costs of the raw input milk. They 'do' more and apparently are able to recoup that in their prices. This 'more' could mean using more additives and treatments, more R&D - which seems to be supported by our earlier table with estimated R&D figures - more marketing, more distribution costs or - in theory - less efficient production. Private firms do more often have multinational production than cooperatives in Europe - Campina-Melkunie and Avonmore being the exceptions in Europe, FFD in the rest of the world.

Cooperatives tend to be either unwilling or unable to fund the more expensive strategies and tend to opt for low-cost strategies combined with some selected niche-units and units that operate on local markets (especially fresh products). Small companies - either private or cooperative - are a mixed bag. Those that operate on the same markets as the (large) private firms do have a potential handicap when it comes to obtaining A-brand status, since the larger firms can more easily recoup their investments in R&D, marketing, promotion and distribution given their higher volume. However, since the cooperatives are less keen on spending large sums of money on R&D, marketing and promotion, small *private* firms have an opportunity in countries dominated by large cooperatives. Small *cooperatives*, linked in long-term supplier relationships with private trading/marketing companies (like Wessanen) may in this way indirectly obtain A-brand status and some of its advantages.

Sometimes, small and efficient firms with low overheads may be able to eat up some of the market shares of large private firms by producing private labels for retail chains (Aldi, Albert Heyn etc.). However, it is also possible that very large retailers prefer to do business with large producers instead of a number of small ones that may be inconsistent in quality.

Small firms can successfully operate on local fresh markets, as subcontractor, low cost producer of private labels or specialised niche-markets. Unfortunately, our database did not focus on small firms. Therefore, we do not have a representative sample of European small dairy firms to base conclusions on in order to differentiate between *small* private firms and cooperatives concerning their performances in terms of turnover/kg milk. However, from our studies so far it appears that size does not seem to play a significant role in determining the result; owner- ship structure does (see also Feka & Kamann, 1994; Kamann Consultancy, 1993; van der Hemsvoort & de Vlieger, 1994).

With respect to the *Dutch* dairy companies, we may also divide these into two segments: private and cooperative firms. The private firms scored high value added/kg, the cooperatives scored low value added/kg, with the first tending to spend more R&D/ton milk processed than the cooperatives.

4. The Dutch dairy industry in Porter's perspective

4.1 General

· The cluster chart for the dairy processing industry contains the following elements:

Final products	butter(oil), cheese, fresh milk, desserts, powder, babyfood, industrial inputs
Machinery	plants, specialised machines and equipment, computer processing control, plant monitoring, packaging machines
Specialty inputs	raw milk, whey, intermediate products, catalysts, fruits
Services	software, R&D, consultants, marketing, distribution, engineering, installation, maintenance, cleaning, trade, transport, printed informa- tion, plant management, laboratory services, financial and legal services

Importance and performance

We described the European industry in section 3. There we already noted that the Dutch industry is rather concentrated, with 70% of the milk processed by only three independent cooperatives. Furthermore, we saw that the Dutch dairy industry is rather prominent in Europe. The European number one in terms of processed milk is Campina-Melkunie - including its German and Belgian subsidiaries Südmilch and Comelco. Also, two other Dutch firms rank high in terms of the volume of milk processed. However, when we rank the Dutch companies in turnover/kg milk among the other larger European companies, we see a different picture (see Table 3; shaded firms are Dutch).

Table 3 gives the value of the national dairy products in million Ecu for 1980 and 1990 and the volume of milk processed in 1990.

The table not only gives the absolute figures for the value (in constant Ecu), but also the percentage change in the value of production and the share of each country in the total value and volume of all countries.

The first striking thing we find in the table is that over the period 1980-1990 the *value* of dairy products *decreased* only in the Netherlands. In *all* other countries it increased. In the large producer countries, France, Germany, and Italy, this was by as much as 82%, 44% and 158%, in spite of major reorganisations in France and Germany. One should also remember that Italy has not obeyed the EC regulation of compulsory volume reduction since 1984.

We also find in the above table that countries scoring a 'share-in-the-total-value'/'share- in-the-total-volume' ratio of more than 1 are (ranked in score) Greece, Belgium, Spain, Italy, France and Portugal. The Netherlands comes out again the worst in scoring[25]. Countries scoring above 1 are net-importing countries.

The table indicates that Dutch products - compared to the products of other countries - score *on average* a lower value per unit of volume. And that, over the years, this position in absolute terms (absolute value) has deteriorated[26]. Reduced subsidies for intervention and export products is one of the main causes. Dutch products are relatively more often found in the bulk segment than is the case with other countries. Most of the subsidized products - cheese, powder and butter - are at the core of this bulk market. One can therefore say that the Dutch were quite successful in producing low cost products for subsidized export, but were caught sleeping when the tide changed.

A dual industry: private versus cooperative

We ended section 3 with the statement that the Dutch dairy industry is - in line with the Eureopean picture - a *dual* industry. One segment contains the *private* firms, with a relatively higher turnover/kg and a higher share of A-brands (Kamann Consultancy, 1993). Some of the private firms have foreign ownership - sometimes completely (Nestlé) sometimes in part (Unigate's stake in Nutricia). Another segment contains the dominant *cooperatives*, with a low turnover/kg and a higher share of bulk products (>80%).

Table 3. Value (mln ECU) and volume (% share) of dairy production in EC countries, (1980 and 1990)

year	B	DK	GFR	GR	E	F	IRE	I	NL	P	UK
	value in million ECU:										
1980	1306	1531	8372	201	2146	9704	1284	2629	5183	285	5709
1990	2554	2643	12073	517	4249	17624	2715	6787	4979	1028	7190
80-90 %	96%	73%	44%	157%	98%	82%	111%	158%	-4%	260%	26%
	percentage share in value of total EC production value:										
share	4.1%	4.2%	19.4%	0.8%	6.8%	28.3%	4.4%	10.9%	8.0%	1.6%	11.5
	percentage share in volume of total EC production volume:										
share	3.0%	4.6%	22.3%	0.5%	4.7%	24.4%	5.4%	8.6%	11.4	1.5%	14.7
ratio	1.37	0.91	0.87	1.60	1.45	1.16	0.81	1.27	0.70	1.06	0.78

Sources:
value: Panorama of EC Industry, Stat. Supp. 1992, p. 15 - 23;
volume: Dairy Ind. Newsletter, nr 8, p. 4.

Although the Dutch industry is important in terms of volume and employment, it presently is undergoing serious criticism (Kamann Consultancy, 1993; A.T. Kearny, 1994) for its apparent lack of innovativeness and unsuccessful marketing performance. In the next section we will use Porter's 'diamond' model to see whether we can find an explanation for *(i)* the success in terms of volume and export position; *(ii)* the lack of success in being market leader and in high value-added producer of the cooperative firms given; *(iii)* the success in being market leader and in high value-added products of the private firms.

4.2 Strong and weak points of the industry in more detail: Porter's 'diamond'

What are the comparative advantages and disadvantages - the strong and weak points - of the Dutch dairy *industry?* Its first and major advantage in fact relates to the *farming segment* that precedes the processing industry already described in section 2. Good quality of soil and favourable climate - or, in other words, a quality of the soil and climate that is most favourable in creating income when used for cattle.

In addition to this, highly skilled human capital and advanced knowledge support put the farming segment in a favourable competitive postition. What about the *industrial* segment? We will discuss this under the various Porter-headings also used in section 2.

4.2.1 Factor conditions

(i) human resources

Two factors play a role here: the quality of the workers and the skills of the management. The *workers*: because of the early start of dairy in the Netherlands, and the early specialisation in the northern regions, a long tradition of craftsmanship especially in cheese-making exists. A well-organised and skilled labour force, with adequate education (the 'Bolsward' education) resulted in good, solid craftsmanship. Working in dairy had enough status to attract young people. The well-organised work force was able to secure relatively higher wages than in other sectors. High job security - to simply reduce the labour force in a factory and sack the workers was not only difficult, it was considered to be 'not done'[27]. This attitude later on was formalised by the unions in agreements and social contracts[28]. This resulted in relatively high wage costs and redundancy payments, which hampered rapid restructuring into low-cost/large-scale production sites.

Management up to very recently was recruited internally. Appointments in the cooperatives - the dominant form of production - were based rather on loyalty to farmers' interests and familiarity than on professional qualities, with the exception of technical knowledge. For most candidates the most determining factor in their attitudes was the fact that they had been brought up as farmers' sons and only had technical training. It resulted in a management class not only with poor marketing skills for the dairy industry but also a more technically production-biased mentality. The trade was characterized by shrewdness rather than intelligent long-term forecasting and planning. This resulted in short-term - often opportunistic - policies. Leadership in industrial terms was reserved for the farmers' representatives on the boards of the firms. Farmers' interests dictated investment decisions[29].

The result of the important role of the farmers in industrial policy was that the 'way of looking at things' - the cognitive maps - of the farmers was transferred to the processing firms. When a farmer faced a problem, he was used to solving it by rationalising, by cutting costs, investing in cost saving techniques and methods and reducing labour costs. His last thought would be to change his output: milk. This way of thinking, when transferred to the processing industry, meant that instead of trying to improve or change products, the focus was on cost-reduction efforts. Investments in R&D, marketing and building up market positions in value-added segments were vetoed by the farmers and condemned as a waste of money. 'There is nothing wrong with our product. It is those stupid consumers who do not realise what they are missing.' that was the standard attitude. New products were evaluated based on the amount of milk that was involved, not the margins made or net profits made. Even hired consultants fell into the trap and advised focussing on bulk since 'cheese was cheese and that's all you can say about it'. The industry was deaf to criticism. Our experience with the industry as consultants dates from 1984. Since then, we have been warning the industry of their fatal course in successive reports[30]. However, it needed hundreds of millions of guilders in losses before the industry realised that the old routines and attitudes were wrong. Only one of the cooperatives - Friesland Frico Domo - has in the past 3 years replaced its senior management with managers from outside the industry[31]. Most of the middle management layers in the industry are still from the old days.

Conclusion: a highly skilled labour force but poor management quality in the cooperatives, which sometimes even borders on the brink of incompetence.

(ii) physical resources

High-quality input - milk - albeit at almost the highest prices in the
EC - resulted in reliable final products, leading to a good name for Dutch
dairy products abroad (evaporated or condensed milk, baby powder,
cheese).

(iii) knowledge resources

The industry itself performs relatively little research. The pre-
competitive research was until very recently performed in a joint dairy
research institute (NIZO; Netherlands Institute for Dairy Research). Some
of the smaller cooperatives, selling to private companies like Wessanen,
have good relationships with university departments. Strangely enough, it
is the Japanese dairy industry that has established a research branch in the
science park of Groningen University because of the knowledge available.
The 'local' industry acts as if these new developments are too far-fetched.
The amount of money spent on R&D in product innovation is extremely
low[32] compared to other food industries, and has low priority. Recently,
the NIZO was considered to be redundant. The argument was that the
companies should do that research in-house. From our observations we
conclude that they do not and never really seriously have. Process innovations are supplied by machine suppliers and consultants. The industry has
a high turnover in management consultants. ASB (now Adstrat),
Beerenschot, Bakkenist Spits & Co, Horringa & De Koning, Kamann
Consultancy, McKinsey & Co., Booz-Allan-Hamilton, Coopers &
Lybrand, to mention a few, have earned tens of millions of guilders in the
industry. Many times the result has been '... at the end of the day: (...) a
new set of lies (...) and pain behind the eyes'[33]. Reports were in many
cases written as alibis for poor management decisions and were unable to
change the mental map of the industry to make it more competitive.

(iv) capital resources

Because of its cooperative nature, two types of capital are available.
First of all there is capital supplied by the farmers in various forms.
Secondly, the cooperative Rabo Bank is another major supplier of capital.
Capital required for modernisation was easily available in the *early* period
of the dairy industry. Pictures of proud farmers and workers in front of
the first steam-driven factory show their commitment to modernisation. In
the late 1980s, attitudes changed. The most modern cheese factory in
Europe of the 60s, in the village of Tuk, recently was closed because of
continuous lack of investment over the past 10 years. Many other
(cheese) factories are suffering from the same phenomenon. Farmers

opted for high immediate personal income rather than to modernise and keep factories and products up to date. This means that capital today is available if, and only if, it results in cost and labour reductions. Investments in markets are rare and are less than the amount going into reorganising and restructuring the companies (into fewer factories and with fewer workers). This can easily be explained by the industry's focus on efficient production rather than on effective marketing. The exceptions in the industry are all either private companies - e.g. Nestlé, Nutricia, Menken & van Grieken, De Kievit - or are strongly demand-driven by private customers - the 'Free cooperatives' and their main buyer, the private company Wessanen. From random visits we even have the impression that it is not only the technologies applied that are more advanced in the private (driven) factories. We also have the impression that the level of hygiene is higher in these private plants and therefore, given increasing requirements by customers, their competitive power in industrial and international markets is stronger.

(v) infrastructure
   The physical infrastructure is good. Internationally speaking one can even say excellent. Both in terms of local roads to the farms and roads leading towards distribution areas, no bottlenecks are present[34].

(vi) factor creation and positive effects of factor disadvantages
   Dairy products are characterized by two important features: they are highly interrelated and most of them are perishable goods. The first element means that a firm cannot specialise in making only cheese or just making butter without having to sell all kinds of residuals or to buy the specific ingredients that only use certain components of the raw material milk. For instance, if one wants to specialise in cheese, the whey remains as a residual. In the old days, this was used as liquid pig feed - as still is done in e.g. Greece. Presently, a number of firms have units that specialise in whey-*derivatives* - a highly profitable industrial market. These units simply process the whey provided by the cheese-units of the same company and/or buy whey on the market. Sometimes, cheese producers have started joint-ventures that process the whey. Because of the interrelatedness of products and residuals, the amount of *milk* going into cheese also determines the amount of whey available. Similarly, the amount of fat used in all products - cream-powder or low-fat powder - directly affects the amount of butter and butter oil produced by the butter-unit. Central coordination of the milk-flow therefore is important. Given our earlier remarks about the ideas cognitive maps fixed on process and

milk-flow, this aspect only reinforces those features. However, the *positive* side of this phenomenon of interrelatedness is that the cooperatives, at a rather early stage, combined their efforts to maximise efficiency in processing residuals. Hence, *negative* factor features like those mentioned above - interrelated intermediate products and goods being perishable - induced *cooperative efforts* for processing residuals jointly and/or acquiring missing components.

The perishable nature of dairy products has resulted in an active exchange of production capacity between competitors. Products, for which each of the three large cooperatives would not be able to obtain sufficient scale effects if all three would produce them, are shared. Company 1 produces product *a* with its own label and the labels of the competitors. In exchange, company 2 produces product *b*, also under own label and competitors' label and so on. One may find in any of the production sites of these companies that butter, desserts and fresh milk products are produced for the competitors.

Both aspects discussed refer to interwoven activity chains that are the result of a tightly knit complex. As such, we may consider this an additional factor created in a situation where, again, efficient production was primarily focused on in a policy to defend *domestic* market position and fight the competitor - foreign penetration - instead of extending the market broadly into Europe.

(vii) selective factor disadvantages: the negative aspects

We described above what we may term the 'positive side' of some factor disadvantages. The negative side is that the cooperative spirit drugged the *competitive* spirit. Together with a strong and well-organised lobby to support interventionism, it enabled the industry to sit back in comfort. It also made it possible that firms with mediocre management survived. Fighting for a market share and a brand position was neither their trade nor their training: conspiring was. The 'MELDOC'-cartel of the major Dutch cooperatives was officially disbanded by ruling of the EC Commission. But the players still meet frequently in secret meetings to discuss the market. Therefore, we would state that *management cognition and skills became a distinct selective factor disadvantage.*

Another selective factor disadvantage is caused by the specific arrangement of supplier (i.e., farmer/owner) relations in the processing industry. The *mission* of the cooperatives was - and still is - to 'process the milk supplied by the members'. This means that the company is discouraged - or even has as its explicit company goal (e.g. Friesland Frico Domo) *not* to buy milk from non-members and certainly *not to invest* in products made from milk - or other inputs - that do not originate from the members' farms. Here we clearly see that the company got its criteria mixed up. Instead of using a return on investment or market position criteria, it uses a criterium that has nothing to do with the market nor with performance, but is politically determined by farmers' emotions.

The 'fights' between the various units of the company for their share of the raw material highlight the supply-oriented policy of the cooperatives, because business units are discouraged - read: simply not allowed - to buy raw material or other inputs (whey) elsewhere. This fixation on exclusive member supplies restricts the long-term planning of the units, since when the production of full cream powder is going well, that of butter is less and so on. Therefore, for the cooperative dairy companies there is a selective factor disadvantage that business units *(a)* cannot make long term arrangements and commitments with clients or markets because their supply in volume is determined by the shadow results of their inputs which implies that they may run short of supplies; *(b)* the same argument, ending in the situation that they are forced to produce *more* than anticipated because the shadow revenues are lower and therefore they receive much more volume than they originally planned.

In other words: the supply-driven character of the units and product groups in the cooperatives differs significantly from the market-driven private firms where the required return on invested capital and cash flows are used as major criteria for expanding efforts in a market or otherwise.

4.2.2 Demand conditions

In this section we will deal with *(i)* the segment structure; *(ii)* the role of sophisticated and demanding buyers; *(iii)* anticipatory needs and finally, *(iv)* demand size, rate, history and pattern of growth.

(i) segment structure

The market is segmented firstly into consumer products and industrial products, then into subsidized products and non-subsidized products. Typical intervention (i.e., subsidy) products are (low-fat) powder and butter. Part of the demand - EU but in particular world market[35] - is in the commodity-type market (cheddar and other semi-hard cheeses, powder, butter). In all segments where the Dutch industry operates, A-brands, B-brands and private labels can be found. In segments where products are imported in the Netherlands - desserts, luxury soft cheeses -

private labels do not occur and the Dutch dairy industry shows weak market performance[36].

The next step is to compare the pressure arising from strong home demand in various countries and the role and position of producers in the various countries in respect to those products. In theory large home demand should stimulate local producers and give them a head start in international competition.

Table 4. Consumption in kg/head of various dairy products in 1989

COUNTRY	MILK	BUTTER	CHEESE	YOGHURT
Germany	70.7	7.4	18.1	10.6
France	79.5	6.7	22.3	15.9
Italy	na	2.4	17.8	2.4
Netherlands	93.0	3.4	14.8	21.1
Belgium	59.5	7.9	16.5	6.9
Luxembourg	na	7.0	12.9	5.4
U.K.	122.5	3.8	8.1	4.1
Ireland	184.6	3.8	5.3	3.2
Denmark	122.6	7.1	14.2	7.9
Spain	na	0.6	5.3	7.7
Greece	na	0.9	22.1	5.5
EC-9	na	na		8.4

Source: Milk Marketing Board, 1991.

The EC production (of 1989) is given in Table 5.

Table 5. EC production of product groups and main producers (1989)

PRODUCT	MAIN PRODUCER	VOLUME (Mil.ton)	EC SHARE
Raw Milk	France	26.2	23.9
	FRG	24.2	22.1
	UK	14.9	13.6
Consumption Milk	UK	6.9	41.3
	France	4.3	17.1
	FRG	4.0	15.9
Butter	France	*0.4*	*27.6*
	FRG	*0.4*	*25.4*
	Netherlands	*0.2*	*11.5*
Cheese	France	1.3	30.2
	FRG	1.1	23.9
	Italy	0.6	13.8
Low fat powder	France	0.4	31.7
	FRG	0.4	30.9
	Ireland	0.1	10.0
High fat powder (>1,5% fat)	France	0.2	26.1
	Netherlands	0.2	21.5
		0.2	19.8
Cream	FRG	0.4	39.7
	France	0.2	19.6
	U.K.	0.1	14.5
Yoghurt and other Buttermilk types	France	0.9	31.6
	FRG	0.9	31.3
	UK	0.2	7.9
Condensed Milk	FRG	0.4	37.0
	Netherlands	0.4	36.0
	UK	0.1	11.6

Source: Milch Marketing 11/1990, p. 21.

We see in the first table - the *demand side* - that the Netherlands has above-average demand (in kg/head) for yoghurt (highest in Europe) and medium demand for cheese. Demand for butter is relatively low, for consumption milk it is higher than in France and Germany.

Yoghurt
When we look at yoghurt *production,* we find the following: Germany is market leader in the EC, producing 962,000 tons or one-third of

the total EC 1990 production. France is second with 941,000 tons, being 32% of EC 1990 production. Spain produces more yoghurt (300,000 tons) than the Netherlands (208,000 tons; only 7%)[37]. Germany is expanding: production of yoghurt in West Germany went up from 157,300 tons in 1970 to 950,000 tons in 1991 for fruit yoghurts, and from 71,400 to 200,000 tons in 1991 for natural yoghurt. German companies like Südmilch (recently taken over by the Dutch Campina-Melkunie) has a market share of 3.6% of the U.K. market (1991), German Müller 16.2%[38]. In Italy, France is the largest exporter (with 11,400 ton or 37.4% of all imported yogurt), the GFR second with 27%, Belgium/ Luxembourg with 23% (surprisingly), Greece with 11% and the Netherlands with 0.5% (only twice the amount imported from Finland)[39].

What do we learn from this? The Dutch are by far the most pronounced yoghurt eaters, hence a good home demand stimulus. In spite of this, the Dutch industry failed to play an important role in this segment of the market. The Dutch industry used to sell yoghurt in 1 liter bottles and packs, rather than the more lucrative single portions. When the industry switched to also providing the 'fancy' types, they had already lost the international markets to the French - Danone, Yoplait - and the Germans. Hence, in spite of a large home-demand for desserts, bulk-packing was the lead formula, also in desserts.

Cheese

From the same table we may conclude that the Dutch are *not* the most outspoken cheese eaters in Europe. Still, almost 50% of the milk of most Dutch cooperatives is processed into cheese. There are two reasons that account for this. The first one is export demand with subsidised prices to make competition easier on the world market. A second reason is that one needs 10 kg of milk for one kg of cheese; hence, it is a nice product to help you get rid of a lot of milk. Demand was more or less a commodity demand which did not require much R&D. Combined with the focus on investing in process production rather than 'fancy' products, the Dutch were able to be out in front in producing standardized products of good quality for a low price, which gave them a leading edge in this segment for many years. Still, according to the above table, the Netherlands is only a small player in the EU context.

Butter

Butter scores low in home demand. In spite of this, the Netherlands is a major player in this typical intervention product; 12% of the EC production. Also, as we will see later on, 40% of the promotional budget goes into butter.

Consumption milk
 In spite of their relatively low-home demand pressure (in kg/head), France and Germany are the main producers, while the Netherlands, with higher consumption per head, is not.

Promotional activities
 We get an even more contradictory picture when we study the promotional efforts of the various countries (Table 6). We have to correct the table in that *collective* promotional expenditure (abroad) does not seem to be included in it. Nevertheless, the table shows some striking differences.
 First of all we note that the amount per head spent in the Netherlands is relatively low and belongs to a middle category.
 The single product group that receives most of the Dutch promotional efforts is butter; a product for which the country shows relatively low consumption per head but it has a strong international position.

Table 6. Promotional expenditures in Ecu/Head and promotional group for 1991

Country	Ecu/head	Liquid milk	Cream	Butter	Cheese	Ice-cream	Others
France	0.24	20%	3%	45%	32%	2%	-
Italy	n.a.	10%	-	12%	75%	2%	1%
Netherlands	0.46	39%	21%	40%	-	-	-
Belgium	0.25	60%	-	30%	10%	-	-
U.K.	0.73	54%	18%	9%	19%	-	-
Ireland	0.58	24%	-	31%	38%	-	7%
Denmark	0.53	100%	-	-	-	-	-
Greece	0.54	10%	-	-	4%	70%	16%
Spain	0.08	62%	1%	1%	20%	6%	10%

Source: Table 119, p. 177 EC Dairy Figures 1991, Milk Marketing Board.

Powder and condensed milk

A typical end-of-life-cycle product is condensed milk. The Netherlands is responsible for more than a third of all EC production. High-fat
powder is a typical subsidized export product. Some production uses
brand names, and Nestlé in particular has many A-brands. Much of the
production is under private labels. A significant part of this product is to
be regarded as a commodity market with tenders from large government
agents. Local demand for both products (condensed milk is used as coffee
creamer) is small.

(ii): sophisticated and demanding buyers

Retail chains have increased their power over the last ten years.
Around 40% of milk and milk products is sold in 4 *national* retail
chains[40]. The largest national retailer, Albert Heyn, has a market share
of around 24% (1992). The 7-8 largest *regional* retail chains have a total
market share of 23-25% (1992/1993). The around 10 so called 'Voluntary
Branches'[41] have a total market share of 24%. Albert Heyn owns the
largest group in this category (Schuitema), with a market share of around
7% (1992).

The question is 'so what?'. Does this situation differ from other
countries? Table 7 shows the market shares of the top 5 retailers for 7 EC
countries.

Table 7. Market shares of top 5 retailers, producers and role of private labels

country	market share top 5 retailers	market share top 5 producers	% of private labels*
United Kingdom	62.0%	66%	30%
France	45.1%	not available	21%
Germany	45.7%	in turmoil	25%
Italy	10.0%	not available	7%
Netherlands	45.2%	70% (top 3)	18%
Belgium	50.0%	60% (top 3)	19%
Spain	20.4%	unknown	7%

Sources: G.R. De Boer, 1994, p. 55; * as % of all sales: p. 59.

In theory we would expect some association between the concentration among retailers and producers to balance the power[42]. However, the concentration among retailers in the U.K. is 30 percent higher than in the Netherlands[43]. Still, the concentration among producers is higher in the Netherlands. This relatively higher concentration among retailers in the U.K. may well explain the high percentage of 'private labels' in that country. However, the concentration among retailers in Belgium is higher than in Germany and France and still, the score on private labels is lower. A hypothesis for Belgium and the Netherlands could be that the relatively high concentration among producers off-sets the power of retailers to some extent, resulting in a relatively lower share of private labels.

Industrial buyers

The large international industrial buyers - Mars, Sandoz, Unilever etc. - are becoming more and more critical when it comes to hygiene and process control. We have evidence of some of the larger cooperatives losing clients because they can no longer meet the required standards.

(iii): anticipatory buyer needs

Many new products are developed in cooperation between the cooperative producer and the customer - either one of the largest retailers such as Albert Heyn or one of the large trading companies, like Wessanen. Many companies, even private ones like Nestlé - produce baby milk powder for trading houses and private foreign labels on specification. Most of the companies in this business - the three cooperatives, and private ones like Nestlé and de Kievit - own modern, automated processing plants.

(iv) demand size, rate, history and pattern of growth

Demand shifts and fluctuates. It fluctuates over the year because of seasonal influences. It shifts from high-fat to low-fat, from sterilised products to fresh products. The market for desserts was - and is - growing. Products like condensed milk, sterilised milk and powder are at the end of their life cycle in the European market. Butter and Gouda-type cheese are increasingly becoming commodity products like cheddar.

Dutch consumers tend to be price oriented rather than quality-oriented. We already pointed at the fact that they tend to buy large quantities - 1 liter of yoghurt, 1 kg of cheese - in order to economise. Jams, sauces or other flavourants to the yoghurt are added to the portions shared out at home, at lower cost. Unfortunately, Dutch consumers also tend to be followers rather than critical leaders. This is reflected in Dutch food legislation, allowable foodstuffs and the quality of Dutch home-market products that seem to lag behind neighbouring countries like Denmark and Germany. This may well influence the attitudes and product innovation policies within the Dutch dairy industry. Hard statistical tests would be welcome.

4.2.3. Related and Supporting Industries

(i): competitive advantage in supplier industries
Suppliers to the dairy industry are on the one hand the farmers, discussed in section 2. In addition, *technical* and *administrative* suppliers play an important role. The technical suppliers were able to build up a lead in Europe in designing and constructing dairy plants. However, lack of modernization plans in the Dutch industry has weakened this advantage. For instance, one can find the most sophisticated all-round plants in Europe these days - e.g. Thessaloniki (Agno) - designed by Italian engineers and Swedish processing control (Alfa Laval). The only Dutch machines come from generator producer Stork. Packing machines, however, come from Italy. In Dutch cooperatives these machines are imported, many times leased from Elopak or Tetra-pak.

Exporting Dutch know-how and constructing factories elsewhere benefitted the Dutch suppliers but caused - and will cause even more - competitive problems for the Dutch industry with their on-average older Dutch factories. This is because the new efficient factories are built according to present standards of technology and hygiene in countries with lower wages, lower prices for raw material (milk) and in many cases with capital subsidies (e.g. the ex-DDR countries). In some cases, these factories are (partly) owned by French or Italian dairy multinationals.

4.2.4 Firm strategy, Structure and Rivalry

Porter (1990, 107) refers in this context to goals, the influence of national prestige, the presence of sustained commitment, the role of domestic rivalry and new business formation.

Goals
We already stated that the goals of the farmers are imposed upon the cooperatives and that the farmers' goals contradict the long-term goals of the processing industry in modern times. The orientation to easy bulk products that earned handsome subsidized incomes thanks to efficient political lobbying put the sector to sleep.

National prestige and political support

The close connection between the ruling Christian Democrats and the farmer lobby ensured durable and sustained commitment and support for a policy that tried to smother competition in dairy products rather than stimulate it. It eliminated domestic rivalry in terms of market share and replaced it with rivalry in terms of the price paid for the raw materials to the farmers. To obtain *that,* necessary investments in R&D and markets were sacrificed.

Domestic rivalry

The previous paragraph already pointed at weak domestic rivalry in terms of products. This lack of competitive spirit was reflected in the MELDOC-cartel of the major cooperatives. They carved up the market and set prices. After the cartel was condemned by the EC, the annual meetings at secret places continued. Only last year (1994), a spirit of competition flamed up when Coberco broke the rule of supplying under private label to certain retailers (Superunie). In spring 1995 the other major cooperatives counteracted by signing an all-fresh dairy products deal with another voluntary retail chain, Unigro, excluding Coberco from any supply to the retail chain[44]. Also, because of Coberco's action, the largest retailer - Albert Heyn - replaced Coberco as supplier by the two other major cooperatives[45]. Hence: Coberco seems to have put up a desperate fight to survive and even is willing to forget the old vows of solidarity. The question is who will benefit from this belated competitive spirit in a rather oligopolistic market.

Strong domestic rivalry is one of Porter's main criteria in explaining export success. However, the Dutch processing industry did *not* have strong domestic competition in the past - the past that made them so successful. The interesting thing is that since the late 1980s domestic competition has grown stronger and this also is the period that we see that the processing industry starts to lose its international position.

Entries

Finally, entry barriers for producers (farmers) are high: they have to buy quota. Entry barriers for industrial producers on the market are low. The Dutch firms do not know how to fight. Recently, a small German firm (Brio, in Wilhelmshafen) was able to penetrate the Dutch fresh produce market with cut-price offers. The dessert market is under attack - and in parts dominated - by German and French suppliers.

Exits?

The Dutch cooperative segment of the industry is withdrawing and losing market shares. For instance, Friesland Frico Domo stated it would focus on the Far East and invested 50 million guilders in Vietnam, roughly the amount one needs to develop and market a single product in the European market. But apparently FFD chose not to do so, admitting it had lost the battle in Europe. The company processes more milk than BSN. It had a chance to cooperate with Sodiaal (Yoplait) but stopped the negotiations[46]. Major product groups (e.g. ice cream in Thailand) have been sold off in order to survive[47]. The company has declared itself to be a 'follower': R&D is minimal. Most products are at the end of their life cycle. The company has an impressive list of failed product introductions and a poor track performance in innovation (Wever, 1988).

Another major player, bulk-producer Coberco, is following Friesland Frico Domo. Coberco recently announced an increased involvement in one of its bulk segments - cheese. Coberco's sole real success is its subsidiary Riedel, producing A-brand fruit juices.

The third Dutch cooperative, Campina-Melkunie, may be the only long-term survivor among the large cooperatives on the European market. It recently took over Südmilch and by doing so stepped into the European dessert market with Europe's most modern plant. Campina-Melkunie also has the national A-brand dessert producer Mona and owns 40% of the successful private fresh milk producer Menken & Van Grieken. Recently it was praised by marketing specialists for innovativeness[48]. However, even this company produces too much in bulk products. It will take an enormous effort to restructure the product line into a more value-added one. In order to raise cash, Campina followed the example of Friesland Frico Domo by selling off its Dutch ice cream operations to Nestlé[49]. Are FFD and Campina-Melkunie two cooperatives selling off their jewelry to private firms to put things in order or simply to satisfy the income needs of their members/suppliers/farmers?

The remaining smaller cooperatives presently are regrouping into larger units. Their focus on more value-added cheese will buy them some time. How long that will last depends on their innovativeness and their major buyers like the private company Wessanen.

The high price of the raw material - milk - in the Netherlands will also affect some of the private firms, especially those in export products with reduced margins. Nestlé started already factories in Poland with similar products as in the Netherlands and has transferred production to its factories in the U.K. because of its cheaper raw materials[50]. At the moment, it still is the high and standardized quality of the Dutch milk that keeps Nestlé in the Netherlands (and Denmark). As soon as Polish and other Central European producers are able to match the same quality, Nestlé, Nutricia and Wessanen will undoubtedly transfer their production, especially since by that time EU export restitution will be minimal so that that incentive will not be there to keep the Swiss in the Netherlands.

The lack of *fighting spirit* of the Dutch cooperatives Friesland Frico Domo and Coberco is also reflected in the Central European market. In Hungary for instance, Parmalat claims to have 80% of the fresh milk market in Budapest. It produces fresh milk and a wide range of milk-based desserts in local plants. Avonmore claims a significant share of the Hungarian market with fresh milk and desserts and German private firms like Alois Müller and Meggle are selling well and carving out their positions in desserts, butter and coffee creamer. Unilever took over ice cream production plants. The Dutch presence in dairy at the recent Foodapest fair was a number of engineering and technical consulting firms and only a combined stand for the Dutch Dairy Association (NZO) representing the entire industry. Visitors could taste poor quality Gouda in cheese cubes of 2 mm by 2 mm. Typical Dutch?

In spring 1995 Friesland Frico Domo announced it would enter the Central European market with less-perishable dairy products (condensed milk, etc.). ERU (cheese-spreads) has decided to build a cheese factory in Hungary. In June 1995, Friesland Frico Domo announced a take over of a Polish dairy cooperative. The company stated that it would not transfer production from the Netherlands to Poland.

4.2.5 Chance

We already have stated that the Dutch industry is rather sensitive to world-market fluctuations and treaties. For FFD and Campina-Melkunie, about one-third of turnover is earned on the domestic market. The GATT agreement, the EU CAP, the decrease in oil incomes in the Middle East and Nigeria, problems in Egypt, the boycott of Iraq - it all affects export possibilities.

5. Superior dairy farming; an inferior dairy industry?

Our industry analysis in fact supports the division made from the beginning into a *farming* segment and a *processing industry* segment. The farming segment of the sector and its support industries have already for some time been leading in the world. Both the actual production on

farms, the technical support industries, breeding, grass and feed producers, soft- and hardware suppliers, robots and so forth, are among the
best in the world and export on a global scale individual products and
turn-key projects (e.g. complete farms).

The position of the processing industry[51] is quite different. While
the industry was quite successful the earlier days, today we find a dual
industry. There is a primary sector with *private* firms that is to some
extent owned by foreign firms, and a secondary sector with *cooperative*
firms owned by the suppliers: the farmers. The first is demand driven, the
second supply driven. This means that the first is product-oriented using
performance - either financial and/or market-related - criteria; the second
is process-oriented using raw material usage and efficiency related
selection criteria.

All (large) dairy companies in the Netherlands - both private and
cooperative - are export-oriented. A relatively small home market forced
the industry to export. Subsidies made certain products attractive. Both
the private sector - Nestlé - and the large cooperatives are heavily
involved in EC export products like (subsidised) milk powder, condensed
and evaporated milk. This makes these producers vulnerable to world
market fluctuations and decreased EC subsidies. Shifting these products
towards the European market is impossible because of their end-of-life-
cycle nature on that market. The *private* industry has better brand positions than the cooperatives and scores a higher turnover/kg milk processed. As true multinationals, they are also better able to apply multinational sourcing and production, as we concluded in section 3.4.

Around 50% of all milk in the *cooperatives* is processed into cheese,
to a large extent for export to the EC market and outside the EC. Again,
this product is affected by reduced export subsidies. Competition on the
European market has intensified since many producers - e.g. from Germany - switched from export products (skimmed milk powder) cheese
production - many times in factories designed by Dutch suppliers.

In high value-added markets Dutch cooperatives do not play a
significant role and private firms do.

Cooperative firms have rapidly lost their competitive edge compared
to their private rivals over the last decade, both in terms of market
position and technical state of the factories. Since farmers ruled the
factories, their way of looking at things and their priorities prevailed. This
induced loyal, technically oriented managers rather than competent
marketing managers willing to oppose farmers' directives. It resulted in
lack of investment - both in plants and markets - lack of R&D and lack
of innovations. It inevitably led to decreased competitive power. Only

very recently cooperatives counteracted the farmers dominance by new legal constructions. It has yet to be decided whether these attempts will be successful.

Support industries of the processing industry suffer from lack of modernization in most of the Dutch cooperatives. Lack of demand from this industry causes suppliers to lose international competitiveness. They try to compensate this by exporting knowledge to Central European and Far Eastern countries. Of course, in the long term this will only be detrimental to the Dutch competitive position. Large Dutch cooperatives do not employ frontier technologies in their plants; competitors and new entrants - usually in countries with cheaper factor conditions - *do* modernize and use more advanced technologies.

In conclusion: entrepreneurial and managerial skills of Dutch *farmers* are well above the European average; management skills of the predominantly *cooperative* processing industry are well below those of its major private competitors.

6. The usefulness of Porter's 'diamond'

6.1 The concept as a check-list

Porter's concept proved to be useful as a *checklist* to describe and analyse the industry. The question is whether it enables us to explain the *direction* of developments and changes or rather the lack of changes, in the case of the processing industry. It transpired that while domestic rivalry was basically absent from both the farming and processing industry in the 1960s and 1970s, both segments of the sector were very successful. Farming is still successful, but the processing industry seems to be losing its past position.

As we have stated, the nature of the regulatory system *per se* is in our view an element in the strategies and policies of the actors involved. It is the result of them and affects them in turn. Because of this, *changes* in the regulatory regime - whether becoming more deregulated in certain aspects because of changes in the EU Common Agricultural Policies and the GATT negotiations as in the EU, or simply because of changing political systems as in transitional economies in Central Europe - *should* require changes in strategies related to any or all 'diamond' factors mentioned. The concept, however, is unable to explain (1) why the regulatory regime *did* change and (2) why *some* of the strategies applied by actors did *not*, and (3) the *direction* of changes.

6.2 The explanatory value of the model

The 'diamond' may explain - *ex-post* - why a certain industry became successful or unsuccessful. The failure of cooperatives to be competitive after some deregulation of the market would fit in with Porter's warning against regulated markets. However, the *farming* segment of the industry was and still is successful, in spite of the regualtions of the past and present. The *private* dairy processors, working under the same regime, also were and are successful. Therefore, it seems that Porter's concept is less able to explain, let alone predict, *bifurcations* in the development path, stagnation or even catastrophies.

One can find this in Porter's own work by comparing *his* example of the Italian shoe industry with Camagni and Rabellotti's (1994) excellent analysis of the three different development paths of three different industrial shoe districts. Or Crevoisiers' (1993) analysis about the different development paths of the Swiss and French watch industries in the Jura. In each of these studies the cognitive elements - the social and technological paradigms - play vital roles as explanatory variables in explaining the differences in strategies.

One of the common elements of the above mentioned studies with the Dutch processing industry is the following: the initial succes of many areas seems to be based on a paradoxical situation. Many geographical areas became successful thanks to the fact that they were *hampered* by some type of relative bottleneck and/or barrier in their development or functioning (Ratti and Reichman, 1993; Kamann, 1993, 1994, 1995). In fact, these are in Porter's terminology stimulating factor disadvantages. By *overcoming* these bottlenecks companies in these areas managed to establish, in fact, competitive advantages - a process that usually took at least a decade and made them for some time rather successful. However, time solved the bottlenecks and/or eroded the competitive advantages. Or the regulatory regime that used to be favourable changed. Lack of proper interpretation of the changing tide by the actors involved - fed by inertia in routines, fixed technical and managerial paradigms and trajectories - resulted in loss of competitive advantage and recession in the areas' activities and their market position. Foreign take-overs, closures and/or loss of activities and jobs are the predictable result.

In all these cases we find that *cognitive elements* that deviated, blocked, or indeed initiated changes, made the difference between 'success' and 'failure'. Also in our industry analysis we find that the transference of the cognitive maps of the farmers - their way of doing, their way of solving problems, their criteria, their goals and values - in fact proved detrimental for the sector. It was a cognitive map or belief-set that pervaded the governmental departments and services and the financial institutions (the cooperative Rabo Bank) for too long. *It paralysed its ability to react to market pressure,* at least in the dominant - cooperative - segment of it.

6.3 Conclusions

Porter's 'diamond' is useful as a guideline or a check-list. Like his '5 forces' it gives us a tool to look at reality. Networks play an important role, but as has been discussed at several places in this book, there is no explicit theory on networks. Consequently, Porter ignores two basic characteristics of networks. *(i)* Relationships are inter-connected. Exchange in one relationship is conditioned (path dependent) by the configuration of relationships in the entire network it is part of. *(ii)* A common cognitive belief-set develops inside the network, reflecting routines and steering the social and technolocial paradigms; they explain and indicate the direction of changes or the lack of adequate change. And more related to the specific market we studied, a third characteristic of networks can be mentioned: *(iii)* regulatory regimes are not a black box, but are related to the network; the regime is affected by lobbies and vice versa; the regime affects and influences the policies and strategies of actors inside the network.

Porter's model is unable to describe and explain phenomena like stagnation or bifurcations. *Why* did the *cooperative* dairy processing industry in the Netherlands fail after initial successes? How come the farmers remained so successful? Why were the farmers in the early days willing to invest in factories, showing long-term planning horizons? Why did their planning horizon 'shrink', resulting in rickety old factories? Why was *private* industry much more successful, resulting in recognized brands and modern factories?

Was it the *process orientation* of the farmers that overruled the market and product orientation of the selling processors? The hybrids - the small cooperatives that are 'steered' by large private buyers who do the marketing - indeed seem to have been more successful in recent years.

The statutory *mission* of cooperatives seems to have forced them into focusing on the best way to serve the farmers' interests: by *only buying* the milk *they* supplied and processing *all* the milk that was offered to them. This was so even when it meant forfeiting sourcing possibilities that would have been cheaper or production of products at zero profits or losses to be able to cope with the supply they were obliged to process. Short-term farmers' incomes became more important than long-term investments in markets, brands and product innovations.

In contrast to this , the mission of the private firms was to serve the market best in order to obtain an attractive return on invested capital using *anybody's milk* and producing whatever product where-ever; as long as it was profitable. No forced production because of compulsory processing, no forced sourcing.

People in the sector *perceive* their thoughts and policies as rational. From an outsiders' point of view, they prove to be not effective in securing long-term viability. Cognition - mental maps - and non-rational behaviour play a much more important role in the direction of development paths than Porter allows for. The fact that the major parts of the Dutch dairy industry became *locked in* to a certain mental map perhaps explains its present state best.

Of course, *in words* the cooperatives claim to be more market-oriented now and persuing higher added value products; hence, the rethoric is now all right. Some are trying to create new legal entities; new hybrids (Kerry Group, Friesland Frico Domo). However, in *acts and behaviour* they still do not seem to believe their own words; they do not make their wallets do what their mouth claims they do.

Changing the mental map *beyond* the level of rethoric is not enough to save the industry. It is too late for that. Time for the cooperatives is running out. Unfortunately.

Notes

1. We confine ourselves to the 1993 member states of the European Union.

2. As far as land-based activities are concerned.

3. Figures in this section are obtained from the following sources:
CEC - *The Agricultural Situation in the Community*. - Report, Brussels/ Luxembourg, var. years
Kamann Consultancy B.V. - *De toekomst van de zuivel*. - Groningen, 1993
LEI-DLO - *Bedrijfsuitkomsten en financiële positie*. - Den Haag, var. years
LEI-DLO/CBS - *Landbouwcijfers 1994*. - Den Haag/Voorburg, 1994
LEI - *Melkkoeien 1987*. - Den Haag, 1987
C.P.C.M. van der Hamsvoort and J.J. de Vlieger - *Recent developments and future trends in the Dutch dairy chain*. - unpublished paper, LEI-DLO, Den Haag, 1994

A.T. Kearney - *De markt gemist?.* - Amsterdam, 1994

4. The term 'sustainability' is *not* used in the environmental sense of non-polluting, but in the sense that the network is *economically* able to stay in existance for a long time.

5. Under pressure of EC rules this system is changing.

6. Also in the light of reduction in EC subsidies on products like butter, a high-fat containing product.

7. Recently, one of the large cooperatives - Friesland Frico Domo - decided that the price it would pay for the milk would equal the average of the 5 highest prices paid in the country.

8. Dutch dairy farmers receive among the highest price per kilogram for their milk, given the fat and protein contents (Kamann Consultancy, 1993). Even after standardizing the milk price, prices are quite high (see the debate about this in *The Boerderij*, 1993). Together with modern production techniques and size, it means that the Dutch dairy farmers have the highest incomes in the EU among dairy farmers.

9. A U.S firm such as Kraft is not explicitly included in the analysis; firms such as Kraft is participating in are included under their original name.

10. Sales, not production.

11. In a way, these strategies fall into the two basic strategies of Porter (1980) - cost leadership or price leadership - combined with spatial focus.

12. Especially when comparing companies in roughly the same area we may assume that price differences in the raw input milk are less than 4%.

13. Source: internal NIZO report EEG Z.0.0.3

14. Other Nestlé subsidiáries, like in the U.K., Denmark, Greece and Italy (Locatelli) have been excluded from this analysis.

15. In 1993/94: 4.3 bil. guilders turnover with 1.8 bil. kg milk.

16. In July 1992 ULN was taken over by Bongrain (AgD 2 July 1992).

17. In 1993/94, the turnover in Sweden reached 2.4 bil. guilders, using 2,135 mil kg milk in Sweden. Arla participates in German companies (AgD).

18. In 1993, Besnier's turnover reached 8 bil. guilders with production in 77 plants of which 11 are outside France (Belgium and Spain). 4.8 bil. liter milk was processed (AgD, 11 Jan 1995).

19. In the book year 1993/94, MD Foods had a turnover of more than 4 bil. guilders. The net result decreased to about 170 mil. guilders (AgD 23 Nov 1994).

20. A slightly different use of the statistics ('quick clustering'), resulted in 5 clusters, where the two largest firms of cluster 2 (Sodiaal and Dairy Crest) were clustered together with Campina-Melkunie (previously individual/cluster 5). The rest of cluster 2 was added to cluster 1.

21. Lower yield than cluster average (lowest of cluster).

22. Higher yield than other cluster members; higher turnover in value terms than other group members.

23. Lower yield then rest of cluster.

24. By statutory requirements, cooperatives in the Netherlands are obliged to accept - buy - the milk of their members; members are obliged to supply - sell - all their milk to the cooperative they are a member of.

25. We also see that the Dutch share in the EC-12 value went down from 13.5% to 8%.

26. Prices are current market prices. When constant prices are used, the Dutch absolute value in Hfl went down 28% in the 1980-1990 period.

27. This originates from the fact that in earlier days, the cooperatives were small village cooperatives where everybody was involved and one does not sack ones neighbour.

28. According to historical reviews.

29. Unfortunately, we cannot give the juicy details of the evidence that supports our observations in this paragraph.

30. Kamann Consultancy B.V. Various reports for the dairy industry.

31. From the paper industry, McKinsey, and two managers from Heineken. Recently the latter company unpleasantly had to become aware it had focused too long on a single product and ignored the changing tide in the market. It is

presently trying to correct that failure by taking over small but successful breweries and conducting massive promotional campaigns.

32. Source: see also the NIZO estimates in Table 2. This is supported by internal confidential information over the last 10 years.

33. '... I go checking out the reports - digging up the dirt; You get to meet all sorts in this line of work. Treachery and treason - there's always an excuse for it. And what have you got at the end of the day? What have you got to take away? A bottle of whisky and a new set of lies. Blinds on the windows and pain behind the eyes...', 1982, Dire Straits.

34. Although some local politicians claim that the infrastructure is lacking, this is not a fact but a perception.

35. World market prices can be lower than inside the EU because of the export-subsidy system of the EU; because of this, prices of milk (and therefore farmers' incomes) can be high with low world market prices.

36. A company like Unilever is in this contribution excluded from the dairy sector, even though it owns specialised cheese factories and is a large ice cream producer.

37. Source: Milch Marketing 4/1992, p. 54, quoting IMAGE.

38. Source: Deutsche Milchwirtschaft, 47/1991, p. 1565.

39. Source: Österreichische Milchwirtschaft 3, 7 Feb 1992, p. 8.

40. 'Groot Winkel Bedrijf'

41. 'Vrijwillig filiaal bedrijf'

42. Compare the horticultural situation in Kamann and Strijker, 1992.

43. In spite of this, the single largest retailer in the U.K. - Sainsbury - has a market share of 18.2% (De Boer, 1994, 44) while Dutch retailer Ahold has between 25 and 30%!

44. Sources: Agrarisch Dagblad, 9th May 1995.

45. From our own observations - using Government Stamping codes on packs - some retail chains had been supplied under private label for already some years (e.g. Nieuwe Weme), but apparantly this did not rupture the friendships.

46. According to the newspapers, Philip Morris subsidiary Kraft replaced Friesland in this deal.

47. While many dairy companies in Europe have attractive ice cream operations, Friesland sold its entire Thai operation including distribution to Unilever using the argument that it was not a core activity. Ice cream operations in Guam, Taiwan, Saoudi Arabia and Southern Korea were *not* sold however. Friesland Frico Domo's subsidiary Foremost was the leading icecream company in Thailand. In 1989 Unilever started the attack on Foremost's position and managed to beat the Frisian subsidiary within three years in the Bangkok area (AgD, 8 July 1992). FFD presently follows a strategy of having abandoned the European market and efforts are put in Asia (Vietnam). The question is whether the company is able to defend itself in *any* market when a real fight has to be put up, given the failure in Thailand to maintain a leading position there.

48. Food marketing journal *Distrifood* awarded second place for the 'most innovative poduct' to Campina-Melkunie (first was a suger-free Cola). In dairy products, Campina-Melkunie received first, second and third places, Danone (BSN) fifth and seventh places and Coberco sixth (no FFD..). In deepfreeze products Campina's - just sold off - division received a first place (AgD, 11 Oct 1994).

49. Lack of required investment to do the job properly was used as an excuse by Campina. Friesland claimed ice cream was not a core activity and therefore had to be sold.

50. In this context, it is interesting to follow the effects of the so called privatisation of the Milk Marketing Board, resulting in increased prices. Already, industry leaders warn of pull outs.

51. Friesland Frico Domo earns quite some money in so called 'TAROs': Technical Assistance and Royalties. The Technical Assisting part is mainly - as the term indicates - technical. Furthermore, these terms usually are used as a pre-tax cost for the foreign company or subsidiary and in fact are a licence fee or straightforward levy (compare Nestlé and its management (etc.) 'levy' on foreign subsidiaries, which is *negotiated* with the local tax inspector.

References

Agrarisch Dagblad, 1992 - present AT Kearny - *De markt gemist?* (Market failure?). - Amsterdam: AT Kearny, 1994

Axelsson, B. and G. Easton (eds.) - *Industrial Networks*. - London: Routledge, 1992

Boekema, F.W.M and D.J.F. Kamann (eds) - *Sociaal economische net werken* (Social Economic Networks). - Groningen: Wolters-Noordhoff, 1989

Boer, G.R. de - *De Britse levensmiddelensector in een veranderende wereld* (The British foodsector in a changing world). - Bureau Landbouwraad London, Dept. of Agriculture and Fishery, 1994

Camagni, R. and R. Rabellotti - *Footwear Production Systems in Italy: a Dynamic Comparative Analysis*. - Paper presented at the IV GREMI Meeting. - Grenoble, June 11th 1994

Capineri, C. and D.J.F. Kamann - *Synergy: concepts*. - Paper presented at the NECTAR Euroconference. - Espinho, Portugal, April 1995

Crevoisier, O. - *Industrie et région: les milieux innovateurs de l'Arc jurassien*. - Neuchâtel: EDES, 1993

Feka, V. and D.J.F. Kamann - The Greek dairy industry in the light of the European developments. - In: W. Biemans and P.N. Gauri (eds) / *Meeting the Challenges of New Frontiers*. - Groningen: IMP/Bedrijfskunde, 1994, p. 779-792

Hemsvoort, van der, C.P.C.M and J.J. de Vlieger - Recent Developments and Future Trends in the Dutch Dairy Chain. - *Draft mimeo LEI*, 1994

Jacobs, J, P. Boekolt and W. Zegveld - *De economische kracht van Nederland* : (The economic clout of the Netherlands). - TNO-Beleidsstudies, The Hague: Stichting Maatschappij en Onderneming (SMO 90-4), 1990

Johnson G. and K. Scholes - *Exploring corporate strategy*. - New York: Prentice Hall, 1989

Kamann, D.J.F. - Actoren in netwerken (Actors inside networks). - In: F.W.M. Boekema and D.J.F. Kamann (eds) / *Sociaal economische netwerken* (Social Economic Networks). - 1989, p. 29-84

Kamann, D.J.F. and F.W.M. Boekema - Netwerken: een introductie (Networks: an introduction). - In: F.W.M. Boekema and D.J.F. Kamann (eds) / *Sociaal economische netwerken* (Social Economic Networks). - 1989, p. 1-8

Kamann Consultancy B.V., authors: Kamann, D.J.F, W. Meiers and D. Strijker - *De toekomst van de zuivel,* (the future of the dairy industry). - Groningen/Utrecht: Kamann Consultancy/Voedingsbond FNV, 1993

Kamann, D.J.F. and D. Strijker - Mechanisms of coordination in the Dutch horticultural complex. - In: *European Review of Agricultural Economics,* 19 (1992) 393-416

Kamann, D.J.F. - Barriers in Business Networks.- In: R. Ratti and S. Reichman (eds). - 1993, pp. 65-102

Kamann, D.J.F. - *The good things out of bottlenecks*. - Paper presented at the NECTAR Workshop Cluster 3. - Molde, Norway, September 1994

Kamann, D.J.F. - Policies for dynamic innovative networks in innovative milieux. - In: R. gordon, D. Maillat and R. Ratti / *Milieux innovateurs*. - GREMI publication, 1995

Kamann, D.J.F. and D. Strijker - The Spatial Differentiation in the Organisation of the European Pork Market. - In: J. van Dijk and R. Florax (eds.) / *Nieuwe Ideeën in Nederlands Ruimtelijk Onderzoek*. - RSA Nederland/GEO Press: Groningen, 1994a, p. 135-148

Kamann, D.J.F. and D. Strijker - *The European dairy industry in turmoil*. - Paper presented at the 34th European RSA Congress. - Groningen, August 1994b

McGee, J. and H. Thomas - Strategic groups: theory, research and taxonomy. - In: *Strategic Management Journal*, 7 (1986) 141-160

Meester, G. and D. Strijker - *Het Europese landbouwbeleid voorbij de scheids lijn van zelfvoorziening* (The European agricultural policy beyond self reliance). - WRR V46, The Hague: Staatsuitgeverij, 1985

Porter, M.E., - *Competitive Strategy: Techniques for analysing industries and competitors*. - Free Press, 1980

Porter, M.E. - *Competitive Advantage*. - Free Press, 1985

Porter, M.E. - The competitive advantage of nations. - In: *Harvard Business Review,* March-April, 1990, p. 73-93; as book: London: Macmillan

Ratti, R. and S. Reichman (eds) - *Theory and practice of transborder cooperation*. - Basel: Helbing & Lichtenhahn, 1993

Strijker, D. - Structural development towards a modern agricultural sector, 1880-1985. - In: W. Huizinga and D. Strijker / Two lectures on the historical development of Dutch agriculture, 1600-1985. - The Hague: LEI, *Mededelingen*, 351, 1986

Wever, E. - *Afzender: ccFriesland* (Sender:ccFriesland). - Leeuwarden: ccFriesland., 1988

Chapter 5

J. KUIJPER, S.R. MALTHA[1]

INDUSTRY COMPETITIVE ANALYSIS IN THE NETHERLANDS
A practitioner's view

1. Introduction

In 1980, Michael Porter metaphorically and literally crossed the
Charles River in Cambridge (M.A.), bringing together the traditions of
Harvard economics with those of its Business School (Kay, 1991, 58).
Since then, his *Competitive Strategy* (1980) is a well-known textbook on
industry analysis and on the influence of the business environment on
firms' profitability. Over the years, Porter enriched his view on long-term
sustainable competitiveness of certain national industries by closely
investigating the broader industry and institutional setting. This experience enabled the author to take a step over the oceans to explain the
competitiveness of nations (Porter, 1990). Fortunately, he did not land in
the Netherlands, leaving ample space for incumbents' research on its
competitiveness (see e.g. Jacobs, 1990; EZ, 1990).

In this chapter, three Dutch sector studies are presented which are
based on the method Porter has introduced in *The Competitive Advantage
of Nations*. The case-studies form part of a broader collection of studies
on Dutch manufacturing and services industries, done at the TNO Centre
for Technology and Policy Studies. The selection of cases supports the
two objectives of this chapter. First, we discuss the applicability of
Porter's industry competitive analysis on the issue of national competitiveness. Two points are addressed: the cluster chart and the 'diamond'
model. Which elements are covered, which get extra attention in the case-
studies? Second, to what extent can industry success be explained by the
determinants of Porter's 'diamond' model?

Three different sector studies are used as exemplary cases of
industries in the Netherlands: the plastics processing industry, the dredging industry (including Flanders) and the telecommunications equipment
industry. The level of analysis differs per case. The case of the plastics
processing industry is most like a business school textbook analysis with
respect to its scope, though within plastics processing the range of
materials and process technologies is large. The second case deals with
three vertically related sectors which form a well-developed value system.
Finally, the third case concentrates on the telecom equipment industry,
but situates this sector in its wider context of related telecom services. All

three case-studies are examples of industry analysis commissioned by industry associations, intermediaries and ministerial bodies.

2. Methodological remarks and interpretations

2.1 Definitions and statistical sources

In *The Competitiveness of Nations* a quantitative and a qualitative method has been applied to determine competitiveness. First, Porter calculates the relative export performance of industrial products and services by comparing the value of gross export of a sector in a given year with the national average. This is done on the basis of UN Standard Industrial Trade Statistics, rev. II (UN, annual). The result is a limited number of competitive product groups. Subsequently, these are classified in a chart involving 16 *clusters* of industries. Following Porter's definition, a cluster is nothing more than an aggregated construct of different successful complementary industries. Porter states that 'the basic unit of analysis for understanding national advantage is the industry. Nations succeed not in isolated industries, however, but in *clusters* of industries connected through vertical and horizontal relationships' (Porter, 1990, 73). A successful cluster links several industries. Within such a cluster, one or more networks of related firms will exist. However, in his cluster-concept Porter does not pay much attention to actual inter-firm relation-ships. Our interpretation suggests that cluster and network are different things. One could even postulate that a cluster cannot be successful without the existence of several interrelated networks of firms. Also, other organisations may form part of such networks, e.g. organizations from the knowledge infrastructure.

The cluster chart follows the general scheme of production from upstream, intermediate level to end-use industries. Within a cluster, four interrelated industries are presented: primary goods, machinery for production, specialty inputs and associated services. The advantage of such a classification is the assignment of the service industries to their manufacturing base. For example, wholesale trade in beer belongs to the Food/Beverage-cluster. The more that export products of all four industry categories are presented in a cluster, the deeper a cluster is specialized in a limited range of products. The larger the number of export product groups classified, the broader the cluster is developed.

This statistical analysis leads to the conclusion that, according to Porter's definition, in the Netherlands few, if not only one, widely and deeply evolved cluster exists: the Food/Beverage-cluster (Jacobs, et al, 1990, 82). All other clusters lack a particular category of industry. The most striking phenomenon is the relative absence of the machinery industry, with the notable exception of the dredging equipment industry and the food processing machinery industry. The export performance of the Netherlands shows a relative specialization in volume-driven process industries like the food processing and chemical manufacturing industries. A comparison with German export figures leads to the interesting conclusion that Dutch and German industries are complementary (Bloemen, et al., 1993, 14). For example, Dutch food processing, paper production and chemical industries are major customers of the German machinery sectors.

The cluster chart boundaries have been rather influenced by the availability of international statistics. Several related product groups have been split rather arbitrarily. For example, in the Dutch case 'cut flowers' and 'live bulbs' have been put into the Personal cluster, while they undeniably belong to the Food/Beverage-cluster, as products of the greenhouse horticulture industry. More criticisms with respect to the interpretation of the statistics are documented by Jacobs et al. (1992).

Subsequently, in Porter's own research the statistical picture is made up of a qualitative analysis focusing on the factors determining export performance. This is the phase for which the 'diamond' model is developed. It is here that the basis for the export performance of certain product groups is specified by analysing the real linkages between industries. This is the phase in which the difference between cluster and network becomes messy. Porter does not refer to both of these terms, but only mentions related and supporting industries in the 'diamond' model. Putting real relationships as the basis for clustering instead of statistical industry or product definitions enables the researcher to identify interrelated economic entities and to construct a cluster chart. This can lead to a different configuration of industries, better reflecting the inter-industry strengths at the national level.

2.2 The 'diamond' model

The internal cohesion of and the actual development of networks within these clusters can only be studied through monographic research. Porter has developed his 'diamond' framework to structure the specific configuration of factors which make an industry 'tick'. As his model is discussed elsewhere in this book, we will not repeat it here, but rather focus on the specific emphasis we place upon the determinants of the 'diamond'. First, within the *factor conditions*, we think the continuous upgrading of advanced factor conditions is most important to determine the dynamics of an industry. Upgrading strategies may very well focus on several issues, such as technological innovation, market expansion or re-organisation. What matters is whether upgrading takes place. Another important focus is the strategic intent of upgrading: is it mainly directed at cost-leadership or are features of differentiation taken into account? In other words, do firms merely compete on the same product basis through achieving lower production and service costs, or do they compete on the basis of product and/or service difference? As for industries in the western industrialised countries, Porter stresses differentiation as the optimal generic strategy in the long term, because runner-up countries elsewhere in the world enjoy far lower costs especially for labour inputs. The delicate balance, however, between cost leadership and differentiation differs per industry. The biggest threat to firms is that without strategic intent, they will be stuck in the middle.

Continuing with the *demand conditions*, we follow Porter in stress-ing the qualitative features of home demand. Are there any demanding customers? In what product features? In what way do national demand patterns reflect those worldwide, so that learning experiences at the home market can be exploited through export? Third, within *related and supporting industries*, the presence is stressed of suppliers and service providers which help an industry create advantages. Especially the ability to exploit economies of scope in export marketing, common technologies and facility sharing is deemed of special interest. Such strategic combina-tions of value adding activities require well developed inter-firm relation-ships, preferably in networks of different kinds. With respect to the fourth determinant, *firm strategy, structure and rivalry*, Porter bundles 'structure' and 'conduct' variables from the 'Structure-conduct-performance' model of 'Industrial Organization' (see Scherer and Ross, 1990). Indeed, the intensity of competition within the regulatory regime is important. But competitors should also be able to cooperate on certain issues which yield mutual benefits, like collective research or joint export marketing. The presence of cooperative behaviour is partly influenced by the business culture. The balance between rivalry and the willingness of competitors to co-operate on mutually beneficial topics is often non-exist-ent. In our case-studies, we find this inability (and unwillingness) of SMEs to invest in joint innovative projects a major obstacle leading to structural inertia. Porter does not pay much attention to this phenomenon in his 'diamond' model.

Finally, the *government* (at all levels) is important for its encouragement effect. Do regulative and administrative actions impede innovation and change in the industry system or do they support it? The only element in the 'diamond' model which is of little direct help in explaining competitiveness is the *'chance'* factor. Not so much the given phenomenon itself is important, but the strategic response it evokes. In our interpretation, the 'diamond' configuration at a certain stage leads to apparent strengths and weaknesses of firms related to factor and demand conditions and related and supporting industries. It also illuminates threats and opportunities that a sector faces. A 'SWOT'-table synthesizes these findings, focusing the response needed from the actors involved.

On the basis of export performance and the geographic scale of production, several industries have been categorized (Jacobs *et.al.*, 1990, 70-71). This is shown in Table 1.

Industries which deserve a 'diamond nomination' in Porter's work fall within the cell bottom-left of Table 1: production takes place in a small region and the firms operate globally. Top-left, industries have global production facilities and face worldwide markets. Such industries have no strong national bindings and become 'footloose', accordingly. Traditional factor advantages alone are not sufficient any more to keep these global industries within the country. Porter therefore emphasizes the presence of more advanced production factors like specialised personnel, supporting industries and adequate research institutes. Such advanced factors enlarge the dependence of global industries from other actors in a cluster and improve the attractiveness of a region as a location for such industries. Bottom-right domestic services and industries are situated, exclusively operating in local markets. Since these industries do not export, Porter does not classify them as competitive sectors. Top-right, only industries with multi-domestic markets operate, like for example sweet manufacturing industries, only slightly adapting their products to local flavours.

160   *Kuijper, Maltha*

Table 1. Geographic scale of production versus relevant markets

Production \ Market	WORLD	EUROPE	NETHERLANDS
WORLD	LP-records Telecom equipment Shipping services		
EUROPE		Plastics processing	
NW-EUROPE	Marine suppliers	Heavy trucks Polymers	
NETHERLANDS	Dairy processing machinery Industrial textiles Yachts (top segment) Greenhouse construction	Dairy products Road transport	Dairy engineering services Yachts (lower segment)
REGIONAL	Cocoa Cut flowers Dredging	Copiers	Construction

Source: Jacobs et al., 1990, p. 70-71.

    The case-studies to be discussed in the next paragraphs are represented in Table 1. Their classification in this table is a result of analysis using the 'diamond' model for real firm activities and relevant markets. These sectors also belong to three different original 'Porter'-clusters in the cluster chart: plastics processing in the upstream chemical cluster and telecommunications equipment manufacturing and the dredging industries, respectively in the intermediate Telecommunications and Transport clusters.

    All three show different industry playing fields with different competitive positions based on the relevant market. With respect to the industries belonging to the dredging cluster, research & development, equipment manufacturing, specialised suppliers and dredging contractors are all regionally concentrated while their relevant market is global. The second phase represents an industry with still growing markets. Though the plastics processing industry can be found all over the world, the sourcing and sales coverage of the Dutch sector is mainly oriented to Continental Europe. The telecommunication equipment industry is a typical global industry.

3. The plastics processing industry

3.1 Definition of the industry

The plastics processing industry in the Netherlands is a relatively young industrial activity, expanding at the end of the 1950s and early 1960s. Nowadays some 1,200 firms belong to the industry, with an annual turnover of more than NLG 7.5 billion and approximately 28,000 employees in 1992 (CBS, 1993). The export performance of 'plastic products' in general is strong: 42% of production in 1991 (CBS, 1993). Yet, the import of plastic products is even larger than the export. In the cluster chart, such product groups do not get a mark for competitiveness, because foreign competition in domestic markets is stronger than the national presence abroad. Unfortunately, in the UN international trade statistics 'plastic products' is not subdivided into specific product groups, making it difficult to assess industry strengths and specialisations on the basis of these data.

Another question is where to demarcate industry boundaries? For example, many producers of end products in the machinery, toys and electronics manufacturing industries are also involved in plastics processing, but they cannot be identified as such in the official statistics, because they are labelled according to other end product features. Moreover, plastics processing involves various process technologies, such as injection and blow moulding, extrusion, spraying techniques, and various virgin materials. This diversity in production methods can lead to extreme specialisation in narrow product niches, but also to multi-technology-based competition in the same broader market segments. A final difficulty for industry segmentation is that injection-moulding machinery enables firms to switch moulds, giving firms swift access to other product markets. In a sense, these are problems customary for supply industries delivering semi-finished products for downstream assembling industries. As we will see further on, the functions such suppliers perform in the supply chain to OEM-firms (Original Equipment Manufacturers) are crucial for the upgrading potential of this industry.

The Dutch turnover accounts for 6% of the EC-wide turnover in plastics processing. The number of plastics processors in the European Community is estimated at 17,000, with an average firm size of 33 employees. The Netherlands have relatively more small-scale producers (< 20 employees) than Germany and France. These small-scale firms mostly act as general jobbers, processing rather simple plastic products. Less than 10% of the industry population designs, produces and sells an end product to the consumer of business-to-business market. This rather underdeveloped specialization pattern is one of the major problems the Dutch plastics processing industry faces.

3.2 Demand conditions

The market demand for plastic products is still increasing in the industrialised world, including in the Netherlands. The Dutch demand pattern shows two major market segments: semi-finished materials and components for civil construction and industrial packaging. Especially in the last market segment, the Dutch industrial and transport specialization is reflected: most of the plastic packaging is used for consumer food and for all kinds of freight containers, buckets and bottles. The export-intensive dairy and food processing industry and the many logistical centres therefore are major customers. Sometimes it is even possible to find a specific cultural characteristic which led to an export niche. For example, according to Dutch producers the development of light domes was stimulated by the architectural interest in the ray dispersion of light. Generally, however, the Dutch demand pattern is of little help for the plastics processing industry, because high-quality professional demand is relatively lacking. In recent years, increasing environmental awareness is even threatening the sustained market growth for plastic packaging and construction material. Such a threat, however, also provokes plastics processing companies to find new and better packaging concepts, leading to less plastic household waste.

3.3 Firm strategy, structure and rivalry

The Dutch market is competitive in most product segments. The majority of the firms are still family-owned and rather small compared to other countries. Competition is strongly oriented to cost-leadership and flexibility, eager as all jobbers are to fill machinery capacity to a maximum. Entry barriers are low, which puts even more pressure on prices. Short-termism is dominant.

The larger plastics processing firms are more inclined to pursue a strategy based on product differentiation. Many of these have had prosperous growth over a number of years in a rather isolated market niche, in which they could develop experience for export. Now that they are facing European competition both in export and home markets, many still struggle with relatively smaller scales in production and sales networks.

Cooperation among competitors is scarce but increasing. The only industry association providing a common platform is the Dutch Federation for Plastics (NFK), organizing 25% of all firms. Fear for an irrational rejection of plastic as a suitable material for a range of products is providing common ground for cooperation, such as in the case of the plastic packaging producers. A more pro-active cooperation with customers upstream in the production chain on e.g. technical innovation is still minimal.

3.4 Factor conditions and upgrading

After World War II, when the plastics processing industry took off in Europe, the Netherlands offered a favourable location for production. Especially in the former textile areas of Twente and Brabant, many plastics processing activities started because of the available low-cost employment. Interestingly, formal education in plastics processing technology was lacking for many years. It was mainly learned 'on the job', while for the large bulk chemical industry a very good public educational system had been created at all levels. The plastics processing industry put great effort into bringing plastics technology into the public technical education. Only at the end of the 80s did these efforts start delivering sufficient qualified plastics processing engineers at the polytechnic level.

With respect to the scientific infrastructure, a similar trajectory occurred. Most research went into the material aspects of plastics, not the processing and design technologies. Within the research on new materials in the semi-public TNO Plastics and Rubber Research Institute, research was biased towards composites, mainly for the benefit of Fokker and some defence and aerospace suppliers. Only the plastics manufacturers with their own application labs and Philips - for internal use - invested heavily in a wider range of processing and application technologies. Diffusion of that knowledge to SMEs is a difficult process, due to the very different business cultures in the scientific bodies and the manufacturing firms. Educational and vocational training institutes, especially at the polytechnic level, try to bridge these differences.

The result of this historical development has been rather negative for the plastics processing industry at large. Contrary to Germany, where plastics processors were always heavily involved in research for the automotive industry, in the Netherlands only the very recent environmental awareness has raised public support for research on plastics processing technologies. Since 1989, work is being done on process simulation and plastic recycling, giving firms the opportunity to tap into university research.

3.5 Related and supporting industries

The plastics processing industry has always largely relied on the plastic material manufacturers which upheld large aftersales services on application techniques. At the same time, the Dutch machinery industry for plastics processing is almost lacking, with Stork as the exception. Also with respect to moulds, the Dutch plastics processing industry has been rather dependent on foreign supply. Hence, we conclude that the cluster of related and supporting industries in the Netherlands is rather thin.

A major structural weakness for the Dutch plastics processing industry is the absence of a strong domestic group of industrial OEM-firms, sufficient in number and active in various high-quality markets. Philips has its own plastics processing division. Copier-manufacturers like Océ and Rank Xerox indeed have national suppliers for plastic components, but their contribution is small. All major players in Europe in plastics processing have strong domestic industrial customers. In Germany and France, this is most visible around the automotive industry. That is why the few Dutch-based OEM-final assemblers in the transport equipment industry, DAF Trucks, Scania, NedCar, largely contract component suppliers from these countries. This competitive disadvantage hinders the transition of the large 'jobber' segment in the Dutch plastics processing industry to more value-adding activities. The difference in average firm size compared with the German and French plastics processing industry may also have a negative affect on co-supplier involvement.

In this respect it is striking that Dutch based plastic material manufacturers like DSM, GE, Dow and Akzo Nobel indeed are successfully integrated in such European industrial supplier networks. Through larger developments projects, often supported by Eureka or EC R&D programmes, these material producers have direct access to the larger European OEM-firms, passing over the plastics processing industry. This phenomenon raises the interesting question whether in the upstream Porter-clusters economies of scale in production and R&D is the major criterion for joining industrial networks, often of an international character.

3.6 Conclusions

The plastics processing industry still profits from sustained growth in very heterogeneous markets for plastic products, enabling many small companies to compete in small market niches. But growing European competition now puts even larger companies under pressure to rethink market position and build up their own technological competences. In terms of the 'diamond' concept serious shortcomings are identified both in the presence of the related and supporting industries and in the interaction with the public knowledge infrastructure. Apparently, the mere presence of advanced production factors (like public R&D bodies) is not enough. Close interaction between industry and supporting advanced institutions is a necessary second condition. It is to be expected that the markets for plastic products will become more mature and integrated, which will lead to less autonomous growth. Our analysis shows that the current 'diamond' factors of the Dutch plastics processing industry are not strong enough to create competitive advantage in the future.

The case exemplifies the usefulness of the 'diamond' concept to explain a lack of competitive advantage in a specific industry. It is a matter of degree whether our emphasis on the public knowledge infrastructure in order to improve the industry's position is in line with Porter or not. Chapter 3 assesses the role of this infrastructure more fully.

4. The dredging industry

4.1 Definition of the industry

From the look of it, dredging is a rather simple activity including surveying, digging and transporting sand, mud and/or rock from one location to another. The term is predominantly used for water-based mud clearing. Dredging is applied for maintaining access in water transport routes, for mining of construction material or as an intermediary process for coast, harbour and shore protection and construction.

The century-long battle against the water in the Low Countries (Flanders and Holland) has enabled local craftsmanship to grow into a competitive industry with global markets, but a very regionally organised production node. We prefer to discuss the structure of this industry in terms of its *cluster*, including the dredging contractors, the specialized shipyards and the marine supply industry. There are approximately 50 contractors in the Netherlands, of which four have worldwide operations.

These are accompanied by two Belgian global players. Together, these six have a share of 70% of the 'open' international dredging market, with an annual turnover of NLG 3 billion. Because of the nautical character of dredging, the production of dredging equipment is largely a shipyard assembly activity, in which less than 10 yards worldwide are specialized. Of these, IHC Holland is the world market leader for custom-made complex dredging vessels and equipment with a global market share of 50% in newly built equipment. Other, smaller Dutch shipyards are specialised in standard dredging equipment in smaller performance ranges. Finally, the marine equipment industry has a more heterogene character and its turnover is unknown. Almost all the special dredging components are either produced by IHC or by local mechanical engineering companies. In total, around 10,000 employees work within the dredging cluster.

4.2 Demand conditions

Historically, coast protection and the generation of new land (polders) commissioned by Dutch government bodies accounted for the majority of work. During the end of the 19th and the first half of the 20th century, major harbour infrastructural works in the Netherlands were always followed by similar large-scale projects in other countries, thus enabling the industry to exploit what it had learned at home. The Dutch Ministry of Transport and Public Works, especially the Department of Public Works, had always played a crucial role as prime customer, critical to price and performance. But it also invited contractors to design new working methods, especially in the large-scale Delta works in the period 1960-1975. This specific project was also very important for the shipyards, for it involved the construction of specially designed work ships.

In recent years, the role of the Netherlands as a demanding home market has decreased. The international dredging companies or their subsidiary civil engineering units are also active in assisting foreign governments and port authorities in their demand articulation. The dredging market has acquired more features of large-scale engineering projects, such as the importance of export credit schemes and strategic joint ventures with national incumbents in 'closed' markets. Of major importance for large-scale infrastructure projects, such as the Hong Kong Airport project, is 'picking the winning' consortium. For this, excellent contacts are necessary with other globally operating civil engineers and contractors active in subsequent phases of construction works.

4.3 Firm strategy, structure and rivalry

Competition among the dredging contractors clearly has two sides. In the Netherlands, the global players share the market with many small domestic competitors which keep prices sharp. Moreover, there is a fierce competition between the four biggest Dutch dredging contractors and the Belgian two for the prestigious main contractorships of large dredging projects. The other side of the argument is that worldwide the global players often are involved in facility-sharing and combined activities. So, cut-throat price competition is avoided among the tight oligopolists. They have learned from the meagre period of 1980-1985 in which several smaller international dredging companies merged into the current six. From the point of financial soundness, it is more important for contractors to have a long-term optimal capacity utilization rate with a reasonable price than a short-term maximum capacity load at peak prices. The power of the government as customer vis-à-vis the contractors is also rather large.

Horizontal co-operation among the contractors and vertical co-operation with suppliers, shipyards and government clients are institutionalised in formal and informal relations. This is especially the case for pre-competitive subjects of interest, conditional to the well-being of the whole dredging cluster. For example: vocational training, recruitment of work force, collective technology programmes and the industry's image.

4.4 Factor conditions and upgrading

Traditional factor conditions

The traditional joke about the Dutch that 'God created the world, except Holland' is undeniably true for dredging. Large parts of the Netherlands could not exist without their protection against rivers and the sea. Proper maintenance of dams, dikes and waterways is needed to guarantee the safety of the country. For more than five centuries, dredging has been a crucial element in keeping the water back. It is a craftsmanship that is indissolubly related to living in the Netherlands. There are several reasons why the dredging industry developed a strong home-base. The location by the sea and the commercial spirit of the Dutch people allowed the country to develop a sophisticated trade and transport infrastructure. The realisation of the 'Nieuwe Waterweg' in 1870, the draining of the Zuyder Zee in the 1930s, the reconstruction of Rotterdam harbour after World War II, the Delta works in the 1960s and

1970s and smaller coastal protection projects created an excellent domestic learning environment for the dredging industry. These works allowed the dredging industry to export the acquired expertise all over the world.

In Flanders (Belgium), it has been the construction of the large harbours in Antwerp and Zeebrugge, and the continuous maintenance of the Schelde-estuary that created the opportunity for several dredging contractors to build up their knowledge and expertise.

Advanced factor conditions: education and research and upgrading strategies

The dredging industry has at its disposal a tailor-made education system. In the Netherlands, specialized training is available at all education levels. There is much interaction between the industry and the education system, which guarantees a good connection between the two. The level of expertise in the field of dredging processes and design and construction of dredging equipment is a clear competitive advantage for the dredging cluster. Nowadays, joint research is permanently done by the 'Combinatie Speurwerk Baggerwerk', which combines expertise from the government, dredging contractors and various laboratories. Dredging-related research is also being conducted at Delft University of Technology and at individual firms like HBG, Ballast Nedam, Boskalis and IHC Holland.

The firms in the dredging cluster have developed several strategies to improve their competitive position through upgrading of production factors. Many firms are involved in product and process development. Most developments concentrate on the issue of faster dredging at greater depth. The weather, the tide and the characteristics of the soil to be moved make dredging a challenge against natural forces. Many product and process developments try to improve the level of precision of the dredging process and to compensate for these difficult production conditions. The vessels that have recently been built are larger than ever, and have been equipped with advanced positioning systems. Process innovations relate to the use of information technology. IHC is also known for its stimulating production organisation, allowing for job rotation and minimum hierarchy.

The dredging cluster follows a clear differentiation strategy in which technological sophistication is the main element. Relative cost disadvantages are made up for by excellent project performance in excavation, within sharp time limits. The second business strategy of the dredging cluster is internationalisation. All larger dredging contractors invest in entering new geographic markets to avoid over-dependence on a relatively small and mature home market and for protection from continental business cycles. Marine suppliers, a few specialized shipyards and the dredging contractors all regard geographical diversification as an important risk-spreading business strategy.

4.5 Related and supporting industries

Upgrading of the activities of the dredging cluster not only takes place because of the innovative attitude of the firms within the cluster, but is also induced by related industries. Offshore oil and gas operators, for example, as customers of suppliers and shipyards, have provided strong impetus for innovation in material technology and logistical operations in the dredging industry. High quality and safety standards in the offshore end market enable equipment manufacturers and shipping companies that work for both dredging and offshore markets to exploit economies of scope.

Another transfer of know-how comes from Dutch civil engineers and contractors' firms and public bodies in the field of coastal and civil construction. Here, the connecting node is collaborative contract research to a select group of specialised laboratories, among which is Delft Hydraulics. This laboratory is also one of the partners of the joint research initiative of the dredging industry: the 'Combinatie Speurwerk Baggerwerk'.

Part of the innovative strength of the dredging cluster is explained by shared cultural backgrounds and the same language, a genuine entry barrier for foreign competitors! The fact that the large contractors would meet each other frequently at large international dredging projects soon created a new type of 'family tie' which is quite as strong as the former regional one. The strength of the dredging cluster is definitely related to a combination of several of these cultural factors.

4.6 Conclusions

Strong historical roots, commitment to technological development, a skilled work force and global operations in a niche market give the dredging cluster in the Netherlands and Flanders a competitive advantage. New opportunities will arise, both in increasing productivity and in capturing new demand. Threats remain vivid. Concentration within the small group of international dredging contractors may dampen internal competition. Low-cost dredging contractors in Southeast Asia may upgrade themselves and attract new vessel and equipment manufacturers.

The cyclical nature of the dredging market needs a clear response of the whole cluster to avoid another round of harsh restructuring when demand sharply declines. A challenge for contractors and equipment manufacturers is to exploit dredging expertise and technology in related markets through careful diversification. It remains to be seen whether such a process will be one in which the Dutch and Flanders' companies act on their own as niche players or as part of bigger foreign building conglomerates. The prospects, though, for an independent course look good.

The Porter concept proved to be quite relevant in describing the industry's competitive position on the world market. The strong cultural (including language) identity of the Dutch/Flanders cluster shows an element of networking which is discussed more extensively in chapter 4. There the conclusion is drawn that the 'diamond' model lacks an indepth analysis of networking relations to be able to understand the importance of clusters better.

5. The telecommunications equipment industry

5.1 Introduction

The telecommunications equipment industry must be seen as a part of a larger telecommunications cluster. The equipment industry is just one chain in the telecom cluster. Its existence is so tightly linked to market success of the services provided by the installed telecom infrastructures, that we cannot make an assessment on competitiveness of the industry without paying attention to the rest of the cluster, especially the telecom services. Therefore we will give a short overview of the performance of the whole cluster, before focusing on the equipment industry.

The telecommunications market in the Netherlands is about NLG 16 billion in size and the industry produces slightly over NLG 15 billion, divided among the segments telecom equipment (switches, transmission, radio equipment, terminals and components), cable, installation and services. The service market is five times as big as the equipment market and is responsible for 85% of the total value added. In total, the Dutch telecommunications industry gives direct employment to 50,000 persons and indirect employment to 10,000 persons in supporting industries. Furthermore, telecommunications has become a cross-cutting technology, a point of intersection where many other industries such as computing, industrial automation, consumer electronics, media, publishing and banking come together. New developments in digital, optical and microwave technology not only lead to convergence of telecom infrastructures - *the Electronic Information Highway* - but of industries as well[2]. We expect the telecommunications industry to expand to a huge multimedia cluster.

Table 2. Key figures of the telecom-cluster

billion NLG	produc-tion	market	trade balance	value added	% GDP	employment
tel.equipment	2.2	3.0	- 0.8	1.0	0.20	8500
cable	0.4	0.4		0.2	0.04	2000
installation	0.4	0.4		0.2	0.04	4000
services	11.7	11.7		8.2	1.52	34500
total	14.7	15.5		9.6	1.8	49000
supplying industry	4.5					10000

Source: H. Schaffers, S. Maltha & G. Fahrenkrog (1993), p. 1-5, 4-28.

The importance for the Dutch economy can be derived from the percentage share of total value added of the telecom value chain in the total gross domestic product. A share of almost 2% can be compared with industries like food, electronics and public utilities (Schaffers, Maltha and Fahrenkrog, 1993, 1-7). The Dutch telecom equipment industry is domi-nated by five (mainly foreign) multinationals: AT&T, Siemens, Ericsson, Philips and Alcatel. The latter, however, has chosen the Netherlands to locate its holding, for fiscal reasons. In 1991, PTT Telecom was respon-sible for almost all service revenues (NLG 10.1 billion, due to its monop-oly positions on most of the service markets). National network services for voice telephony is the main sub-market and will remain monopolized until 1998. Especially in the markets for Value Added Services (NLG 0.5 billion in 1993), international voice telephony, datacommunications and mobile services, competition is increasing.

To examine international competitiveness Porter uses the share in world export. If we look at the top-50 of best exporting Dutch industries, the telecommunications industry is not on the list[3]. To determine the level of competitiveness of the Dutch telecom industry, we are dependent on international trade statics. These are available for telecom equipment

but not for services. Therefore, we concentrate on the Dutch telecommunications equipment industry[4].

Table 3. Trade balance for Dutch telecom equipment (mln Ecu)

	1988	1989	1990	1991
switching equipment	77,596	100,898	1,501,265	25,129
transmission equipment	-59,931	-50,171	-65,641	-24,654
radio equipment	-5,262	-4,966	-10,706	-8,800
telecom components	-47,338	-50,078	-41,261	-39,656
telecom terminals	-302,279	-335,243	-295,841	-256,858
total equipment	-337,214	-3,339,560	-263,184	-304,839

Source: Eurostat-Comext / DG XIII.

The trade balance for telecom equipment - defined as the difference
between the market value of exported and imported goods - shows us a
structural deficit of 0.3 billion ECU in the late 1980s and early 1990s.
Only for switching equipment was a surplus realised, for which AT&T
NSI was almost completely responsible. in contrast to the Dutch deficit,
the European Union generated a surplus of 0.5 billion ECU in 1991 and
0.75 billion Ecu in 1992. The Dutch world-export share for telecom
equipment was 0.4% in 1990[5]. In comparison with Jacobs' top-50,
telecommunications is not very impressive in terms of export share, even
if we were to include the service market[6].

On the basis of the (relatively poor) trade statistics on telecommunications, and our study, we can draw some initial conclusions. On the
one hand this Dutch industry is a very small player on a global market,
with competitive threats to its relatively weak equipment industry. But on
the other hand its importance for the national economy is substantial. The
tension between these findings is one of the reasons that often other than
world-export shares are used in internationally comparative telecom
studies as an indicator for industry performance. In Porter's case, export
shares were used for mainly practical reasons, in order to make consistent
comparisons on a global basis possible. Nevertheless, it seems to be a
good instrument to identify globally competitive industries, independent
of their absolute size. Using this indicator, often less obvious, or less

well-known industries appear to be competitive success stories. However, the availability of trade statistics on services remains in many cases an obstacle. Therefore, other indicators for economic performance of industries have been used in recent telecom studies, summarized in the table below.

Table 4. Indicators for telecom industries' performance

- value added as % of GDP
- market revenues as % of GDP
- market growth
- productivity growth
- tariffs
- investments as % of total national investments
- degree of digitalization
- degree of liberalization

Source: H. Schaffers and G. Knieps, 1994.

For the Dutch telecommunications industry, the trade figures show a structural trade deficit for equipment. Moreover, the equipment segment suffers from increased competition. Its competitive strength has become weaker and it does not play a significant role in the world telecom equipment market. The reasons behind this are analysed below.

5.2 Demand conditions

The equipment industry is operating on a global market. A strong home market is, in the case of the Netherlands, only of little importance. The national market is too small for scale-economies in the development of national standards. But a well-developed home market can normally contribute to the nation's industry competence. PTT Telecom is the most important buyer and its sophisticated demand stimulates the production of high-quality equipment. However, PTT Telecom is among the smaller buyers in Europe.

The export of equipment is concentrated on Germany (16%) and Spain (13%). According to Porter, extraordinary intensive export to neighbouring countries can be seen as a relative competitive weakness. Attempts to penetrate the advanced North American and Japanese markets have been unsuccessful as yet. New services are the driving force behind new demand for equipment. With the introduction of competition in services, new potential buyers will enter the national market. New operators have to build their networks and will create a new national demand for infrastructure and terminals. We can think of mobile communications (GSM, two licensees), mobile datanetworks (Traxys and Mobitex, already operational) or new networks for public safety services (TETRA). But also the provision of new interactive services and in the future telephony via CATV, requires interconnection and upgrading of the local cable networks.

5.3 Firm strategy, structure and rivalry

The Dutch telecom equipment industry is very concentrated and completely dominated by five multinationals, of which only one is Dutch. The concentration ratio is much higher than the average in Europe and much higher than the world average.

Table 5. Concentration ratio's for telecom equipment production in 1989

	World market	European market	Dutch market
C 5	32%	65%	85%
C 10	49%	81%	-
C 20	62%	92%	-

Source: Eurostrategies (Estel)/STB-TNO.

AT&T NSI, Ericsson, Siemens, Alcatel and Philips were responsible for 85% of the Dutch equipment production. Under pressure of increasing capital requirements, concentration is expected to increase even more in the next years. Higher investments are needed for the development of management systems and software in order to control ever increasing telecommunications networks, but also for fibre in the local loop (the last part of the network connection to the home), as well as for mobile and satellite communications. The necessity for strategic alliances has been fed by the increase in R&D- expenditures, but also by the wish to penetrate new markets. Recently it has been announced that AT&T Netwerk Services in Huizen and Philips PKI in Germany will start a joint-venture for the production of base-stations and terminals for GSM-networks.

AT&T NSI is the main provider of digital public switches and transmission systems for the Dutch PTT, which are the biggest national submarkets next to the terminal and mobile market. Also Ericsson and Alcatel are suppliers for national infrastructure. Development of new generations of digital equipment is so costly that the national subsidiaries of the foreign companies need to operate internationally in order to survive.

The market for terminals has been liberalized since 1989. In the beginning, this created chances for the smaller national terminal manufacturers. But with the internationalization of telecommunications markets and the installation of pan-European telecommunications networks, the role of the smaller equipment manufacturers has shifted more and more to engineering and system integration. Development of new digital equipment, only for the Dutch market, is too costly. This is one of the main reasons why Porter's argument for a strong home-market in the Dutch telecom case is less relevant.

5.4 Factor conditions and upgrading

The presence of production facilities for telecom equipment in the Netherlands depends more on positive factor endowments than on national demand.

Traditional factor (dis)advantages
The Dutch PTT can be seen as a sophisticated operator which built up an advanced infrastructure and pursued a technically modern policy. In this demanding environment, manufacturers were given the opportunity to follow the newest technological developments. Looking at the degree of digitalization of the public infrastructure, we must conclude that the Netherlands compared to other European countries is not in a front position, but somewhere in the middle (Den Hertog & Jacobs, 1990, 15).

The traditional high penetration of CATV is likely to become a factor advantage in the future, more than it has been in the past. In the past the cable networks were only used for one-way transmission of television signals. For new interactive services, upgrading of existing equipment is necessary. In contrast with the Nordic countries, the weak Dutch position on the mobile equipment market can mainly be explained by the fact that the geographical circumstances did not form substantial obstacles for installing a widely spread wired infrastructure. In general, one can find a telephone booth within 10 minutes' walk or drive. The role of Philips in telecommunications is partly due to chance. After World

War II, production facilities of Siemens - who was at that time the
biggest supplier of switching equipment for the national PTT - went over
to Philips. Philips became PTT's home-supplier along with Ericsson and
ITT (Den Hertog & Jacobs, 1990, 15).

Other traditional factors that attracted a lot of international companies and stimulated the provision of good telecom facilities in general
are:
- the focus of the Dutch economy on distribution, trade, services;
- the attractive tax system on this point; and
- the geographical location.

That telecommunications traditionally have never been a national competence or a nationally driven industry, can be seen as the most important
disadvantage. The Netherlands does not have a history in telecommunications as it does in electronics, shipbuilding, agriculture, trade and distribution. Neither has it had a huge military apparatus that could accelerate
telecommunications' development, like the Defense industry has done in
the United States.

Knowledge infrastructure, education and upgrading

The major part of R&D has been performed by the main manufacturers themselves. However, a significant part of this R&D takes place
abroad. The R&D labs of the foreign multinationals are concentrated in
the countries of their origin. Additional R&D efforts are customer-led
from PTT Research and to a lesser extent through public funding to the
three technical universities, TNO, and the Telematica Research Centre.
Co-operation between PTT Research and manufacturers is mainly
restricted to pre-competitive research, which is in most of the cases linked
to major European and EC research programmes like EUREKA, RACE
and ESPRIT[7].

In sum, the research is strongly diversified and often focused on
technologies and systems for niche markets. PTT Research is a telecom
generalist with special interest in services, and can be considered as the
most important knowledge centre for telecommunications in the Netherlands. The co-ordination between the industry and education is limited.
The technical universities have been reproached that their research is too
dispersed, and too fundamental, with only little interest for new applications (Den Hertog & Jacobs, 1990, 17). Lack of education is considered a
factor disadvantage. The main problem is a shortage of electronic engineers. In 1990, the demand for telecom engineers was almost two times
the actual supply. Moreover, the technical expertise often did not suit the
specific wishes of the manufacturers. Therefore, seven manufacturers

participated financially in the foundation of vocational training courses in Telematics at the polytechnic level.

The development of a *national electronic information highway* - in short: interconnecting existing and new infrastructures - will become a driving force for upgrading of existing networks in the near future. The CATV penetration of 95% can be considered very attractive for new American companies (operators) to enter the European market. But with respect to CATV we expect more new entrants in the service than in the equipment market. For the national CATV equipment market Siemens and Philips are the main providers. In general, the Dutch telecom equipment industry is a technology follower. To play any role of importance in a world telecommunications niche market, a concentration in know-how and excellence is necessary. In the Netherlands we can distinguish three competence centres for different submarkets:
- AT&T (switching equipment);
- Philips (private access branch exchange); and
- Ericsson (paging equipment).

Only to a very limited extent can we speak of *Dutch* niche production markets, where the specific competence is dependent on only a single company. Upgrading in terms of development of new applications for a world market will remain difficult.

5.5. Related and supporting industries

Because telecommunications is becoming more and more an enabling industry, close connections to many other industries exist, eg transport, banking, industrial automation, even agriculture. However, when we look at the related industries, like datacommunications, automation, consumer electronics and office machines, we must conclude that main suppliers for electronic components are almost absent in the Netherlands. There are many national and some international companies specialized in trade and services (engineering, system integration, installation) but production of components is limited to electro-mechanic parts (feeders), metal-ware, cables and plastics (Jacobs *et al.*, 1994). In 1990 only 10-20% of the components bought by the telecommunications industry had been produced by national suppliers (Den Hertog & Jacobs, 1990, 25). Most of the chips and modules came from the mother-company or were bought on the world market. In the Netherlands, no machines for the production of telecom equipment are produced. In general, the Dutch suppliers are too small to be a driving force for innovation for the telecommunications industry.

5.6 Conclusions

The relatively weak competitive position of the Dutch telecommunications equipment industry can very well be explained with the determinants for national advantage of Porter's 'diamond'. From the previous analysis, we can draw the following conclusions:

1. Upgrading of factor advantages is difficult, because they are all most absent.
2. The home market is too small to develop efficiently national digital systems and technology.
3. The domination by foreign manufacturers limits research activities in the Netherlands. The majority of R&D is performed in the countries of the manufacturer's origin.
4. Related industries such as the component and the computer industry do not significantly support the telecommunications equipment industry.

An aspect not tackled by the 'diamond' model is the global nature of competition in telecommunications. While Porter describes a growth path from factor-driven domestic competition towards international innovation-driven competition, the industry has never been a national driven industry.

The overall conclusion, however, is that the model is well-suited to explain, in this case, the 'negative dynamics' of the disadvantages of the Dutch telecommunication industry.

6. Concluding remarks

Although Porter's aim was to provide a new concept for determining national competitiveness, he actually developed a new method for industry analysis. Or should we consider his method as an upgraded form of his former analysis derived from the 'structuralist stream' in industrial organization theory, in which he incorporates the advantage of national resources? In the 1980s, he broadened the scope from industries to clusters of industries and stressed the importance of the dynamics, and upgrading, of national (dis)advantages. The importance of a supporting and stimulating cluster environment for the competitiveness of industries makes his analysis more suitable for industrial policymaking on the meso and macro levels. Nevertheless, although the national authorities can contribute to improvement or consolidation of national resources, it is still the individual entrepreneur who is responsible for the valorization or capitalization of these national advantages. It is the entrepreneur who has to develop and upgrade his company's distinctive capabilities, making use of all cluster characteristics available to him. This point will be discussed more extensively in chapter 7.

So the major contribution of *The Competitive Advantage of Nations* to industrial organisation and strategic management is the acknowledgement of the importance of the cluster of related and supported industries. In sum, a specific industry may derive its strength from the specificity of the whole cluster in which it is embedded. According to Porter, two mechanisms function as the main engines for competitiveness: domestic rivalry and geographic industry concentration (1990, 131). The former 'promotes upgrading of the entire national diamond', the latter 'elevates and magnifies the interactions within the diamond'. Our final comments concentrate on these two points. While the case-specific conclusions were written in the context of the Porter model we make some more general statements here which also criticize the model itself. We first discuss domestic rivalry, then we take a side-step concerning the importance of the 'diamond' factors separately and in combination and finally we comment on the geographic concentration aspect.

The three case-studies support the importance of domestic rivalry but not unconditionally. In the Dutch plastics processing industry, competition among the many small producers is abundant but strongly focused on cost efficiency. In contrast, the larger dredging contractors pursue differentiation strategies in a cost-dominant market. The rivalry in the Dutch telecommunications equipment industry is one situated at a different scale of playing field, namely the multinational. Important is the effect rivalry has on the strategies firms follow. It should not lead to competition based on the same parameters, but to variety. The cases also show that the quality of the determinants in the 'diamond' model is not always equal. If several determinants show weaker points, then the gross effect on industry dynamics is negative. Porter, however, does not pay much attention to the relative weights of the determinants. In his model, it is the total effect which counts. This remark relates to the more fundamental point which questions to what extent the 'diamond' can explain the competitiveness of all kinds of sectors. We come back to this with our last point about concentration (but see also chapters 4 and 7).

With respect to the emphasis Porter places on geographic concentration and its effect on the dynamics, we would like to add some comments based on our case experience. The case-study of the dredging industry clearly supports the value of the two driving mechanisms. But the industries in which both requirements are valid are scarce nowadays. Internationalisation of marketing and supplier involvement make it more and more difficult to develop geographically concentrated industrial clusters. Here, the findings summarized in Table 1 may lead to an extension of Porter's theory for the European situation. Geographic concentration need not necessary fall within national boundaries. Concentration could well be considered in terms of the balance between the geographic scale of production and the scale of the relevant market. The yield of several industry case-studies in the Netherlands leads us to the conclusion that sustained competitiveness of specific Dutch industries may very well depend on the strength of a cluster of related and supporting industries spread all over Northwest Europe. When both markets and production networks start globalising, then the geographic concentration changes and the linkages between the major industries within the cluster may become less tight.

Strong clusters evolve over a long period of time. The aspect of time brings us to a second comment. What to do with new technology-based industries, in which the evolutionary path of production system and market has almost immediately led to global business? This is for example the case for the Dutch telecom cluster. It leads us to the interesting observation that in terms of export performance an industry may be overlooked, but in terms of relative position in the national network the industry fulfils a strategic role, enabling other - more traditional - industries to flourish. In the Netherlands, this is the case for telecom in relation to the road transport service industry, the main port of Rotterdam and the agrofood industries.

Related to this topic is another theoretical element Porter somewhat neglects: the type of interactions between actors (including firms, intermediaries, research institutes) within a cluster and the relative positions necessary in a network. Here, relevant theory is being developed in the network-schools of Håkansson c.s. and the French 'filière' approach (see for example Beije, Groenewegen and Nuys, 1993). The cluster-concept that Porter uses is of a more aggregate level than the concept of interfirm networks. Porter indicates the type of industries to be included in a cluster, but he does not refer to the type of relations between these types of industries. Nor does he pay attention to the minimal set of actual networks which make a cluster successful, for example co-developing and co-engineering supplier-involvement and knowledge brokerage and diffusion. It would be interesting to analyse per industry what minimum configurations of individual firms are necessary and which type of interactions are needed to construct a fertile context for a cluster. Would there be any difference between more up- or downstream sectors? For example, it may not be necessary for manufacturing industries to be closely located to the machinery equipment producers, but it may be vital to the sector to have easy and frequent access to the final customer and designers. Kay refers to the value of these network-related concepts when stressing the importance of 'relational architecture' as one of the foundations for corporate success (Kay, 1994).

Finally, Porter's theoretic framework and the empirical case-studies lead to interesting policy issues. How to incorporate national available resources into the specific national industry structure is the main question addressed in 'national innovation system' studies and is a major challenge for advanced industrialised countries. The central government is one of the key players in this setting. Principally, through different means, government is capable of influencing all four determinants of the 'diamond'. As a 'network broker', a term attributed to Reich (1992), government could help bring a supply of publicly funded research and education to the business community in a certain market by regulatory or financial incentives. Developing customership for own governmental use is another more direct way to become directly involved in a cluster. In defense and civil engineering related industries, this is a frequently used instrument. Whether the organisational characteristics of government are now well moulded to perform such activities efficiently remains a subject for coming debates in innovation management.

Notes

1. Both authors work as researchers at the TNO Centre for Technology and Policy Studies within the field of industrial organisation, innovation economics and technology policy and regulation. Areas of interest include construction, metal and plastics engineering, telecommunication services.
Address: P.O. Box 541, NL-7300 AM Apeldoorn. E-mail: Kuijper@stb.tno.nl or Maltha@stb.tno.nl.

2. For examples of converging telecom infrastructures see for instance S.R. Maltha (1994), 'Spectrum use for mobile communications instead of television broadcasting', *Telecommunications Policy*, Volume 18 Number 4, May/June.

3. This list gives an overview of 50 Dutch industries with more than 15.5 % share of relevant world export markets in 1986. Jacobs et al. (1990, 29).

4. EuroStat recently requested the Central Buro for Statistics (CBS) and the Telecommunications and Postal Department for data on telecom services in the Netherlands. Further detailed research on this point will be needed. Hopefully

in the near future international comparisons of the service sector will be possible.

5. Schaffers, H., S.R. Maltha & G. Fahrenkrog (1993, appendix, BL 2-2).

6. The partly monopolized service market is mainly domestic orientated. This counts to a lesser extent for Value Added Services.

7. EUREKA: European platform for stimulating international cooperation of European companies and research institutes in the field of advanced technologies. RACE: Research in Advanced Communications Technologies. ESPRIT: European Strategy Platform for R&D Information Technologies.

References

Beije, Groenewegen, Nuys, (eds.) - *Networking in Dutch Industries.* - Garant/SISWO, 1993

Bloemen, E., Kok, J., J.L. van Zanden - *De top 100 van industriële bedrijven in Nederland 1913-1990.* - Achtergronddocument 3, Den Haag: AWT, 1993

Hertog, P. den, D. Jacobs - *De Nederlandse sectoren telecommunicatie-appara tuur en telematica-installaties.* - Apeldoorn: STB-TNO, 1990/1991

Jacobs, D., P. Boekholt, W. Zegveld - *De economische kracht van Nederland.* - The Hague: SMO, 1990

Jacobs, D., M. de Jong - Industrial clusters and the competitiveness of the Netherlands : Empirical results and conceptual issues. - In: *The Economist,* 1992, nr. 2, p. 233-252

Jacobs, D., H. Vethman, A. de Vos - Michael Porter en Nederlands economi sche kracht. - In: *Holland Management Review,* 1992, nr. 33, p. 7-16

Jacobs, D., J. Kuijper, H. Vethman, M. Zegveld - *De kunststofverwerkende industrie in Nederland: klaar voor de volgende stap?* - Leidschendam: NFK, 1993

Jacobs, D., I. Limpens, J. Kuijper, B. van de Ven - *De economische kracht van de baggerindustrie.* - Sliedrecht: IHC/CB, 1993

Jacobs, D. et al. - *Clusters in de metaal-elektro.* - Apeldoorn: STB-TNO, 1994

Kay, J. - Economics and business. - In: *Economic Journal,* Special issue 1991, p. 57-63

Kay, J. - *Foundations of corporate success* - London: Oxford University Press, 1994

Maltha, S.R. - Spectrum use for mobile communications instead of television broadcasting. - In: *Telecommunications Policy,* Volume 18 Number 4, May/June 1994

Ministry of Economic Affairs (Ministerie van Economische Zaken) - *Economie met open grenzen (Economy with open frontiers).* - Den Haag: SDU, 1990

Porter, M.E. - *The competitive advantage of nations.* - Boston (MS): Free Press, 1990

Reich, R.B. - *The work of nations.* - New York: Vintage Books, 1992

Schaffers, H., S.R. Maltha, G. Fahrenkrog - *Economische betekenis van telecommunicatie voor Nederland, deel 1 : Hoofdrapport.* - Apeldoorn: STB-TNO, (1993)

Schaffers, H., S.R. Maltha, G. Fahrenkrog - *Economische betekenis van telecommunicatie voor Nederland, deel 2 : Bijlagen.* - Apeldoorn: STB-TNO, 1993

Schaffers, H. and G. Knieps - *Competition and regulation in network-based industries: the role of interconnection and access regulation.* - Paper presen ted at the ITS Tenth Annual Conference 'Beyond Competition' - Sydney: 3-6 July, 1994

Scherer, F.M. and D. Ross - *Industrial Market Structure and Economic Performance*. - 3rd edition, Boston: Houghton Mifflin, 1990

United Nations - *International Trade Statistics Yearbook*. - New York: UN, 1986-1991

F. BOEKEMA, H.J. VAN HOUTUM

REGIONAL ECONOMIC COMPETITIVENESS; PORTER AND BEYOND

1. Introduction

Empirically tested concepts of competitiveness have always been best-sellers, for the simple reason that they sell success. Michael Porter's 'The Competitive Advantage of Nations' is no exception to this rule. On the contrary, it is an outstanding example of it. The book addresses a question which lies at the very heart of economic science and politics: economic welfare. Both economic theory and policy have hardly received a greater stimulus since Adam Smith's 'Wealth of Nations'. For theorists in the Netherlands involved with competitiveness Porter's concept offers no doubt an inspiring new avenue. Policy makers and economic practitioners have taken up the challenge as well, partly because the book provides a handle for national governments to evaluate and stimulate their national economy, despite the growing importance of internationalization of economic activity. For the Dutch government the book has been even more appealing because the concept fits the tendencies of decentralization of government and local initiatives to sustained regional economic growth. This can clearly be seen in the report of the Ministry of Economic Affairs, called 'Economics with Open Borders', which, to say the least, is very much inspired by Porter's work (Ministry of Economic Affairs, 1990).

As has been argued at several other places in this book, Porter's title, 'The Competitive Advantage of Nations', is in itself not unequivocal. Porter explicitly argues that competitiveness cannot be used to compare countries. Firms compete, not nations. Nevertheless, later in the book it becomes clear that he uses the phrase 'the competitive advantage of nations' to indicate the economic strength of globally operating firms. This strength is determined by the national 'diamond', the home base of the firm. Secondly, the home base of the firms is, as he argues, very often of a regional or local character. He explicitly states that because of the regional agglomeration of firms and people, the regional economic level in particular is probably the most appropriate level on which to analyze competitiveness:

This book is about why nations succeed in particular industries, and the implications for firms and for national economies. Its concepts, however, can be readily applied to political or geographic units smaller than a nation. Successful firms are frequently concentrated in particular cities or states within a nation. (...) What I am really exploring here is the way in which a firm's approximate 'environment' shapes its competitive success over time. (Porter, 1990, 29)

The emphasis on the regional level is even more clearly stressed as he states:

While economic geography has not been seen as a core discipline in economics, my research suggests that it should be. (Ibid., p. 791)

The very challenge that he issues to regional economists and economic geographers with these lines has been an impetus for us to study his work in more detail. For that matter, it would be worthwhile to find out what impact Porter has had on the work of regional economists and economic geographers. Nevertheless, his approach is mainly focused on nations, as the home base for competitive industries. In his book only little attention is given to the application of the concepts on the regional level. We want to find out if his method could indeed be applied on a geographical level lower than the nation.

In this chapter we will address three questions:
1. What is 'the economic competitive advantage of regions' according to Porter?
2. What is the added value of Porter's work for regional economic theories?
3. Can Porter's view on the measurement of competitiveness be interpreted on a regional level?

The first question is discussed in the second and third section, thereby presenting an extensive regional empirical study, which was conducted in line with Porter's approach. In the fourth section the second question is answered. After the explanation and application of Porters' concept an evaluation is given (second and third question). In section five Porter's theory is evaluated. In the final section the measurement problem is addressed. Moreover, in this section a new kind of measurement is presented.

2. Economic performance and competitiveness

The *first* question implies an analysis of the way Porter interprets and uses the term 'Regional economic competitiveness'. The discussion could be split up into two aspects, namely the *indicator* (the how) and the *explanation* (the why) of regional economic competitiveness (Van Houtum, 1991). Since Porter's insights have received so much attention in the literature, we will treat his concept rather briefly, thereby focusing on some key elements of his study which are required to understand the regional application of his concept.

Porter's book is basically a mix between the meso and macro-level. He recognizes that seeking to explain competitiveness at the national or regional level as a whole would be to answer the wrong question. Therefore he tries to focus not on the economy as a whole, but on specific clusters within a nation or region. As we interpret it, he defines a cluster as a set of related and supporting industries on the product-group level, ranging from raw material to consumer product (five-digit level)[1].

The indicators he uses for competitiveness are export and foreign investments. However, he does not distinguish international competitive advantage based upon exports from that based upon direct foreign investment. National competitive advantage, in his view, is measured as the share of a sector in the world export market or the share of direct foreign investments by the specific cluster. National competitiveness is considered to be the sum of the world competitive clusters present within its territory. For the national level, he designed a cluster set of 16 different groupings of economic activities (table 1).

Table 1. Porter's classification of clusters

Upstream industries
1   Materials and metals
2   Computers and semi-conductors
3   Forest products
4   Petroleum and chemicals

Industrial and supporting industries
5   Diverse (multiple business)
6   Transportation
7   Office
8   Energy
9   Telecommunication
10 Defense

Final consumption
11 Food and beverage
12 Household and housing
13 Entertainment and leisure
14 Health care
15 Textiles and apparel
16 Personal business

Source: see Porter 1990, p. 742.

The international competitive product groups are allocated in this cluster chart, in which per cluster a further division is made into primary goods, machinery for production, specialty inputs and associated services. This technique leads to a completely different sector division than the Standard Industrial Classification, which is in fact based on production technologies and features of products, resulting in the main division between agriculture and fishery, industry, commercial and non-commercial services. As we will see in section 3, the application of this method in the Netherlands by TNO yielded surprising, new results and recommendations for the national economy (TNO, 1990).

In regard to the explanation of competitive advantage, it can be said that the whole notion of competitiveness is actually derived from the micro and meso-economic level. At the micro-level of firms, competitiveness is regarded as the capacity of a firm to compete with other firms in the same branch; at the meso-economic level, this would be the capacity of a sector in a nation to compete with the same sector in another nation. At these levels of analysis, several explanations and indicators have been put forward in the literature.

The meso-economic notion of competitiveness made it possible for the discussion to be raised to the macro-economic level. The need for this 'translation' of the concept to a macro-economic level was speeded up at the beginning of the eighties when some sectors of the East-Asian countries developed themselves very rapidly. Based on the so-called 'Revealed Comparative Advantage' (RCA) method (Balassa, 1965) an assessment was made of the strong sectors in the East-Asian countries followed by a comparison of these countries with other countries based on the 'sum' of the strong domestic sectors' economic strength. The alternative concept for evaluating a country's competitive advantage would be the well-known Heckscher-Samuelson-Ohlin theorem following from Ricardo's work. This theorem concentrates on production costs derived from a given set of production factors.

The essence of the RCA approach is that at the level of branches or product groups a given measure for export performance is used as an indicator of the comparative advantage that is gained in the branches or groups concerned. The level of analysis is therefore the main difference between the approach of RCA and the 'factor difference approach'. Furthermore, by analysing it in this way, the empirical effort to pin down the 'competitiveness of a nation' comes before the theoretical point of view. This is why this approach seems useful in making up a strengths-weaknesses-opportunities-threats (SWOT) analysis of a particular country or region. However, the application of the RCA approach in itself is not an easy task. According to Tettero (1987) a tradeoff has to be made between scientific purity and analytical pragmatism in assessing the competitiveness of nations. From a scientific point of view the level of analysis at which competitiveness should be measured and explained is the market level where individual firms 'compete to gain advantage'. Limited availability of data is often a problem at this level.

Porter implicitly follows the RCA approach in his empirical work. Furthermore he tries to fulfil the need for a theoretical foothold for the inductive RCA approach by providing a theoretical concept. Balassa's approach lacked a theoretical explanation. This part of Porter's work has received most attention in reviews and publications. The explanation comes down to the question of what the driving forces of competitiveness are. We would like to argue that the term 'competitiveness' can only be applied at the territorial level in the comparison of different countries in terms of their attractiveness for firms' investment. But this is not the meaning Porter is after, namely, competitiveness in the sense of economic performance, for he himself states that firms compete, not nations. There-fore it can be concluded that competitiveness of firms is a consequence of or merely a contribution to the economic performance of a nation. To avoid confusion, we will only use the term *'economic performance'* at the territorial level and not 'competitiveness' (Van Houtum, 1991).[2]

According to Porter, it is the nation or region itself, or as he calls it, the 'diamond' that shapes the international competitive performance of firms over time. So the clusters are location-bound. Since firms mostly develop within the domestic proximate environment prior to expanding internationally, Porter argues that the specific configuration of the 'home base' plays a key role in determining the character of the human capital, the resources and the identity of the firm. In his view, the typical national or regional 'diamond' factors which determine the environment of the firms influence the success of the firms and thereby the growth-path of the region[3]. Historical and cultural values of a region are not mentioned separately, but do in Porter's opinion play a vital role in influencing the characteristics of the factors mentioned. According to Porter, the regional competition and the nature of the regional demand can serve as testing fields for the initial development of firms in a region. To the extent that they are flexible, the existing and rising linkages in the region are import-ant in that they can permit an efficient and fast entry to the necessary goods and services, information and insights. The interaction between the firm and its subcontractors can hence be profitable and self-enforcing. The production factors, divided into basic and advanced factors, should be upgraded continuously. It is not the stock itself that is important, but rather the rate and efficiency with which they are created, upgraded and deployed in particular industries. Governments should only play an indirect, not a direct role, for they are not believed to be able to create competitive industries themselves; only firms can do that.

This view is illustrated by several case-studies of the most successful industries in different countries. In short, Porter has built institutional elements into the theory of international trade which until then was basically focused on cost differentials. We will discuss this further in section 4.

3. The empirical application of Porter's approach in the Netherlands

As a consequence of the success of Porter's book 'The Competitive Advantage of Nations' both in the United States and in Europe, the Dutch government was very much interested in the application of the model to the national economy as a whole. The Dutch research institute TNO/STB was asked to produce a SWOT analysis of the Dutch economy right at the start of the new cabinet's term 1990-1994. It was emphasized that for this task, the Porter-approach should be used. The results of this study were published in a report called *The economic clout of the Dutch economy*, which has been discussed in chapter 1. Following Michael Porter's methodology the ranking of the strongest product groups of clusters of the Dutch economy was very surprising, at least if we compare them to traditional approaches. If the position in the home-market is considered to be very important as Porter suggests, the 'diamond' concept must be able to explain the success of the Dutch agricultural sector which contains all of the most-exported products. This cannot be done very easily, as Kamann and Strijker argue in chapter 4 of this book . Coming back to the list, the natural oil and chemical cluster was very well represented. The first electrotechnical sector was only to be found in the 14th place of the ranking list. Another remarkable feature of this list was that most of the strong clusters are dominated by small-scale enterprises. In almost all of the first twenty clusters, the combination of smallness of scale, craftsmanship, a good network within the Netherlands, and a fair amount of technological capability is present. In this respect, these clusters remind us of a move towards flexible production in the Netherlands at the cost of bulk and serial production in the industries. In the fifth section, we will go into more detail on the comparison of Porter's theory with the realm of present regional economic theories.

After the brief discussion of the application of Porter's concept at the national level, we now turn to the regional level. One of the most extensive try-outs on a *regional* economic level was the study by the Economic Technological Institute of North Brabant (ETIN), called 'Brabantse Economie met Open Grenzen (BEMOG)', which could be translated as: Brabants' economy with open borders. Inspired by the great emphasis that was put on the Porter analysis at the national level, the regional authorities in the Province of North Brabant decided to adapt the Porter approach as the method to be used.

First the most important socio-economic indicators are presented in the following table, namely, population, gross domestic product and unemployment. The differences with neighbouring provinces in the Netherlands and Belgium and Germany are shown.

Table 2. Socio-economic indicators

	Pop.	GDP	GDP		Unemployment	
	1989	1989	1989	'85	'90	'91
	mill.	Bill.	x1000	%	%	%
		(ECU)	(inhab.)			
NL	14.8	203	13.7	10.3	8.0	7.2
Belgium	9.9	139	14.0	11.3	7.1	7.6
Luxembourg	0.4	6	15.0	3.0	1.5	1.7
Germany	61.9	1080	17.4	7.3	5.2	4.5
France	56.2	870	15.5	9.9	8.8	9.3
UK	57.2	760	13.3	11.5	6.3	9.0
Ireland	3.5	31	8.9	18.3	15.3	16.9
EU 12	325.2	4407	13.6	10.8	8.4	8.8

Source: BEMOG, p. 8.

The most relevant feature of the Porter approach is the important role attached to economic clusters. Therefore it is useful here]] to identify all the economic activities which are related to each other, with emphasis on the common final product. The Porter approach focuses only on those parts of the regional production structure[4] which are able to compete with other economic activities outside the region itself. In other words, in his approach the strengths and weaknesses of a region can only be shown in relation with other regions. In the research by ETIN it appeared that it

was very hard to pin down the relative export and direct foreign investment performance of North Brabant, since at this detailed geographical
level, it is hard to obtain these kinds of data. In addition, the export and
direct investment to the rest of the Netherlands had to be taken into
account, a figure that does not exist on a regional level either. Therefore,
as already stated, it is questionable whether this indicator is a good
estimate of the economic performance of the sectors of a region. Besides
this problem, Porter's cluster chart had to be rearranged for this province,
   since for certain clusters it was not possible to fill them with meaningful data in terms of turnover and employment. The cluster 'Forest
Products' was left empty, the clusters 'Office' and 'Diverse' were added
to a new cluster 'Firm Support' and the cluster 'Telecommunication' was
added to the cluster 'Computers/semi-conductors'. Two other clusters
were made, namely, 'Government/non profit' and 'Textile' to capture the
whole economic reality in North Brabant.
It was found that, although Porter stipulated that his approach was also
meant, and maybe even more appropriate, for the regional economic
level, the translation to the regional level was not at all without difficulties. The ETIN solved the indicator problem by taking the relative
under or overrepresentation of employment of sectors on a four-digit level
as a measure of regional economic performance, compared to the rest of
the Netherlands. Furthermore, those clusters were gathered which are
internationally active and of direct importance to the regional economy in
terms of employment.
   Throughout the research it was learned that the grouping of economic activities in clusters at this level gives the impression that tight
network relationships exist within clusters. That need not be the case. It is
only an indication, a selective view on reality. An empirical network -
analysis would have to be necessary to show the real in- and out-going
lines between firms within a region. But such a complete analytical
picture of a network is not easy to set up (Ummels, 1993). If no a priori
limitation of the research population is made, a 'snowball sampling'
would have to be the proper method for networking analyses, which
could be infinite. The ETIN approach resulted in ten rather than 16
clusters. Table 3 shows the specific relative under or over representation
of employment in the different relevant clusters for North Brabant,
measured in location coefficients[5]. The coefficients are compared with
the Dutch situation as a whole. The figure 100 is the overall Dutch
average. A further distinction is made with regard to four different
regions[6] in North Brabant.

Table 3. Location coefficients[a] of the clusters of North Brabant, measured in employment

Region/Cluster	West (Breda)	Central (Tilburg)	North-East ('s-Hertogenbosch)	South-East (Eindh./Helmond)	Total
(1) Materials/metals	134	130	91	158	128.5
(2) Computers/semi-conductors	64	53	81	163	90.3
(3) Petroleum/chemicals	176	105	43	46	92.5
(4) Business support	83	73	68	99	80.8
(5) Transportation	100	93	65	111	92.3
(6) Food and beverage	140	95	175	90	125
(7) Housing and household	132	121	127	129	127.3
(8) Entertainment/leisure	97	268	79	498	235.5
(9) Health care	78	83	271	133	141.3
(10) Textile and apparel	100	478	176	190	236

Source: BEMOG
[a] Location coefficient is defined here as the value of sector X in region Y compared to the value of X for the Netherlands as a whole.

In terms of relative specializations, measured in employment, it is clear that especially the clusters 'materials and metals', 'food and beverage' and 'housing and household' are overall strongly represented in North Brabant, compared with the Netherlands as a whole. In addition, these clusters are more or less equally spread over the four regions. 'Textiles and apparel' and 'recreation (entertainment/leisure) and health care' are also over represented, but more regionally concentrated. 'Recreation' can mostly be found in central Brabant (photo/film, audio/video) and southeast Brabant (audio/video). 'Textiles and apparel' are mostly concentrated in central Brabant. 'Health care' is primarily present in northeast Brabant (medicines/bandages, wholesale trade) and southeast Brabant (medical measuring equipment). Another noticeable feature of this table is the apparent under representation of 'business support', which includes, among other things, business services and research. These services are not predominantly present in Brabant, compared with the Dutch overall average.

Sections 2 and 3 make clear that 'regional competitive advantage' merely implies looking at the 'diamond' factors at the regional level according to Porter. Our discussion of a specific regional 'application' of the 'diamond' shows that the pattern of competitive industries differs from the results of the analysis at the national level (see chapter 1).

4. Evaluation of Porter's theoretical concepts

The *second* question was if and, if so, to what extent Porter's approach has an added value for regional economic science. This is basically a question concerning the evaluation of Porter's theoretical framework. We are particularly interested in the theoretical thinking behind his cluster approach. We come back to the indicator Porter used to determine national or regional competitiveness in section 5.

4.1 The place of economic clustering in economic geography

Economic clustering is a popular concept in contemporary regional science as well as in corporate geography. It appeals to a cross-fertiliz-ation between the contextual approaches, by which the mainstream of regional science and the primarily organizational approaches of corporate geography could be characterized (Vaessen, 1993). But it is certainly not a new concept. As early as 1890 Marshall (1890, 1920) found that econ-omic regions are mainly created by co-operative production among firms. He called the resulting regions 'industrial districts'. It enabled firms to gain economies of agglomeration. Various regional economists have also tried to explain the grouping of firms. The grouping principle Porter refers to is what French regional economic scientists used to call 'filière-configurations', which has a comparable purpose to Porter's clusters. A filière is a french term for family relationship or genealogical tree. In this approach central focus is on the value chain of a product, ranging from raw material to consumer product. Further, the different relations of every producer in this value chain are taken into account. In other words, in such a tree economic relations are not only horizontal but also vertical. Such a 'filière configuration' is able to show the linkages between different kinds of producers and services, grouped in a chart by end-use application, and to show the roots of certain kinds of activities. Further-more, it shows how difficult it is to change a given structure through economic policy (Lambooy, 1992).

Another principle of grouping economic activities was followed by Chardonnet (1953). Central in his analysis is the 'key firm', a large enterprise with different kinds of dependency relationships in a certain region. In line with this notion, Perroux developed the growth pool concept, using the same principle of key firms, which he called growth pools (Perroux, 1955). He referred to the different relations with supplier industries as 'economic space'. For Myrdal these lines of thinking constituted the basis for the development of his principle of 'cumulative causation' (Myrdal, 1957), with which he tried to make clear what effects are to be expected for the (regional) economy when a key firm is installed at a certain location.

These somewhat older approaches tried to stress the presence of interlinkages in the economy. That is what Porter has tried to do with his cluster chart. But, a chart alone is not able to show the kind of networking that really exists. It is static, not dynamic. It is for this reason that his 'diamond' is of such importance in his book: the 'diamond' is the dynamic logic behind the economic processes in a region. The combination of an empirical tool to tackle the networking in a region and theoretical logic to explain the economic dynamism is what makes Porter's work interesting to analyse in further detail. In a way, Porter's book has hence caused a resurgence of regional economic network studies. Nevertheless, there are also other recent theories about this topic which have become very important in the literature. It is interesting to analyze where Porter is to be placed among these other new theories. We look at this in the next section.

4.1.1. The new theories of economic clustering

The new theories we are pointing at are part of what Best refers to as the 'New Competition' (Best, 1990). With Old Competition he means the former dominance of the economy by largely vertically integrated, highly routinized mass-production processes. This strategy of vertical integration, or internalization, was to prevent bottle-necks and thus inefficiency in the supply of key components in rapidly expanding markets. Producing output and lowering the costs of production are seen as the central issues of the organizational strategy. The assembly-line technologies, standardization of work routines and the rigid labour relations involved, helped to boost such industries as automobile, machinery, and domestic appliances (Lagendijk, 1993). This type of production is usually called Fordism (Gramsci, 1930) and it is characterised by much emphasis put on the production process itself. The environment is not regarded as crucial to the continuation of the firm. It is, to put it differently, a mechanical and closed system. The spatial implication of this trend was and is to some extent still to be found in the Manufacturing Belt in North America and in the industrial regions of Northwest Europe, which stretch from the English Midlands through the southern parts of Holland, Belgium, Northern France, the Ruhr area of Germany, with outliers in northwest Italy and southern Sweden (Scott and Cooke, 1988).

The most important argument for accepting the relative shift in the methods of production towards a system dominant in the New Competition is the following. In the market sphere the increasing volatility in technological developments and the growing importance of globalization within capitalist systems has led to an increase in international competition. This competition has led to the growing sovereignty of consumers (Ohmae, 1990). The range and availability of products is seen as wider, since it is global. The demand is therefore seen as more volatile, quality-conscious and differentiated. As a consequence, price has lost its decisive role in purchasing decisions (Pyke, 1992). In this sense, pure mass-production in consumer durable sectors is said to have lost much of its attractiveness and is gradually being replaced by more flexible
industries, with a stronger emphasis on market orientation. The system is *first* of all less mechanical, more dynamic, and open. That means that there is more room for information flows from suppliers and from customers, more room for chance and uncertainty factors, quality drives, and organizational and technological learning. It also implies, and this is the *second* fundamental distinction vis-à-vis Fordism, that the difference between the 'environment of the firm' (the external organization, and the internal organisation) of the firm is gradually losing importance. The decision to make or to buy, which was characteristic of the former type, has now become to make, to buy, or to collaborate (Richardson, 1972).

Within the flexible production or the new competition, as Best calls it, a distinction can be made among three types of restructuring approaches. These types of production could be called ideal types. Exact copies of these organization structures in regions where the types were originally founded are hard to find. In the actual practice of firms, various combinations often can be found, and more often than not different strategies co-exist within a single firm (Cox, 1994).

(1) The first type of restructuring is *'lean production'*, which stems from the Japanese economic system and was put forward by Womack et al. (1991). The way in which lean production is organized is fundamentally different from other types in regard to the degree of dependency on suppliers and subcontractors (Ruigrok and Van Tulder, 1993). In fact,

lean production is often called 'postfordism' or 'superfordism'. There is a structural control of the assemblers and everything is focused on productivity. But the key difference is that within lean production, the 'just-in-time (JIT) production' and 'total quality' concepts have an important role to play in making the system flexible (Krafcik, 1988; Dankbaar, 1994). By JIT production it is meant that products are ready at the exact time they are needed. This facilitates profitability by reducing buffer-stocks. The core firm is highly routinized, but much 'leaner' than the mass-production-like firm. There are many relations with subcontractors and they all tend to be long-term. Total quality refers to the attempt to avoid wasted effort on the assembly-line and to maintain an ongoing consultation with the subcontractors regarding manufacturing processes and product design (Cox, 1994). Power of centralization, time-management and governance are therefore keywords in the establishment of this organization form.

(2) The second type are the theories put forward by Hymer (1972, 1976) and Froebel, Heinrichs, and Kreye (1977) regarding *'the New International Division of Labour'*. This research put forward a line of thought that focuses on the spatial pattern of a vertical hierarchy in labour, in which the cost of labour is considered to be crucial to its locus. According to this view, multinationals are concentrated in core cities of developed countries, higher-order labour activities are grouped in secondary cities, and lower-order activities are moved to peripheral, backward regions or developing countries. Recently, it is Reich who has contributed to this theory. He contends that the skills and capacities of people have become the primary assets in the economy. He argues that corporations themselves are losing their national identities, since they are becoming global operators. Others, such as Amin and Thrift (1992), have used the theoretical concept of the New International Division of Labour to advance the explanation of the emergence of transnational corporations. In this last respect, economies of scope and governance of international network relations are the new keywords.

(3) The last type to be mentioned here is *'flexible specialization'*. This idea stems from the 'Italian district' way of organizing and was introduced by Piore and Sabel in the mid 80s (Piore and Sabel, 1984). The flexible specialization was originally a spatial interpretation by Scott of Williamson's transaction costs theory, but it was gradually subsumed under the concept of 'technological district'. This concept broadened the discussion of flexible production in such a way that it included the possibility of having an economically prosperous region without corporate giants. In terms of dynamism and breadth of approach it is perhaps the

most flexible method of production of the three. Because it has much in common, as we will see, with Porter's concept, we will discuss it in more detail here.

In the flexible specialization approach, in essence, production is organized according to a model which we would like to call a *Cooperation-Competition-Community-model* (see figure 1)[7]. The line of interpretation of this conceptual schema of the flexible specialization theory is the following. The higher level of quality demanded by customers and made possible by technology has led to increased specialization and vertical disintegration. *Competition* is driven by highly specialized, small firms within the industrial district. This postulated trend of vertical disintegration and specialization, the peeling off of the onion of the firm, may lead to the increasing importance of subcontractors and suppliers and therefore to a growing relevance of networks. It was Scott who introduced the link with agglomeration (Scott, 1988ab). He argued that to the extent that transactions have geographically sensitive cost structures, the increased level of external transactions in a production system would lead to a clustering of producers in order to minimize time and cost of transacting. Other authors like Storper, Walker, and Schoenberger have elaborated further on this assumed positive relationship between the existence of networks and the geographical agglomeration of important parts of the production system[8]. These authors contend that this relationship in flexible specialization exists especially in technologically dynamic industries. The kind of agglomerations that evolve in this way Storper calls 'technological districts (Storper, 1992; 1993). He argues that flexible production and agglomerative tendencies are to be considered as two of a kind. In other words, flexible production was not grounded on 'flexible space'. On the contrary.

Figure 1. Cooperation-Competition-Community-model of flexible specialization

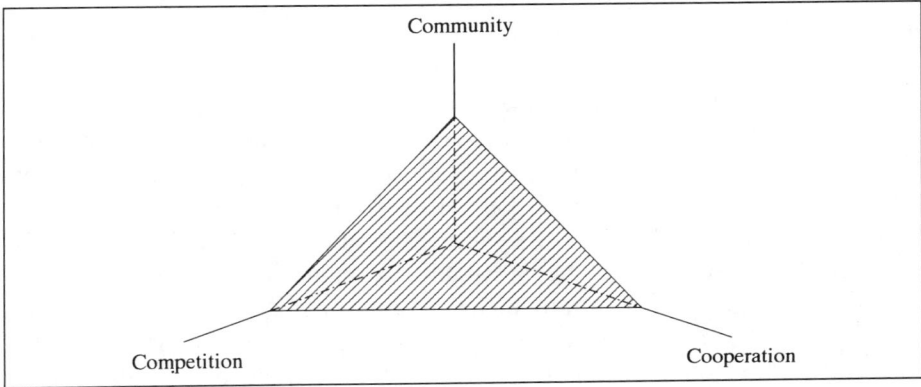

Essential to the element of *cooperation* in the principle of flexible specialization is the consultative behaviour of firms in the production chain. Receiving information from customers, suppliers, and the institutional context enables firms to create a technological learning process. In order to be fuelled with the adequate information about new insights and innovation of the technology that is used, the contracted suppliers of a firm would have to specialize on an industry-wide level and be wholly independent. While full dependency of one core company does have the short-term positive impact of reducing uncertainty, the long-term negative impact would be to reduce the stimuli for innovation, resulting in a 'lock-in' to a given technology (Miles and Snow, 1992, Krugman, 1991). The price and quality of the product of the suppliers should hence be tested in a wider market. The 'lock-in' of the suppliers and contractors, of which only the price components and a reasonable assurance of uninterrupted supply are important, is shunted off to a type of external networking. Continuous technical change constitutes the new competitive standard. In order to let information flow freely within such a district a special link exists between the nature of cooperation and competition and the path-dependent cultural background of its locus. Terms like trust, commitment, mutual involvement, and common history between the critical agents in the production system are considered to be crucial, for they are able to facilitate technological learning. These principles are in fact inversely related to the height of the transaction costs, since transaction costs are costs that derive from the seeking and contracting of business partners.

These feelings represent what Storper calls the 'conventions' of identity and participation (Storper, 1993). By conventions he means practices, routines and agreements and their associated informal or institutional forms. The set of these conventions he defines as a 'local world of production'. It helps create an economic *community*-feeling'. This institutional setting of networking is strikingly different from the other two methods of flexible production.

There has to be a balance between the conventions or community-feelings and transaction costs in order to be able to explain the agglomeration of economic activities. Cooperative community-feelings are not in themselves enough to explain economic grouping, since for individual entrepreneurs it would not be profitable to do so in the long run. They would be outstripped by more efficient enterprises[9]. Competition would then drive out cooperation. On the other hand, the sole factor of transaction costs is not enough either to explain the grouping of activities, since the contacts of entrepreneurs are not limited to a certain region. In fact, it might be more profitable for certain entrepreneurs to seek partners outside the region. Henry, in particular, has argued that there is 'no logic of agglomeration' when one bases one's arguments solely and simply on the transaction cost approach (Henry, 1992). In his view, the process of agglomeration should not be defined simply in terms of an efficient combination of factors, but rather as a logic of interaction. Agglomerative tendencies may then be an outcome, when basing one's ideas on the transaction cost approach, but not a necessary result of this mechanism. Different mechanisms may produce the same result.

Furthermore, there is a balance between the competition and cooperation within a technological district in the flexible specialization approach. Competition is often seen as the single and best drive for economic growth. Nevertheless, within the flexible specialization approach, cooperation is also a major factor in explaining the relative success of the technological districts. Establishing a group strategy, which builds and acts back upon the individual enterprise, is, within the 'flex spec model', perhaps the most characteristic way to explain the assumed paradox between cooperation and economic growth (Best, 1990).

The proponents of the flexible specialization approach have put forward a concept which is said to be especially evident in industries like electronics, designer clothing, craft products and other light industrial consumer products (Amin and Thrift, 1992). These industries have been faced with pronounced volatility and production innovations and hence shortened product-life cycles in their niche markets. The spatial examples which are most commonly used in the Western literature, although quite a few differences can be noticed among them are Third Italy, the US Sunbelt region (including Orange County, Silicon Valley, Dallas, Fort Worth), Boston's route 128, the M4 Corridor in England, the Jura Region in Switzerland, and Baden-Württemberg in Germany (See, e.g., Scott, 1988ab; Amin and Thrift, 1992).

4.1.2. Porter's cluster concept

What is Porter's place in these agglomerative networking theories? It could be argued that his theory of the clusters is indeed a type of networking with spatial implications. We have seen that the central focus of his theory, the networking of economic activities, is not a new concept. The question now is whether his cluster concept is all-encompassing, for he tries to explain the competitiveness of any region.

If we try to interpret Porter's view, his cluster concept could be seen as a spatial concentration of vertically or horizontally related economic activities. This clustering is most profitable, especially in the beginning of the life-cycle of a sector, when the clustered firms are home-based. Some of Porters' clusters consist of a number of cooperative small and medium-sized firms. But not all of them. In this respect, Porter doesn't make a difference between large or small-scale enterprises such as 'key firms'. Further, Porter does not make a distinction between the nature of clustering, be it communal as in the technological district or be it ownership as with the lean production principle. Porter states:

> We observed sharp differences across nations, as well as across industries, in how, and how well, clusters work. (...) Nations gain an important international advantage where national attributes are supportive of intracluster interchange. (Porter, 1990, 152)

In other words, the institutional settings of a nation (region) are a crucial stimulus for the development of economic performance. In this respect, Porter's theory about the networking itself greatly resembles the flexible specialization approach, since in this approach the community has an important role to play in determining the economic behaviour of the entrepreneurs. In the networking chart, the filière-approach is perhaps the closest to the cluster approach, as it is based on the same principle of summing up all activities that are interrelated or supporting from producer to consumer.

An argument that Porter uses quite often in his book, and in which he is correct, is that his concept of clusters is broader. An important reason for this is that Porter's grouping of economic activities is more clearly embedded within a 'diamond', a configuration of a regional or national economy, and that the other principles of networking are in fact only production-oriented. Porter, in his explanation of the strength of clusters, clearly and explicitly takes the customers, the resources, the government, and the chance factor into account, whereas the other regional economic theories are only concentrated upon the nature of networking and the competitive interplay between firms. One could say that the other principles are focused upon a dual relationship within the 'diamond', namely, the element of firm strategy, structure and rivalry, and the element of related and supporting industries. It is, as stated above, the flexible specialization approach which argues for a community, a location-boundedness of economic activities.

It may be considered a serious criticism that in the regional economic approach of flexible specialization, no explicit attention is given to the role of customers, chance, government, or human and natural capital (resources). Porter's theoretical reasoning is schematized in Figure 2. Data stands for the empirical findings, warrant stands for the correspondence in the findings, the backing stands for the theoretical assumptions about reality and claim is a term for the assertation that has been done for a certain case[10]:

Figure 2. Porter's concept

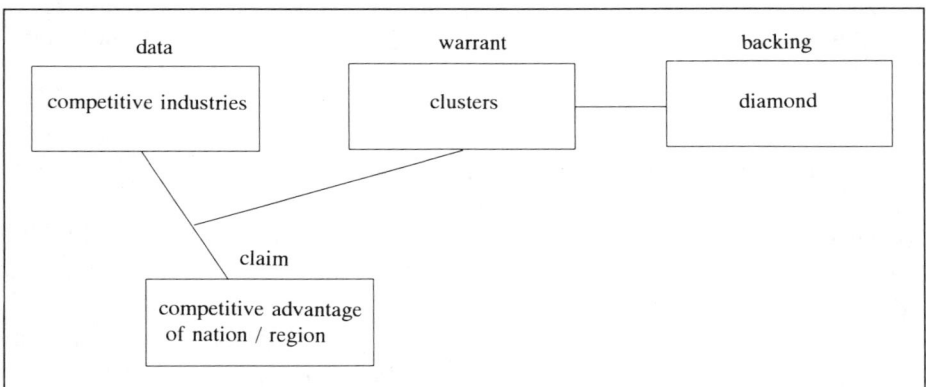

This concept of Porter's has more to say about economic perform-ance than the other new approaches, which only indirectly aim at explaining economic performance. It is to Porter's credit that he is trying to link the network approach more directly with economic performance. Nevertheless, the breadth of the approach has also led to a lack of precision, when his ideas are translated to a regional economic level. Moreover it can be said that although the theory seems all-encompassing it is still probably not rich enough to capture the whole regional economic reality. Thus, in its broadness it is not complete. What is even more important, it is not a theory, not a prescription for policy, but merely a line of thought, a conceptual schema.

Support for this view can be found by closely examining the weak spots in Porter's line of reasoning.

(1) The essence of action and interaction

The first major shortcoming in Porter's approach is that within his cluster approach, no attention is given to the character of interaction between the economic actors in a region. He emphasizes there are different patterns and there is a location-boundedness of the (f)actors. Nevertheless, a growing number of commentators emphasize the relevance of the social factors and the interchange of technological, qualitative information within the interaction patterns (Gertler, 1994). His network concept does not contain socio-economic action. The major principles of interaction, including questions like trust, rationality, perception, dependency, status, power, attitude, commitment, and economic motives for networking are not included in his theory. These network principles are said to be striking features of most modern economic networks. So it is not made clear particularly why and how interaction between firms is set up.

In addition, no attention is paid to the actor, the modus operandi of economic behaviour, the individual behaviour of firms, or, as some authors say: *entrepreneurship* (See, e.g., De Jong, 1986)? To put it differently, firms and entrepreneurs are regarded as 'black boxes'. The emphasis is placed on the environment of the firm, and not on the human factor within the firm. The approach is therefore essentially meso. The book does not give full weight to differences on the micro-level, although that was to be the main focus of it, considering the opening key statement:

> Our central task, then, is to explain why firms based in a nation are able to compete successfully against foreign rivals in particular segments and industries. (Porter, 1990, 10)

(2) Lack of predictive power of the 'diamond'-theory

There is room for opportunism and societal ideologism in the application of his theory. His 'theory' legitimates and challenges policy-makers, since the theory is rich and seems to sell success. The reason for the opportunism is that Porter's claims of competitive advantage lack qualifiers and modifiers. In other words, there are no hypotheses to be tested. Ambiguity in regard to the signs of relationships, the puzzle of the relative importance of the different factors, the complexity of interactions, and dual causation actually renders his 'diamond' unproductive in generating predictions and in advising policy (see, e.g., Grant, 1991).

(3) The cluster approach versus network reality

The cluster approach with which he tries to master the networking within a territory is hard to translate to the regional economic level many smaller-sized non-American countries are used to.

It is hard to distribute the different competitive branches in an economy over clusters and regions. Moreover, he does not give a measurement method for the clustering, the networking among firms. He merely redistributes the competitive branches ex post. That means there is nothing other than a presumed logic behind the linkages in the different clusters and that is the key weakness in his backing of the 'theory'. The relevance of the in and outflow of physical goods, on the one hand, and non-physical goods (e.g. information, power, trust), on the other hand, are not taken into account. What good there is in Porter's approach, the concept of clusters, is not new, and what is new, not factual. It appears that it is still hard to grasp the nature of networking.

(4) Translation to less developed and declining regions and nations

It is not clear what conditions are necessary to achieve the status of a cluster.

His theory is focused on success. The unanswered question is what are the possibilities for the feasibility of fostering dynamic growth based on the cooperative networks in less developed or declining regions and nations. As the philosophy of promoting growth on the basis of flexible production and clusterlike systems is gaining ground, it should be made clear whether, and under what conditions and why, an upgrading of a region can be done. It seems that these conditions still are hard to pinpoint.

Amin, Robins and Thrift have done a lot of research on this question of the success factors (Amin and Robins 1990; Amin and Thrift, 1992). They hold the pessimistic view that not all regions have the same chances. In their view, some regions might have to abandon the ideal of the possibility of self-sustaining growth and might have to rule out the ideal of complete independence. The process of increasingly globally-integrated industrial development and growth would delineate the constraints or possibilities of developments of these regions (Amin and Robins, 1990). So, this view opposes the view of the 'flex spec' model and Porter's concept, which argue for a belief in the regional (and national) embeddedness of economic activities and a mosaic of self-propelling regions (see Van Houtum and Boekema, 1994).

As to the matter of declining regions and nations, it can be argued that Porter does not give a complete picture of the evolution of a region or nation. The clusters, the networking in a region are a result of the past. There is no guarantee that the proper functioning of the network will continue in the future. Any region or nation will have certain fluctuations in development over time. Porter does appeal for a continuous upgrade of the conditions of success. The question is, nevertheless, how this can be done. Further he states: 'a factor disadvantage in a static model of competition can be reversed in a dynamic one' (Porter, 1990, 78). The possible reverse outcome, a dynamic into a static effect, has not been considered.

Nevertheless, it is clear that also for a regional economy, 'trees do not grow to the sky', that there seems to be a natural stop to the growth of an agglomeration. Besides, it is often very difficult to change the regional economic path (Lambooy, 1988). In some core areas, for instance, with a high density of infrastructure and the best attainable agglomerations, some 'old' manufacturing areas are still present. Wallonia in Belgium and the Ruhr area are two striking examples. These areas have problems adapting to the changed economic environment and are suffering from what could be called 'involution' (Whyte, 1965). Development in these regions is restrained by the governing and fixed structure of the declining industry.

Other, mostly metropolitan, areas in the 'Banana' region of Europe suffer from what could be called *agglomeration diseconomies*, of which inner-city problems such as criminality, ethnic problems, congestion, unemployment, and environmental problems are the best known. Thus, the regions with the highest density of (extra and intra) information flows and infrastructural links are not automatically the most promising or prosperous regions.

However, some authors state that it is possible for 'new' industries to suddenly pop up in these 'disabled' regions (Ayadalot, 1984; Amin and Thrift, 1992, Lambooy, 1993). This is what Storper and Walker called *'leapfrogging'* (Storper and Walker, 1989) or what Lambooy referred to as *'spatial jumping'* (Lambooy, 1993) and is essential in the evolutionary point of view: mutations take place in the margin of the large group. So, they then declare that rising industrial areas tend not to be in the largest centers of a nation's urban hierarchy, but in the periphery of these agglomerations. In this way, they try to make it clear that economic development is not dependent on logical locational conditions alone.

(5) Local versus global

In Porter's plea for striving for competitive advantage, he emphasizes the importance of the home base. However, it may be questioned, taking the emphasis on the ongoing internationalization processes in the economy into account, how regional/national the home base can be. How regional/national are industries within a country?

Many commentators on Porter's book have criticized this idea of the home base. Compared to the mainstream of strategic management, Porter does indeed take a distinctive point of view in this matter. Porter's view runs counter to most prevailing thinking which emphasizes the coming of a global economy[11] (see, e.g., Levitt (1983), Reich (1991), Dicken (1992), Bartlett and Ghoshal (1989) on this point). A role model of the proclamation of globalization is, for instance, Kenichi Ohmae, director of Mc Kinsey in Japan. His professional career seems dedicated to describing the trend of globalization. The deposit of his efforts can be found in his most famous books: 'Triad power: the coming shape of global competition' (Ohmae, 1985) and 'The borderless world' (Ohmae, 1990). In the latter, he states that on a competitive map, one showing the real flows of financial and industrial activity, boundaries have largely disappeared. The world has become one market, one village. The central message of these authors is that the world economy is increasingly governed by a few firms with looser ties with their home bases.

In Porter's approach, as in the flexible specialization approach, it is contended that nations and regions do matter. That geography and history do matter. In their views the spatial manifestation of the modern economic system can be seen as a movement in two directions: on one hand, a further globalization of control by transnational corporations and, at the same time, the spatial agglomeration of creative and innovative networks of linkages. What is more: *International linkages and strategies are explained by the regional pattern and formation of linkages and interfirm relationships*. It is this explanation, in the juxtaposition of global and regional networks, that can be seen as characteristic of Porter (Van Houtum and Boekema, 1994).
Porter:

The more competition becomes global, ironically, the more important the home base becomes. Differences in values, traditions, histories, economic structures and institutions are not threatened by the increasing globalization of competition, but they are vital to success in it (Porter, 1990a, 145).

Furthermore in Porter's approach, cooperation with firms from other nations should be selective:

A firm must selectively add to its advantages or offset home-based disadvantages through activities in other nations. That is what global strategy is all about. (Porter, 1990, 606)

It is in this direction that he argues elsewhere:

Alliances, or coalitions, are a final mechanism by which a firm can seek to tap national advantages in other nations. Alliances are long-term agreements between firms from different nations that go beyond normal market transactions but stop short of merger (Porter, 1990, 612).

However several commentators have questioned to what extent the home base can be completely autarkic, even in the beginning of the growth of the firms (see, e.g., De Jong, 1986; Dunning, 1993; Rugman and Verbeke, 1993). Three major points of criticism are mentioned here. Firstly, some industries may indeed be national or regional, while some others, like the computer business, are almost directly of supra-national relevance (as will be argued in chapter 5 for the telecom industry). In this respect, as Dunning argues, Porter's 'diamond' might be an underestimation of the significance of the globalization of production and markets (Dunning, 1993). Secondly, for large economies, like those of the United States, Japan, and Germany, it may be argued that a home base is very fundamental in shaping a business. It seems much less relevant for small and open countries. In that case, for some industries related and supporting industries and clients should be more internationalized. Then networking can also be a global phenomenon. There is more interdependence between the firms than Porter wants us to believe. This interdependence is stimulated by countries as well. They are trying to attract capital and labour to the 'home bases' for they believe *inbound* foreign direct investment could be profitable for the national 'diamond' as well. Especially Rugman and Verbeke have elaborated further on the inbound foreign direct investment movement in the global economy. In the case of small open countries they would rather speak of a mosaic of 'diamond's instead of a single 'diamond' approach. Dunning adds to this, for the case of the EC:

> Integration inevitably means national diamonds have to be replaced by supranational diamonds. (Dunning, 1993, 12)

Thirdly, Porter's view on internationalization is hard to combine with his own cluster approach. Clustering, networking, is in his view to be seen as an important factor in achieving competitive advantage for some industries, but networking with firms from outside the home base should only be done selectively. In his view competition and not collaboration between firms from different nations should be the driving force in economic behaviour.

> Alliances are frequently transitional devices. They profilerate in industries undergoing structural change or escalating competition, where managers fear that they cannot cope. They are a response to uncertainty, and provide comfort that the firm is taking action. (Porter, 1990, 67; see also Porter, 1990b)

In other words, according to Porter, coalition between firms is more an indicator of mediocrity than of progressive corporate practice. The combination of world-wide competition and selective tapping in foreign 'diamonds' is hard to maintain. This kind of internationalization process may well lead to a certain lock-in process, that is, 'a focus of the network on the network itself'. It denies the actual importance of outward-looking networking on the one hand, and, on the other hand, the influence of developments along the global intra and intercorporate networking within which an individual regional network is positioned. International networking is to be considered a new form of internationalization, alongside market and hierarchically oriented forms of internationalization. Porter's ideas on this matter bring into question the persistence in his plea for intensive interchange and cooperation, based only on home base factors, as set out in his 'diamond' approach. This discussion of local versus global is surely not conclusive yet.

Concluding this section on the theoretical value of Porter's concept, we can assert that because of Porter's work the importance of the geographical reconcentration of production is again being stressed in economic science. His theory of 'regional economic competitive advantage' reminds us of several elements of older and newer theories within the field of regional economics and corporate geography. Especially the 'filière-configurations' model and the 'flexible specialization' model have a lot in common with Porter's work. Furthermore, his approach stresses the relevance of institutional elements in the theory of international trade. By doing this, he has made this theory not only more dynamic and more complex, but also more realistic. Yet there still remain some major shortcomings in Porter's theory. For one thing, he has not succeeded in specifying the uniqueness of the actors and factors responsible for the explanation of economic performance. The reasoning on which he claims to have based the method for predicting the competitive advantage of nations is certainly not yet sound. We believe that the players in the field are overpowered by his emphasis on the importance of field itself, the home base. The actors are overwhelmed by the factors. The theory is out of balance. Networks may well be used to explain economic strength but then a more complex network analysis is needed. Moreover a network approach in itself is, certainly on a regional economic level, merely a derivation of the action and interaction modes of individual actors. In Porter's book the driving forces for individual economic behaviour, be it networking, be it exporting or 'upgrading' in a region have not been explored.

5. Evaluation of Porter's measurement of regional economic performance

In the second section of this chapter, it was mentioned that competitiveness is actually a micro-economic concept. The translation to the territorial level is difficult. Porter uses the concept to segment the nation into industries and segments of industries and he suggests that this method could readily be applied to *'units smaller than a nation'*[12]. Nevertheless, we have seen in section 4 that this application is not made without difficulties. The most important problems are the following:

(1) The first critical issue is the use of the term 'competitiveness'. This term might be misleading as it is also used as an indicator of the attractiveness for foreign investors of the territory compared with other nations or regions. In this sense, nations compete with each other. Not in any other sense. We suggest the use of the term economic performance instead.

(2) The indicators used, export and foreign direct investment, are not useful on a regional economic level. In this case the flow of physical and non-physical goods within the country are not reckoned with. Moreover,

210 Boekema, Van Houtum

by using only outflow indicators nothing is said about the non-outward industries in a region, which may well be important for regional economic performance as a whole. Lastly, these indicators cannot tell us anything about the economic health of the industries in the future. They merely report past performance.

(3) Porter's main interest is the measurement of the 'environmental' component of regional economic performance. In such a method regions are assessed on the presence and the quality of the regional characteristics relevant for the different types of firms. The specific aspects of the production structure and the production milieu are then assessed on their presence and quality, after which the distribution of sectors empirically found in the region is explained and predicted with the help of these regional aspects. This principle has its roots in the Revealed Comparative Advantage (RCA) principle developed by Balassa, which we discussed in the second section. Nevertheless, there are a few weaknesses related to the meso-economic approach. By choosing such a high aggregation level, the unavoidable takes place: one loses sight of the details, the micro-economic level. That is what is generally called the *aggregative fallacy*. Even in the most successful sectors, weak firms are present and vice versa. Tettero, in his investigation of the economic performance of the Netherlands, states that it is therefore necessary to seek the relative weaknesses and strengths on the lowest aggregation level, especially in highly developed countries (Tettero, 1987).

Secondly, a *composition fallacy* is often made when using the meso-economic approach. It is possible that on a micro-economic level all kinds of factors and actors are important in determining the economic potential of the firm that on a higher aggregated level are not, or are in a different composition of relevance. The characteristics of competition within a specific industry between two countries can differ from competition between two firms from the same industry in the two countries.

(4) The application of Porter's approach on a regional economic level has shown that the availability of relevant data needed to make the cluster chart of a region is problematic. More importantly, the cluster approach cannot be used as a direct tool for the measurement of economic performance. The cluster division is a mechanism for the theoretical handling of his concept of competitiveness. The networking method is 'input' and can be useful in the (statistical) search for the elements responsible for the results, but it is not 'output'. A clear distinction has to be made between input and output indicators.

(5) In an economic sense, national borders are not easier to cross than regional borders, since national borders are also the borders of

influence of national government. The institutionalization of economic developments is consequently more restricted nationally than regionally. It is from an economic point of view more difficult to limit space to a region than to a nation. The concept of a region is therefore less easy to define. This even holds for a large federal state like the United States. Nevertheless, in that case regions are, first of all, bigger and, secondly, much more independent. Regional economic competitiveness is therefore in a territorial sense partly dependent on the definition of 'region'.

Porter argues that his theory could be applied to any kind of geo-graphical level. But, in his book, attention for the regional economic level is overpowered by emphasis on the national level. For evaluation of the economic performance of a 'unit smaller than a nation', without an 'American bias', it is much more appropriate to stick to the micro-economic level. But, as argued in point 2, data-availability then becomes a problem.

In other words, the trade-off between scientific purity and empirical pragmatism then becomes apparent. The statistical information on a micro-economic level, necessary to make qualified statements, is often more privacy-sensitive, differentiated, and labour intensive.

A second problem is that it is difficult to aggregate the findings. An important criticism of analyses on the meso-economic level is, as we have seen, that it is difficult to go beyond (statistical) associations and integrate the single 'outliers', whereas on a micro-level, it is often difficult to go beyond the case-study level.

This dilemma in the choice of analytical level is characteristic of the measurement of territorial economic performance. One has to bear in mind that full conceptual certainty cannot be obtained with any of the measurement methods. In order to measure, one always has to limit one's scope.

The sometimes large differences in point of view between the various studies are in that respect imaginable. A new and different view on this topic and the subsequent fundamental debate is for that reason more than welcome. We have been working on a new model to measure the econ-omic performance of regions (EIT, 1993; 1994). We have developed a so-called economic barometer, whereby the results obtained directly from firms, the micro-economic level, are further analyzed on a meso-econ-omic level. By using this model as a supplementary dataset at the regional level, it is possible to give an accurate judgement of the actual economic situation and the regional economic development for the coming year, assessed by the firms themselves. We will discuss this measurement tool in more detail in the next section.

5.1 Towards a new measurement of regional economic performance

For the measurement of regional economic performance, we will have to put more emphasis on the actual and future economic strength of firms in the regional economy. In the central Brabant region, with Tilburg as its most important city, an attempt has been made to measure the concept of regional economic performance with this in mind (EIT, 1993; 1994). Using data from the so-called 'Enquête Regionale Bedrijfsontwikkeling'(ERBO) research project as a basis, two indicators have been developed: the 'ERABO-ther' and 'ERABO-bar'[13]. The ERBO research project is a very large field study which is undertaken each year by the Chambers of Commerce in about 70,000 enterprises all over the country. In recent years some attempts have been made to construct a model to give an actual and detailed presentation of economic performance and at the same time a prediction of the regional economic performance. Most recently, Chambers of Commerce and INRO/TNO developed the so-called 'ERbo INdicator'(ERIN) and Erbo VITAliteits-meter (EVITA) indicator. These two indicators, however, make no clear distinction between the actual situation and future developments. In our view, the ERABO indicators do not have this shortcoming. ERABO-ther (thermometer) is used to measure the actual economic situation, whereas ERABO-bar (barometer) predicts the economic situation for the coming year.

In the ERABO indicator, three micro-economic aspects have been distinguished: the development of the turnover, the investments, and the gross profits of the firms. We have chosen to weigh the employment factor as well, since investments alone is not seen as a sound indicator for the growth of an enterprise, especially not in the case of labour intensive firms.

The total indicator is composed as follows:

ERABO = 0.5x Turnover + 0.2x Gross profit + 0.3x Investment/ employment

It can be ascertained that in our performance indicator, growth-factors are dominant, for, in fact, two growth components are involved, turnover and investment/employment. The emphasis is put on growth, for the reason that these factors have the largest spread-effects to the region as a whole. Size and growth of turnover are, at the same time, the basis for the ultimate performance of enterprises. As a consequence of growth in turnover, it may be assumable that business profit, investments, and employment are positively influenced as well.

In 1993 and again in 1994, a telephone-interview was conducted with firms in the region. The firms had 10 or more employees and were mainly from the industrial, construction, transport, business service, and wholesale trade sectors. In order to get a high number of respondents, 1,086 firms were contacted. The response was about 55% (592 firms). The firm results were segmented into sectors of industry. These results have been transformed into two different scales from which it is easy to read and understand the economic performance. Actual economic performance is ranked on a scale from 0 to 10: '0' means very bad and '10' means excellent. The mark '6' means sufficient, whereas '5' means insufficient. In the next table, the scores for central Brabant from the thermometer are presented for the two years.

Table 4. The thermometer scores for the central Brabant region

Branch of industry	Thermometer			Mutation '92-'93
	1991	1992	1993	
Food industry	7.59	6.99	6.41	-
Textiles and clothing industry	6.17	5.85	5.79	-
Paper and graphic industry	6.63	6.61	6.66	+
Chemical industry	7.64	7.64	6.44	--
Metal industry	6.21	6.35	5.91	-
Other industries	6.48	6.50	5.34	--
Construction industry	6.31	5.94	5.62	-
Wholesale trade	6.68	6.40	6.21	-
Retail trade	6.45	6.13	5.95	-
Catering ind. & reparation bus.	6.43	6.10	5.54	-
Transport, communication	6.50	6.63	5.44	--
Business services	6.53	6.50	6.05	-
Central Brabant	6.53	6.36	5.91	-

Source: EIT, 1994

Clear differences exist among the industries in central Brabant. On the whole, performance has decreased. The largest decrease could be found in the chemical, the transport, and 'other' industries. Furthermore, in 1993 some of the industries had a figure lower than 6, which clearly indicates a stagnation in their growth.

We used a different ranking-scale for the barometer, which is based on the firms' expectations on the four elements mentioned in the ERABO indicator. The range of ranks is limited to between '-1' and '+1'. These figures can be interpreted as follows: '-1' means that very poor economic development is expected, while '+1' means that the economic expectations are very optimistic. If the barometer score is '0', no change in the actual situation is expected (table 5).

Table 5. The barometer scores for the central Brabant region

Branch of industry	Barometer			Mutation '93-'94
	1992	1993	1994	
Food industry	0.53	0.47	0.29	-
Textiles and clothing industry	0.24	0.10	0.07	0
Paper and graphic industry	0.54	0.29	0.30	0
Chemical industry	0.47	0.26	0.24	0
Metal industry	0.37	0.21	0.11	-
Other industries	0.38	0.18	0.01	-
Construction industry	0.19	-0.05	0.09	+
Wholesale trade	0.27	0.23	0.36	+
Retail trade	0.25	0.21	0.16	-
Catering ind. & reparation bus.	0.23	0.18	0.04	-
Transport, communication	0.28	0.32	0.12	-
Business services	0.25	0.38	0.20	-
Central Brabant	0.30	0.21	0.16	-

Source: EIT 1994

Although the actual situation in 1993 was a bit pessimistic, the firms still see the future (1994) optimistically. All assessments are still above zero. Net-profits are expected to be positive again. The growth of investments and employment, however, was expected to be negative.

This ERABO indicator could be seen as the sum of individual performances of firms. It is valuable together with a more traditional SWOT analysis of a region. It should not be seen as an alternative, but an addition to the present regional standards. Now not only from a researcher's point of view, but also from the side of the firms a valuation of the regional economic performance can be given. It may be an impetus for renewed attention to the importance of the micro-economic level in the measurement of regional economic performance.

6. Conclusion

The application of the Porter approach at the regional level is difficult and results in many theoretical as well as operational problems. We have summarized the most important problems. In regard to Porter's theoretical point of view, it can be concluded that it is insightful, to a certain extent useful, but not yet explicit enough. The ideas themselves are certainly not new, but they are now used in a more analytical way. Both the breadth and apparent practicability of his approach, together with outstanding marketing of his concept, has challenged theorists as well as politicians to translate the ideas in their own terms. This has in a way caused a resurgence in the study of regional economic processes in the economy. Perhaps we might say that Porter was the inspiration for reviving interest for internal relationships in the regional economy. In our view, the increased attention to his work could be truly justified if his ideas had set the pace for a more accurate theoretical approach.

The same holds for the indicator Porter uses. Although the concept of national/regional competitiveness is already old, no unambiguous definition/indicator has been found yet. Porter's approach to the measurement of regional economic performance is essentially input-oriented and does not measure the results of the economic developments for a region.

In our view, more attention should be paid to the actual performance of firms in a region. It is for this reason, in recent years, we have attempted to construct a model that is more suitable for measuring the regional economic performance in this respect. The development of the ERABO indicators is a first step towards such an approach. By consulting the thermometer and the barometer of one region one gets a distinctive view of the competitiveness of the *firms in a region.*

Acknowledgment: The authors wish to thank Willem de Graaff for his technical help in preparing the figures in this contribution.

Notes

1. Porter does not give a definition of the term cluster in his own book.

2. An interesting question of another order is to what extent the creation of a welfare optimum in a region is also a societal optimum. The definition of economic performance would then even have to be broader. The 'competitiveness' of the Netherlands would have to be seen in a more comprehensive, not purely economic way. In this contribution, however, we will focus only on the smaller welfare definition of economic performance.

3. See Chapter 1 for further explanation.

4. The regional production structure stands for the composition of economic sectors and enterprises within a region.

5. Necessary to say is that an overrepresentation in relative terms (compared to the Netherlands) does not have to imply that a specific cluster in a particular region is the largest cluster in absolute terms. ETIN did go into more detail in their report, but we are merely focusing here on the relative specializations.

6. These regions are so-called COROP-regions, a division which is often used in regional geography.

7. It should be stressed here that this model is a meta-model of reality. It does not involve all factors and actors relevant for a certain region, nor does it reflect our view on regional economic structuring. It is merely a conceptual schema showing how individual firms are interlinked within the flexible specialization approach.

8. It is acknowledged by various authors that flexible specialization and economies of agglomeration can be the result of clustering of small firms or the clustering of small firms around large industries (see, e.g., Schmitz, 1989).

9. See also Granovetter (1985). He stated that it is important to avoid under-socialized and oversocialized models of action, and to recognize that actors

have social as well as economic motives. Their actions have an impact on and they are influenced by the networks of relationships in which they are embedded.

10. See Toulmin et al. (1984) for a further explanation of validity of a theoretical framework.

11. Their view on global corporations is in fact restricted to the three world markets: EC, Japan and United States, the so-called Triad Power.

12. Of course, Porter is not the only one trying to find indicators for territorial competitiveness. The actual number of studies on this subject is very large and so is their heterogeneity (See Van Houtum, 1991; Ummels, 1993). Time seems ripe for an unequivocal indicator, which can be used as a definition as well.

13. The development of these indicators and application to the central Brabant region are partly financed by the RABObank. This is why it is called Erbo RABObank (ERABO).

References

Amin, A., Robbins K. - Industrial districts and regional developments: limits and possibilities. - In: Pyke F., G. Beccatini and W. Sengenberger (eds.) / *Industrial districts and inter-firm co-operation in Italy.* - Geneva: ILO, 1990

Amin, A., N. Thrift - Neo-Marshallian nodes in a global network. - In: *International Journal of Urban and Regional Research*, 16 (4), 1992, p. 571-587

Ayadalot, Ph. - Reversal in spatial trends in French Industry since 1974. - In: J.G. Lambooy (ed.) / *New spatial dynamics and economic crisis.* - Tampere: Finnpublishers, 1984, p. 41-62

Balassa, B. - Trade liberalization and revealed comparative advantage. - In: *Manchester School of Economic and Social Studies*, vol 33., no 1, 1965, p. 103-123

Bartlett, C.A., S. Ghoshal - Managing across borders: the transnational solution. - Harvard Business School Press, Boston, 1989

Best, M.H. - *The new competition, Institutions of industrial restructuring.* - Polity Press: Cambridge, 1990

Chardonnet, J. - *Les grands types de complexes industriels.* -, Paris: Librairie Armand, 1953

Cox, K.R. - *Period and place, capitalist development and the flexible specialization debate.* - paper for the Conference on Flexible Accumulation, Indiana University, 1994

Dankbaar, B. - *Economic crisis and institutional change, the crisis of Fordism from the perspective of the automobile industry.* - Maastricht: Universitaire Pers, Maastricht, 1993

De Jong, H.W. - Markteconomie: ondernemerschap en economische theorie. - In: *Economenblad*, jg 8, april 1986

Dicken, P. - *Global shift, The internationalization of economic activity.* - London: Paul Chapman, 1992

Dunning, J.H. - Internationalizing Porter's diamond. - In: *Management International Review*, vol. 33, 1992, p. 7-16

Economisch Instituut Tilburg (EIT) - J. Dagevos, W. van Zwol, H. van Houtum, F. Boekema - *Sociaal-economische Barometer, Midden-Brabantse en Tilburgse economische verkenningen 1993.* - Tilburg

Economisch Instituut Tilburg (EIT) - W. van Zwol, F. Boekema - *Sociaal-economische Barometer, Midden-Brabantse en Tilburgse economische verkenningen 1994.* - Tilburg

Economisch Technologisch Instituut Noord-Brabant (ETIN) - *De Brabantse Economie met open grenzen.* - in cooperation Buck Consultants International, Tilburg/Nijmegen, 1992

Froebel, F., J. Heinrichs and O. Kreye - *The new international division of labor.* - Cambridge: Cambridge University Press, 1977

Gertler M.S. - *In search of the new social economy: collaborative relations between users and producers of advanced manufacturing technologies.* - Paper for the Regional Science Association International, Niagara Falls, Ontario, 1994

Grant, R.M. - Porter's 'competitive advantage of nations': an assessment. - *Strategic Management Journal,* 1991, vol. 12, p. 535-48

Granovetter, M. - Economic action and social structure, the problem of embeddedness. - In: *American Journal of sociology,* 91 (3), 1985, p. 418-510

Gramsci, A. - *Prison Notebooks.* - 1930

Henry, N. - The new industrial spaces: locational logic of a new production era? - In: *Journal of Urban and regional research,* vol 16.3, 1992, p. 375-396

Houtum, H.J. van, - *The competitive advantage of regions- A critical view and application of the analysis of Porter 'The competitive advantage of nations' on Dutch regional level.* - doctoral thesis, Tilburg: Tilburg University, 1991

Houtum, H.J. van, F. Boekema - Regions seen as laboratories for a new Europe: the applicability of the flexible specialization approach. - In: *Changing Business Systems* / J.J.J. van Dijck, J.P.M. Groenewegen. - Brussels: VUBpress, 1994

Hymer S. - The multinational corporation and the law of uneven development. - In: J. Bhagwai (Ed.) / *Economics and world order.* - 1972, New York: Free Press, p. 113-140

Hymer S. - *The international operations of national firms, a study of direct foreign investments.* - Cambridge: MIT Press, 1976

Krafcik, J.F. - Triumph of the lean production system. - In: *Sloan Management Review* 30 (1), 1988, p. 41-52

Krugman, P. - *Geography and trade.* - Cambridge: MIT Press, 1991

Lagendijk, A. - *The internationalization of the Spanish automobile industry and its regional impact, the emergence of a growth-periphery.* - Tinbergen Institute Research Studies no. 59, Rotterdam, 1993

Lambooy, J.G. - *Regionale economische dynamiek.* - Muiderberg: Coutinho, 1992

Lambooy, J.G. - Regional economic development in Europe: external or internal sources? - In: *Steden en regio's in Europa* / J. van Dijk en M.W. de Jong (red.). - Nieuwe ideeën in Nederlands Ruimtelijk onderzoek, papers van de RSA Nederland dag 1992, Geopers, 1993

Levitt, T. - The globalization of markets. - *Harvard Business Review,* May-June, 1983, p. 92-102

Marshall, A. - *The principle of economics.* - Mac Millan Press: London, 1890, reprinted in 1920

Miles, R., C. Snow - Causes of failures in Network Organizations. - *California Management Review,* 34 (4), 1992

Ministry of Economic Affairs (Ministerie van Economische Zaken) - *Economie met open grenzen (Economy with open frontiers).* - Den Haag: SDU, 1990

Myrdal, G. - *Economic theory and underdeveloped regions.* - Duckworth, London, 1957

Ohmae, K. - *Triad power: the coming shape of global competition.* - New York: Free Press, 1985

Ohmae, K. - *The borderless world, management lessons in the new logic of the global marketplace, power and strategy in the interlinked economy.* - Harper Business, 1990

Perroux F. - Note sur la notion de pôle de croissance. - In: *Economie Appliqué 8,* 1955, p. 302-320

Piore, M.J., C.F. Sabel - *The Second Industrial Divide; possibilities for prosperity.* - New York: Basic Books, 1984

Pyke, F. - *Industrial development through small-firm cooperation, theory and practice-International labor office.* - Geneva, 1992

Porter, M. - *The competitive advantage of nations.* - Mac Millan Press: London, 1990

Porter, M.E. - Europe's companies after 1992: don't collaborate, compete. - In: *The Economist,* 9 June 1990, p. 17-21

Reich, R.B. - *The work of nations, preparing ourselves for 21st century capitalism.* - Alfred A. Knopf: New York, 1991

Richardson, G.B. - The organization of industry. - In: *Economic Journal,* vol. 82, 1972, p. 883-96

Rugman, A.M., A. Verbeke - Foreign subsidiaries and multinational strategic management, An extension and correction of Porter's single diamond framework. - *Management International Review,* vol. 33, 1993, p. 71-84

Ruigrok, W. and R. van Tulder - *The ideology of interdependence, the link between restructuring, internationalization and international trade.* - Amsterdam, 1993

Schmitz, H - *Flexible specialization in third world industry: prospects and research requirements.* - industrialization seminar, Institute of Social Sciences, The Hague, 1990

Scott, A.J. - *Metropolis, from the division of labor to urban form.* - University of California Press, 1988

Scott, A. - *New Industrial Spaces.* - Pion: London, 1988

Smith, A. - *The wealth of nations.* - 1937, 1965, New York: Modern Library (first published in 1776)

Storper, M. - The limits of globalization: Technology districts and International Trade. - In: *Economic Geography,* 68 (1), 1992, p. 60-91

Storper, M. - Regional worlds of production: learning and innovation in the technology districts of France, Italy and USA. - In: *Regional Studies,* vol. 27.5, 1993, p. 433-455

Storper, M., R. Walker - *The capitalist imperative, Territory, Technology, and Industrial growth.* - Basil Blackwell, Oxford, 1989

Tettero, J.H.J.P - *Het concurrentieprofiel van Nederland, Een analyse van het concurrentieprofiel van Nederland in vergelijking met Zweden en Oostenrijk.* - Kanters: Alblasserdam, 1987

Technologisch Nederland Onderzoeksinstituut (TNO), Jacobs D., P. Boekholt, and W. Zegveld - *De economische kracht van Nederland, Een toepassing van Porters' benadering van de concurrentiekracht van landen.* - Stichting Maatschappij en Onderneming: 's-Gravenhage, 1990

Toulmin S., R. Rieke, A. Janik - *An Introduction to reasoning.* - New York: Mac Millan Press, 1984

Ummels, G., - *Perken voor netwerken.* - doctoral thesis, University Tilburg, 1993

Vaessen, P. - *Small business growth in contrasting environments.* - Nijmeegse Geografische cahiers no 40: Nijmegen, 1993

Whyte, L.L. - *Internal factors in evolution.* - London: Tavistock Publications, 1965

Williamson, O.E. - *The economic institutions of Capitalism.* - New York: Free Press, 1985

Womack, J.P., D.T. Jones, and D. Roos - *The machine that changed the world.* - New York: Rawson Associates, 1991

Chapter 7

M.T.H. MEEUS, L.A.G. OERLEMANS

THE COMPETITIVENESS OF FIRMS IN THE REGION OF NORTH BRABANT
An exploratory analysis of Porter's theory of competitiveness at the level of firms

1. Introduction

In 'The Competitive Advantage of Nations' (1990, 19) Porter aims at the development of a new theory which explains why firms from a particular nation choose better strategies[1] than those from others for competing in particular industries. *So, Porter's central question is: why do firms based in particular nations achieve international success in distinct segments and industries?* To answer this question, Porter developed an, at first glance, attractive methodology and a theoretical framework. Porter's 'diamond' proved to be a valid explanatory framework. The theoretical and methodological evaluation presented in this chapter proves that the empirical claims of Porter's theory are restricted to a specific methodological level and a specific set of 'diamond' factors explaining competitive advantage.

This evaluation consists of two elements. The first element is methodological. Here the question is answered: what is the level of analysis of Porter's theory of competitive advantage? Is it the level of firms, industries or nations? The second element is theoretical and focuses on questions regarding the consistency of Porter's theoretical framework. The questions are: 1) Is there a clear conceptual distinction between factors determining the competitive advantage of nations and the factors determining the competitive advantage of firms?; 2) Which set of factors is analyzed empirically?; 3) Does Porter's theory explain how factors determining the competitive advantage of nations are related to factors determining the competitive advantage of firms? By answering these questions, the empirical claims of Porter's theory can be assessed.

Broadening the empirical claims of Porter's theory to other levels of analysis requires answers to the aforementioned questions and a modification of Porter's theoretical framework so that it is applicable at other levels of analysis. This latter concern is precisely what this chapter is all about. In fact we are trying to *validate Porter's theory as a cross-level* dent and dependent variables at *different* levels of analysis (Rousseau, 1985, 20).

2. An evaluation of Porter's theory

2.1 A methodological problem: levels of analysis

At first sight Porter's level of analysis is the *nation*. He examines the decisive characteristics of a nation that allow its firms to create and sustain competitive advantage in particular fields. The reason for this choice is simple. Porter asserts that competitive advantage is created and sustained through a highly localized process which is shaped and influenced by government policies (Porter, 1990, 620). These policies provide the local resources[2] (production factors) and incentives necessary to compete. Differences in national economic structures, values, cultures, institutions, and histories contribute profoundly to competitive success. In other words, at first sight the competitive advantage is produced at the level of nations.

In chapter two, Porter refers to several other levels of analysis. In the introduction Porter puts forward that: 'Firms, not nations, compete in international markets.' (Porter, 1990, 33). However, in the following paragraph on 'Competitive Strategy' the basic unit of analysis for understanding competition shifts to the level of *industries*. Apparently the solution to this problem is found in the introduction of chapter three. Here Porter tries to explain that the competitive advantage of nations cannot be understood by analyzing the actions of nations.

> The way that firms create and sustain competitive advantage in global industries provide the necessary foundation for understanding the role of the home nation in the process. (Porter, 1990, 69)

When Porter (1990, 29) argues that the underlying issues are even broader than the role of nations (or locales) and that what he is really exploring is the way in which a firm's proximate 'environment' influences competitiveness, his position regarding his unit of analysis becomes rather ambiguous. The reason for this ambiguity is that Porter does not describe whose (nations, firms, industries) competitiveness is meant.

The solution to this methodological problem is found in Appendix A (Methodology for Preparing Cluster Charts) (Porter, 1990, 739). Each nation's chart was constructed by identifying all the industries (both product and service) in which the nation has achieved success in international competition. Summarized, Porter's theory is based on data gathered at the level of firms, aggregated to the level of industries whose competitive advantage are compared at the level of nations. In other words the starting point of his analysis is the competitive advantage of industries.

The conclusion of this methodological evaluation is that Porter's research question suggests a methodologically broader scope than he could claim for with his methodology. His empirical statements are limited to industries of several nations. The implication is that Porter ought to avoid the suggestion that his theory explains why *firms* are competitive. His empirical claim has to be limited to the level of industries aggregated at nations.

2.2 The theoretical framework: factors determining competitiveness

In Porter's review of the theoretical foundations of competitive advantage the causes of competitiveness are discussed. Porter (1990, 29) describes that theoretically a lot is known about what competitive advantage is and how particular actions create or destroy it. So that is not the object of his study. Instead Porter focuses on the fact that much less is known about *why* a company makes good choices instead of bad choices in seeking a basis for competitive advantages, and *why* some firms are more aggressive in pursuing them. The object of Porter's study seems to be redefined again with a shift to another level of analysis: the level of the firm. This causes some serious theoretical problems especially regarding the theoretical range of the concepts describing factors determining competitiveness of firms and nations.

We proceed with an evaluation of Porter's theory of competitiveness in order to assess the problems that arise because of his continually shifting level of analysis. First a short review of Porter's theoretical framework is given. Subsequently the theoretical clarity of the framework will be discussed.

In chapters three and four of his book Porter describes a static and dynamic model of interacting determinants of national advantage. The description of his famous 'diamond' is guided by a short introduction:

Why does a nation achieve international success in a particular industry? The answer lies in four broad attributes of a nation that shape the environment in which local firms compete, that promote or impede the creation of competitive advantage... (Porter, 1990, 71)

Because firms, not nations, compete in international markets, the first part of Porter's theoretical framework consists of an overview of the forces in the internal and external environment of the firm that determine the competitiveness of firms in industries. These factors can be called factors determining the Competitive Advantage of Firms (caf-factors). Caf-factors consist of (Porter, 1990, ch. 2):
- an overview of forces that facilitate competition;
- aspects of firms' strategies, e.g. positioning within industries, organization and performance of discrete activities;
- acts directed at creating competitive advantage broadly defined as acts of innovation and forces facilitating innovation, e.g.: technological changes, new or shifting buyer needs, the emergence of a new industry segment, shifting input costs or availability, changes in government regulation.

The second part of Porter's theoretical framework consists of a group of factors described as determinants of the Competitive Advantage of Nations - the famous 'diamond' (can-factors). These can-factors are defined as 'four broad attributes of a nation that shape the environment in which local firms compete that promote or impede the creation of competitive advantage.' (Porter, 1990, 71). Porter distinguishes the following can-factors:
- *Factor conditions.* The nation's position in factors of production, such as skilled labour or infrastructure, necessary to compete in a given industry.
- *Demand conditions.* The nature of the home demand for the industry's product or service.
- *Related and supporting industries.* The presence or absence in the nation of supplier industries and related industries that are nationally competitive.
- *Firm strategy, structure and rivalry.* The conditions in the nation governing how companies are created, organized, and managed, and the nature of domestic rivalry.

The can-factors create the context in which a nation's firms are born and compete: the availability of resources and skills necessary for competitive advantage in an industry; the information that shapes what opportunities are perceived and the directions in which resources and skills are deployed; the goals of the owners, managers and employees that are involved in or carry out competition; and most important the pressures on firms to invest and innovate.

The theory of the competitive advantage of nations consisting of can- and caf-factors seems to be a clear conceptual framework. However, a closer look reveals some serious theoretical problems.

The first problem in the conceptual framework is the overlap in the two sets of can- and caf-factors. The clearest example of the theoretical concordance between the can- and caf-factors can be found in the caf-factors creating competitive advantage e.g. technological changes, governmental policies. In fact those factors can just as well be called can-factors, because the external environment of a firm can also be considered as a set of attributes of a nation. In our opinion those caf-factors can be considered as can-factors because they too create the context in which a nation's firms are born and compete.

The second problem is that Porter's empirical analysis is restricted to can-factors while his statements regarding the caf-factors are made in the form of implications of the analyses of can-factors. Porter reports four studies in national competitive advantage in industries and services and tries to reveal, with several trend-analyses of indicators for competitiveness[3] (1950-1987), patterns of competitive advantage of nine nations. The results are mainly analyses of can-factors, while results of analyses of caf-factors are lacking.

The background of both problems is hidden in the implicit way in which Porter transforms the environmental conditions (can-factors) into caf-factors. However, because Porter considers can-factors as attributes of a nation which shape the environment of firms, it is theoretically not obvious that they are converted into caf-factors (attributes of firms). Probably this theoretical problem is not only caused by the theoretical concordance between the specific can- and caf-factor we just mentioned. The conversion of attributes of nations - the external environment of the firm - into attributes of firms presupposes a theoretical notion about the strategic actions of firms necessary to use or internalize the available resources. The point is that the external environment is a set of resources that might as easily enable as restrict the competitiveness of firms. But the enabling and restrictive functioning of the resources in the external environment can only be deduced from the nature and direction of strategic action of firms which describe how resources and which kind of resources were internalized. This theoretical level is omitted in Porter's theory. Astley and Van de Ven already took account of this problem. According to them in his former publications Porter conceptualized for example market conduct and firm strategy merely as a reflection of the environment (Astley and Van de Ven, 1983, 250). This seems to be a deterministic orientation toward the relation between economic structure

and strategic action. The following lines illustrate vividly Porter's theoretical position. Porter (1990, 71) supposes that firms *gain* competitive advantage:
- when their home base *allows and supports* the most rapid accumulation of specialized assets and skills;
- in industries, when their home base *affords* better ongoing information and insights into product and process needs;
- when the goals of owners, managers, and employees *support* intense communication and sustained investment.

Yet Porter seems to be aware of this theoretical problem of determinism without solving it. He restricts himself to some remarks about the fact that, in nations where the can-factors are the most favourable, national industries are most *likely* to compete successfully. Porter adds - and here the omitted theoretical level is introduced - that not all a nation's firms will achieve competitive advantage and that in fact some firms will fail because not all have equal skills and resources nor do they exploit the national environment equally well (Porter, 1990, 72). Porter did not deal with this problem. For then Porter should have written that firms *are enabled to gain* competitive advantage if *resources would had been internalized* instead of the rather absolute statement according to which *firms gain* competitive advantage if *resources are available*. It just is not obvious that resources will be internalized[4]. The applicability and eloquence of Porter's theory *at the level of firms* is severely restricted by this omission.

To address this theoretical and methodological problem, Porter's theory ought to explain how firms are able to act upon the environment consisting of can-factors and how firms are able to internalize them, thereby converting can-factors into caf-factors. Only by adding this theoretical layer to Porter's theoretical framework, would there be an adequate conceptual framework to explain the conversion of can-factors (attributes of a nation) into caf-factors (attributes of a firm).

Porter does not add an explicit theoretical framework providing a clear set of concepts to show how firms benefit from resources within the organization and resources in the proximate environment of the organization. In the theoretical analysis of his 'diamond' he proves to be an extreme contingency theorist, because all variables in his 'diamond' are conditional upon the other variables. In fact he is schematicising sets of configurations of variables which interact and produce a fertile substratum for creating factor advantages. This also explains why Porter does not provide us with a clear set of hypotheses in which competitive advantage is causally related to factor conditions. Porter just emphasizes that competitive advantage depends on the mutual reinforcement of can-factors possibly facilitated by national governments. The theoretical conclusion must be that competitive advantage is a result of a complex interaction between the presence of factor advantages and the capability to internalize them in firm strategies and structures. In fact, Porter describes the interaction between government policy and firm strategy. Porter's hypothesis is that the rate of factor creation and upgrading determines the potential rate at which a national economy can advance (Porter, 1990, 733).

Summarizing this theoretical evaluation our conclusion is:
- can- and caf-factors lack a sound conceptualisation that makes it possible to distinguish them from one another;
- Porter's theory lacks a theoretical layer explaining the conversion of can- into caf-factors;
- only the can-factors were analyzed empirically.

3. Toward a theoretical model

3.1 The research question

In the introduction we argued that our aim was the empirical validation of Porter's theory as a cross-level theory. To broaden the theoretical claims of Porter's theory on the one hand to the level of the firm, and on the other hand to the caf-factors, a theoretical and methodological problem has to be tackled.

The solution of this problem in our perception consists of the development of measures validly representing can-factors at the level of firms, or as caf-factors. Caf-factors ought to represent the variation in which firms anticipate or react successfully to possibilities to use or internalize resources provided by the external environment. In this way the theoretical layer lacking in Porter's theory is designed.

The theoretical argument for this methodological approach is that factor creation and upgrading can only be facilitated by government agencies, while firms are the actors to implement strategies for factor creation and upgrading. So can-factors must be internalized in firms' strategies and structures, and as such become caf-factors before they can explain why firms vary in their competitiveness. As such, the indicators used for the caf-factors have to measure the conversion of can-factors into caf-factors. This was done by a search for indicators which can be interpreted as measures, transforming attributes of nations (the can-factors) into attributes of firms (caf-factors). Consequently our research question was formulated as:

> Which caf-factors explain the variation with which firms based in the region of North Brabant[5] achieve international success in distinct industries?

Empirically our research question is threefold: which of Porter's factors - factor conditions, demand conditions and industrial networks - are empirically related to the competitiveness of industrial firms located in the region of North Brabant? The search is for decisive characteristics of a population of industrial firms that allows its members to create and sustain competitive advantage in particular fields i.e. the competitive advantage of *firms*. Compared to Porter's central question the main difference is that while Porter directs his attention to nations, we direct our attention to industrial firms in one specific region.

3.2 The theoretical model: making Porter's theory applicable at the level of firms

Before presenting our version of Porter's model we want to explain how it differs from Porter's approach. First, the model developed in this paragraph has to be considered as conceptually inspired by the work of Porter, bearing in mind the aforementioned critique. However, the lower level of analysis, in comparison to Porter (firms versus industries), makes it necessary to use other measures than the aggregate measures Porter uses. We will describe the indicators used to operationalize the 'diamond' factors as caf-factors. Second, our analysis is not based on data gathered at different moments in time. So we cannot make dynamic analyses. Third, our model contains fewer factors than Porter's 'diamond'. Three factors of Porter's model are used as independent variables (factor conditions, demand conditions and network features) to explain the competitiveness of firms in a region. Because *economic conditions* governing how companies are created, organized and managed do not vary within one region, the variable 'firm strategy, structure and rivalry' is omitted in our theoretical model[6]. Fourth, our population contains not only firms from highly competitive industries. Our sample contains all industrial sectors in a specific region.

Our theoretical model is an adaptation of Scherer's structure-conduct-performance model. The alterations regard the performance aspect which is simply left out because Porter did not explore this aspect. The second change in our model, compared to the variables indicating 'structure', are not restricted to 'market structure' as in the theoretical frameworks of Bain (1956) and Scherer (1970) (See also Scherer and Ross, 1990) in which only the market characteristics determine the ease or difficulty with which new firms could successfully come into a market. The theoretical centrality of condition of entry can be considered from an institutional point of view as a too restrictive approach for understanding competitiveness of firms. In this sense our Porterian model can be interpreted as an institutional version of the structure-conduct model.

Figure 1. A conceptual model for caf-factors related to export quote

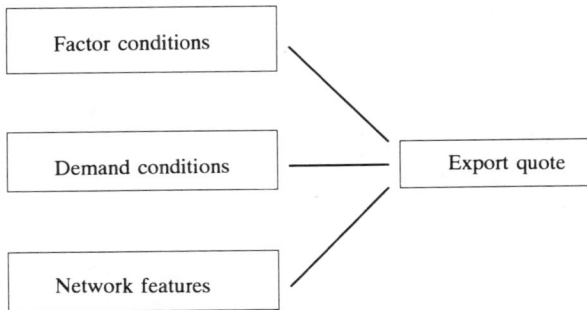

The indicators used to measure *caf-factors* in Figure 1 all represent the extent to which firms successfully used or internalized the resources provided by the external environment. In Table 1 the indicators used to measure the *independent variables* in the theoretical model - factor conditions, demand conditions and network features - are described.

The indicators for *factor conditions* refer especially to *advanced factors* (Porter, 1990, 77). Those advanced factors are the most significant in order to achieve higher-order competitive advantages such as differentiated products and proprietary production technology. The indicators used in our research fit well the factor categories distinguished by Porter (1990, 74). For instance several aspects of R&D activity indicate knowledge resources, capital resources (loss/profit in 1992), human resources (e.g. the percentage of higher educated employees), internal sourcing of innovation, and infrastructure (e.g. the number of automated processes). The indicators we have used were chosen because they are predominantly features produced by firm strategies rather than by governmental policies.

The indicators for the *demand conditions* refer to active and effective anticipation of demand size and patterns of growth (Porter, 1990, 92). The change of strategic position from 1988-1993 indicates the effectiveness of anticipation to changing demands, while the proportional change in turnover between 1988-1993 indicates how far firms succeeded in holding their market position. The indicators referring to the occurrence of product innovation and the orientation toward product innovation show if firms anticipate changing buyer needs (Porter, 1990, 91). In this way the demand conditions were operationalized as attributes of firms.

The *network features* can be considered as indicators for the can-factor 'related and supporting industries' (Porter, 1990, 100-107). However in this study we did not direct our attention to the presence of competitive advantage in downstream industries. Instead of this we focused on:
- the extent and type of networks in which firms are embedded indicated by number of economic relations, number of R&D relations, number of relations with several suppliers, number of customers and the number of relations with knowledge infrastructure;
- the activities organized in networks of customers, focal units and suppliers, e.g.: R&D, knowledge transfer, external influence on innovations;
- the strength of networks with the dependency of firms on their suppliers;
- the regional embeddedness of networks.

The competitiveness of firms - the *dependent variable* - was measured with the export quote: the percentage of annual turnover that is exported.[7]

Table 1. An overview of the indicators used to operationalize can-factors measured as attributes of firms or as caf-factors[8]

Factor conditions	Demand conditions	Network features
- economic performance (loss/profit in 1992) - percentage of higher educated employees - source of ideas for innovation - use of R&D subsidies - occurrence of R&D - R&D department - informal R&D - intensity of R&D - number of automated processes	- proportional change in turnover 88-93 - change in strategic position from 88-93 - occurrence of product innovation - orientation toward process or product innovation	- number of economic relations - number of R&D-relations - dependency of focal unit on suppliers - regional embeddedness - number of suppliers of raw material - number of suppliers of components - number of suppliers of machines and tools - knowledge transfer with supply - number of customers - external influence on innovation - number of relations with knowledge infrastructure

4. Research design, population, research questions and models of analysis

4.1 Research design

In this study a within- and between-subjects design was used. The within-subjects analysis permits researchers to infer the relative importance of particular variables to estimate the export quote within the total population of firms in our sample. In the between-subjects-analyses groups of firms are distinguished with attributes of firms such as: company size (in numbers of workers), type of industrial sector[9], modernity of the industrial sector (traditional or modern)[10] (Kleinknecht and Poot, 1990). For the different subgroups three models were estimated and the results were compared. The three models were: 1) factor conditions and export quote, 2) demand conditions and export quote, and 3) network features and export quote.

4.2 Region and population

A survey was administered to industrial firms with more than five employees in the region of North Brabant (the southern part of the Netherlands). The data gathering took place between December 1992 and January 1993.

The analyses were carried out in only one region, which has specific features. This region, North Brabant, was at the time of the survey in a severe economic crisis. Large firms such as DAF, Volvo (automotive) and Philips (electronics) were confronted with extreme losses which resulted in massive loss of jobs and radical reorganisations. Of course the small and medium-sized organizations, often supplying the larger firms, felt the consequences too. Sales volumes decreased which forced the SME's to search for new markets. In other words, their competitiveness was challenged. These specific conditions signify that Porter's aforementioned question has to be reformulated: *can competitiveness of firms* located in a region confronted with a severe industrial crisis be explained with the 'diamond' factors?

The region of North Brabant has an industrial population of firms which consists of a mix of small, medium-sized and large firms. Furthermore the industry and services in this region have shown a relatively high performance in R&D and export (Kleinknecht and Poot, 1992; Boeckhout and Verkennis, 1993; Den Dunnen, 1993; Roos, 1993, Meeus and Oerlemans 1995).

Table 2 shows that the survey response is a reliable representation of the population of industrial firms in the region of North Brabant. The maximum deviation between the percentages of population sample and the response is within 5% -boundaries except for the metal industry. The mean deviation between the percentage of the population sample and the percentage of responding firms is 2.6%.

Table 2. Population sample and response for sectors

Industrial sectors	Absolute number population sample	Percentage of the population sample	Percentage responding firms (N = 689)
- food and allied products	311	8.9%	6.5%
- textile, apparel and leather goods	370	10.6%	7.5%
- wood products and building materials	480	13.7%	12.7%
- paper, publishing and printing	323	9.3%	5.3%
- chemicals and allied products	227	6.5%	8.1%
- metal manufacturing, metal products, machinery, electronics and electrical appliances, transportation equipment	1,266	36.3%	43.6%
- other manufacturing (incl. business services)	514	14.7%	16.1%
Total	3491	100.0%	100.0%

4.3 Research questions and analyses

The *within-subjects analysis* aimed at the explanation of competitive advantage within the total group of firms in a specific region. In the first step we analyzed whether the indicator-sets for the separate caf-factors are good predictors for the export quote of firms in North Brabant. The research question was:

1. To what extent do caf-factors explain the competitive advantage of firms in North Brabant (within subjects)?

The analysis is done by an estimation of *three models*: factor conditions, demand conditions, and network features regressed on the export quote. The results of these analyses will be compared for the statistical power of the estimated models with the percentages of variance explained.

In the second step all indicators for the caf-factors are used in one model to estimate the export quote of firms in North Brabant. In this analysis the indicators are mutually compared for their predictive power, without separating them into sets as in the aforementioned analysis. The research question was:

2. Which indicators predict the competitive advantage of firms in North Brabant when all indicators for caf-factors are estimated in one model? Is this consistent with the results of the first analysis?

The analysis consists of an estimation of *one model* in which all indicators for caf-factors were used as predictors for the export quote. The results will be compared for their consistency with the results of the first analysis.

The *between-subject analyses* aimed at exploring empirical relations of factor conditions, demand conditions, network features with export quote *between subgroups of firms* distinguished for firm size, type of industry, and modernity of industry.

The results of the estimation of the first model - caf-factors with export quote within firms in a region - will be compared with the statistical power (percentage variance explained) and consistency of the empirical relation (sign of the ß-coefficients) between predictors (caf-factors) and criterion (export quote) for several subgroups of firms. In this way the explanatory power of Porter's theory is tested at several levels. The research questions were:

3. To what extent do the caf-factor models apply for subgroups of firms (between-subjects)?

These evaluations must give an impression of the validity and empirical power of the theoretical model of caf-factors within firms subdivided into differing firm size, different sectors and difference in modernity. If percentages of variances explained or the ß-coefficients differ, one can say that our theoretical model is valid.

4. Which indicators for caf-factors are the best predictors for export quote and are the ß-coefficients in estimated models for subgroups consistent (negatively or positively with export quote) with those in the estimated models in the total sample?

The answer to this research question must give an understanding of the empirical relevance of indicators for can-factors to explain competitiveness of firms. So in this section attention is displaced from the *level of estimated models* and percentages of variances explained to the *level of empirical relevance of indicators*.

5. Is the export quote of firms in differing industrial sectors explained by different indicators for the sets of caf-factors?
6. Is the export quote of firms with differing firm size explained by different indicators for the sets of caf-factors?
7. Is the export quote of firms differing in modernity explained by different indicators for the sets of caf-factors?

Until now our analyses aimed at validation of our version of Porter's theoretical model. However, it is interesting whether a comparison between subgroups e.g. small, medium-sized and large firms, modern and traditional industries reveals different patterns of caf-factors explaining the export quote. This is empirically relevant because Porter is making a number of generalizing statements about the competitiveness of *industries of nations*. Our aim with research questions 5 to 7 is to illustrate that general statements about factors determining *competitiveness of industries in nations* are easily falsified if one takes into account specific criteria for subdivisions within industries. Competitiveness of small firms might be explained by other factors than the competitiveness of large firms, etc.

Our analyses aim at uncovering differences or similarities in the indicators for caf-factors explaining competitiveness for firms differing in firm size, firms from different sectors and firms differing in modernity of their products. The results will be reported in the following way:
- first, for every category distinguished within sectors (1-8), firm size (small-large) and modernity of industry (modern - traditional) the total number of indicators contributing to the explanation of competitiveness is counted;
- second, the number of indicators contributing to the explanation of competitiveness in more than one category (e.g. in large and medium-sized firms) is counted. If a larger proportion of indicators contributes to competitiveness in a larger number of categories, then there is more resemblance between the explanation of competitiveness of categories within a subgroup. The more resemblance there is between categories within a subgroup, the more generalizing statements about the explanation of competitiveness can be made;
- third, the number of indicators that contribute to the explanation of competitiveness within one category (e.g. only in small firms) is counted. The larger the proportion of indicators that contribute to the competitiveness in one category within a subgroup, the more differences there are in the explanations of competitiveness of categories within a subgroup.

These steps in the analyses are made for sets of indicators for every caf-factor and for every criterion to distinguish categories within a subgroup (firm size, sector, modernity of industry). Step 2 produces a measure of similarity for the explanation of competitiveness of firms between categories of firms within e.g. firm size. Step 3 produces a measure of difference for the explanation of competitiveness between categories of firms within e.g. firm size. A combination of the similarity-measure with the difference-measure for the explanation of competitiveness produces a contingency-index. This contingency-index formalizes the distinctive character of competitiveness of categories of firms in different sectors, of firms with a different size, of firms that differ concerning the product-life cycle. If the difference-measure is larger than the similarity-measure this means that the possibilities for firms to internalize resources which produce a higher competitiveness are more dependent on more or less unique conditions and that this unique situation cannot be neglected, and this is exactly what the contingency perspective stands for.

We call this measure 'contingency-index' because diverging predictors for competitiveness can be interpreted as a confirmation for the contingency-perspective in which the specific configuration of caf-factors have to be taken into account to understand the differences in competitiveness. An implication is that researchers cannot easily formalize and aggregate their research models. Broad sets of indicators have to be used to be able to explain patterns of competitiveness. Firms with different size, firms in different sectors or firms whose products are in different stages of their product-life cycle (the modernity of the industry) might be confronted with completely different possibilities to internalize external resources, so that the caf-factors explaining their competitiveness differ as well.

5. Results

5.1 Within-subjects analysis

1. To what extent do caf-factors explain the competitive advantage of firms in North Brabant?

Tables 7, 11 and 15 show that the percentage variance explained in the export quote within firms is:
- 30% for the factor conditions;

- 20% for the network features;
- 1% for the demand conditions.

The implication of this result is that an effective anticipation of demand conditions can be ignored in the explanation of the export quote at the level of industrial firms. Effective anticipation of demand conditions has no predictive value for the competitiveness of firms. Of course this is an important finding in the light of Porter's theory, because he emphasizes the combination of innovativeness and the ability to strategically change (measured by change in turnover, change in strategic position) in sustaining advantage (Porter, 1990, 49-52).

2. Which indicators predict the competitive advantage of firms in North Brabant when all indicators for caf-factors are estimated in one model? Is this consistent with the results of the first analysis?

If all caf-factors are combined in one model to assess their empirical relation with export quotes the outcome is[11]:
- the percentage variance explained is 33%;
- R&D department is positively related to export quote (ß: .27; sign. t-value p.001);
- the number of automated processes is positively related to export quote (ß: .20; sign. t-value p.001);
- the extent of the R&D network is positively related to export quote (ß: .21; sign t-value p.001);
- if sources of ideas for innovation are internalized in the firm, export quotes are higher (ß: .19; sign. t-value p.01);
- the regional embeddedness is negatively related to the export quote (ß: -.15; sign. t-value p.05).

Caf-factors from the factor- and network features model are entered in the regression equation. This confirms the results of the aforementioned analysis of the demand conditions model which indicated a low level of variance explained. In Porter's assumptions regarding the sources for creating competitive advantage e.g. the number of automated processes[12], the linkages are confirmed too.

5.2 Between-subject analysis

3. To what extent do the caf-factor models apply for subgroups of firms?

Tables 8, 12 and 16 illustrate that when the regression analysis is repeated for firms in industries that:
- the factor conditions model is applicable for 4 of 8 industrial sectors;
- the network features model is applicable for 2 of 8 industrial sectors;
- the demand conditions model is applicable for 2 of 8 industrial sectors.

The caf-factor models proved to be applicable only once to the sector of business services (for factor conditions). The caf-factor models fitted most frequently to the chemical sector and the metal manufacturing sector.

The implication of these results is that the caf-factors show a severe limitation in explanatory power when applied at the level of firms in industries. Porter's conclusion that the determinants of competitive advantage are important in understanding global competition of national industries are not confirmed at the level of firms within different industries.

Tables 9, 13 and 17 contain the results of the regression analysis for firms subdivided into different size categories. The results show that:
- the factor conditions model is applicable for all groups of firms with different size categories;
- the same goes for the model for network features;
- the demand conditions model gives no solution for the firm > 100 employees, and the percentages of variance explained are relatively the lowest (7% and 3%).

Tables 10, 14 and 18 illustrate that when the regression analysis is repeated for firms in the traditional industry and firms in modern industry the impression regarding the explanatory power of the three sets of caf-factors is confirmed. The factors explored in the demand conditions model show no empirical relations with the export quote of firms in those different types of industries.

4. Which indicators for caf-factors are the best predictors for export quote and are the ß-coefficients in estimated models for subgroups consistent (negatively or positively with export quote) with those in the estimated models in the total sample?

A comparison between the results of the analyses of the relations between *demand conditions and export quote* (Table 3) reveals the following patterns:

Table 3. An assessment of the empirical relevance of indicators for factor conditions (based on Table 7-10)

Indicators for caf-factor: factor conditions	Frequencies* in which indicators were entered in the regression equation:	Consistency of signs ß-coefficient
economic performance (loss/profit in 1992)	0	
% higher educated employees	0	
source of ideas for innovation	5	all the signs were consistent compared to the estimated model for the total sample
use of R&D subsidies	6	
occurrence of R&D	0	
R&D department	7	
informal R&D	1	
intensity of R&D	2	
number of automated processes	5	

* 14 models were estimated. The figures in this column show how often every indicator contributed to the statistical explanation of competitiveness.

It is obvious that human and capital resources are relevant in explaining competitiveness of firms in a specific sense. It is interesting that not the education level of employees but their function of providing internal resources for innovation is important in our understanding of competitiveness of firms. Another important point is that organizational facilities regarding R&D (R&D department), and innovation-output (in numbers of automated processes) prove to be good predictors of competitiveness of firms, while the 'intensity of R&D' is not a very good predictor. Finally, it is important to emphasize that an indicator that might be the best example of an internalized can-factor - use of R&D subsidies - is one of the best predictors for competitiveness of firms.

In Table 4 a comparison between the results of the analyses of the relations between *demand conditions and export quote* is reported.

Table 4. An assessment of the empirical relevance of indicators for demand conditions (based on Tables 11-14)

Indicators for caf-factor: demand conditions	Frequencies* in which indicators were entered in the regression equation:	Consistency of signs ß-coefficient
proportional change in turnover 1988-93	0	all the signs were consistent compared to the estimated model for the total sample
change in strategic position from 1988-93	0	
occurrence of product innovation	1	
orientation toward process or product innovation	3	

* 14 models were estimated. The figures in this column show how often every indicator contributed to the statistical explanation of competitiveness.

If the highest frequency in which indicators for demand conditions were entered is 3 while the number of estimated models was fourteen, there is only one conclusion. Effective anticipation or reactions of firms to demand conditions is not an adequate factor explaining competitiveness of firms.

A comparison between the results of the analyses of the relations between *network features and export quote* (Table 5) reveals the following patterns:

Table 5. An assessment of the empirical relevance of indicators for network features[13] (based on Tables 15-18)

Indicators for caf-factor: network features	Frequencies* in which indicators were entered in the regression equation:
number of economic relations	0
number of R&D relations	6
dependency of focal unit on suppliers	2
regional embeddedness	4
number of suppliers of raw material	2
number of suppliers of components	2
number of suppliers of machines and tools	3
knowledge transfer with supply	0
number of customers	1
external influence on innovation	0
number of relations with knowledge infrastructure	0

* 14 models were estimated. The figures in this column show how often every indicator contributed to the statistical explanation of competitiveness.

Table 5 illustrates that only two of the 11 indicators for the network features are empirically relevant predictors for the competitiveness of firms: 'number of R&D relations' and 'regional embeddedness'. These results reveal that it is not evident at all that large networks with a variety of activities improve competitiveness of firms. Most indicators prove to be bad predictors for competitiveness.

We proceed with answering the next questions:

5. Is the export quote of firms in differing industrial sectors explained by different indicators for the sets of caf-factors?
6. Is the export quote of firms with differing size categories explained by different indicators for the sets of caf-factors?
7. Is the export quote of firms differing in modernity explained by different indicators for the sets of caf-factors?

Table 6. Differences and similarities in caf-indicators predicting competitiveness between categories of firms within subgroups

Evaluation criterion regarding differences between subgroups of firms	Factor conditions:	Demand conditions	Network features
Sectors (Tables 8, 12 and 16)	5 of 9 indicators entered in a regression equation for four sectors: 1 indicator in three sectors 1 indicator in two sectors 3 indicators in one sector	2 of 4 indicators entered in a regression equation for two sectors: 1 indicator in sector 3 1 indicator in sector 5	5 of 11 indicators entered in two regression equations: 1 indicator in two sectors 3 indicators within one sector 1 indicator in one sector
Firm size (Tables 9, 13 and 17)	5 of 9 indicators entered in a regression equation for three classes of firm size: 1 indicator in two classes 2 indicators for one class 3 indicators within one class	2 of 4 indicators entered in a regression equation for two sectors: 1 indicator in <10 employees 1 indicator in 10-99 employees	4 of 11 indicators entered in three regression equations: 2 indicators within one firm size 2 indicators separately in two other classes
Modernity of industry (Tables 10, 14 and 18)	4 of 9 indicators entered in a regression equation for traditional and modern industry: 3 indicators in both classes 1 indicator in modern industry	0 indicators entered into the regression equations	5 of 11 indicators entered in two regression equations: 1 indicator in both classes 3 indicators within modern industry 1 indicator in tradition industry

Looking at Table 6 there is no reason to discuss research question 5, 6 and 7 separately. Regardless if one considers subgroups of firms differing in firm size, industrial sector or in modernity of the industry, the number of common indicators between classes within subgroups is systematically smaller than the number of different indicators explaining competitiveness between subgroups of firms. So, the contingency-index is indicating that competitiveness of small, medium-sized and large firms is explained by different indicators for almost every caf-factor. The same goes for categories of firms from different sectors and traditional and modern firms.

On the one hand these results confirm the contingency-perspective that Porter uses to develop his theory of the dynamics of national advantage at the level of firms. On the other hand this means that general statements about factors explaining competitiveness of firms ought to be avoided. This is the price to be paid for institutional analysis.

6. Summary and conclusions

The within-subjects analyses (questions 1 and 2) reveal that the factor conditions and network features contribute to the competitiveness of firms, but this is not the case for the demand conditions. Effective anticipation of demand conditions does not explain the export quote at the level of industrial firms. Of course this is an important result in the light of Porter's theory, because he emphasizes the combination of innovativeness, with the ability to strategically change in the explanation of competitiveness.

The between-subjects analyses (question 3) confirm this impression regarding the explanatory power of the caf-factors. At the level of sectors the caf-factors show a severe limitation in explanatory power. In a large number of sectors the caf-factors did not fit the data at all. So, Porter's conclusion that the determinants of competitive advantage are important in understanding global competition of national industries are not confirmed at the level of firms within different sectors. At the level of subgroups of firms in traditional industry and firms in modern industry, the demand conditions have no explanatory power for competitiveness. Comparing firms different in firm size this impression is confirmed. Factor conditions and network features contribute to the explanation of competitiveness of firms, demand conditions do not.

Looking at the empirical relevance of indicators (question 4) we face the difficulties of economic research at the level of firms and the well known difficulties of institutional analysis. The number of indicators with much predictive value is very small (Table 3, 4 and 5). The emerging picture is that the factor conditions contain the best predictors for competitiveness (highest number of frequently entered indicators), followed by the indicators for network features. Indicators for demand conditions again show poor explanative power.

Our test of the tenability of the contingency perspective (questions 5, 6 and 7) shows that, regardless if one considers subgroups of firms differing in firm size, industrial sector or in modernity of the industry, the number of common indicators between classes within subgroups is systematically smaller than the number of differing indicators. Our contingency-index indicates that competitiveness of small, medium-sized and large firms is explained by different indicators for almost every caf-factor. The same goes for categories of firms from different sectors and traditional and modern firms. This means that the contingency perspective is confirmed. The abilities of firms to internalize resources necessary to compete internationally prove to be very different.

Summarizing, our conclusion is that our version of Porter's theory of competitiveness of firms is partially confirmed. This implies that Porter's theoretical framework for the explanation of the competitiveness of firms is vulnerable. Factors which, according to Porter, explain the differences in competitiveness of industries at the level of nations do not explain competitiveness of firms as well. So, statements about the competitiveness of firms in industries require a careful analyses of factors in the internal and external environment enabling firms to internalize resources necessary for successful competition.

Annex

In this overview of tables the asterisks indicate the following levels of significance:
*   sign. t-value p.05
**   sign. t-value p.01
***   sign. t-value p.001

This annex contains three sections of tables describing the estimation of models of the relation between:
1 export quote and the indicators for factor conditions;
2 export quote and the indicators for demand conditions;
3 export quote and the indicators for network features.

Section 1. Export quote and the indicators for factor conditions

Table 7. Regression analysis of the relation between factor conditions and export quote

independent variables	model for total population ß-coefficients (sign. T-test)
economic performance (loss/profit in 1992)	--
percentage of higher educated employees	--
source of ideas for innovation	.18***
use of R&D subsidies	- .20***
occurrence of R&D	--
R&D department	.23***
informal R&D	--
intensity of R&D	--
number of automated processes	.23***
R multiple correlation	.54
R² variance explained	.30
N number of cases	689

Table 8. Regression analysis of the relation between factor conditions and export quote for industrial sectors[14]

independent variables sectors	1	5	6	8
economic performance (loss/profit in 1992)	--	--	--	--
percentage of higher educated employees	--	--	--	--
source of ideas for innovation	--	--	.18*	--
use of R&D subsidies	-.51*	--	-.22**	-.42**
occurrence of R&D	--	--	--	--
R&D department	--	.44*	.20**	--
informal R&D	--	--	--	--
intensity of R&D	--	--	--	.31*
number of automated processes	--	--	.30***	--
R multiple correlation	.51	.44	.58	.53
R^2 variance explained	.26	.19	.34	.28
N number of cases	44	55	295	97

Table 9. Regression analysis of the relation between factor conditions and export quote for small, medium and large industries

independent variables	< 10 employ-ees	10 - 99 employees	> 100 employees
economic performance (loss/profit in 1992)	--	--	--
percentage of higher educated employees	--	--	--
source of ideas for innovation	.41*	--	--
use of R&D subsidies	--	-.16*	--
occurrence of R&D	--	--	--
R&D department	--	.31***	.36**
informal R&D	--	.15*	--
intensity of R&D	--	--	--
number of automated processes	--	.18**	--
R multiple correlation	.41	.44	.36
R^2 variance explained	.16	.19	.13
N number of cases	149	423	114

Table 10. Regression analysis of the relation between factor conditions and export quote for traditional and modern industry

independent variables	traditional industry	modern industry
economic performance (loss/profit in 1992)	--	--
percentage of higher educated employees	--	--
source of ideas for innovation	.26**	.17**
use of R&D subsidies	--	-.21**
occurrence of R&D	--	--
R&D department	.32**	.22**
informal R&D	--	--
intensity of R&D	--	--
number of automated processes	.24*	.25***
R multiple correlation	.50	.55
R² variance explained	.25	.31
N number of cases	217	460

Section 2. Export quote and the indicators for demand conditions

Table 11. Regression analysis of the relation between demand conditions and export quote

independent variables	model for total population ß-coefficients (sign. T-test)
proportional change in turnover 1988-93	--
change in strategic position from 1988-93	--
occurrence of product innovation	--
orientation toward process or product innovation	.11*
R multiple correlation	.11
R² variance explained	.01
N number of cases	689

Table 12. Regression analysis of the relation between demand conditions and export quote for industries

independent variables	sectors	3	5
proportional change in turnover 1988-93		--	--
change in strategic position from 1988-93		--	--
occurrence of product innovation		-.35*	--
orientation toward process or product innovation		--	.40**
R multiple correlation		.35	.40
R² variance explained		.12	.16
N number of cases		86	55

Table 13. Regression analysis of the relation between demand condition and export quote for small, medium and large industries

independent variables	< 10 employees	10 - 99 employees	> 100 employees
proportional change in turnover 1988-93	--	--	--
change in strategic position from 1988-93	--	--	--
occurrence of product innovation	.27*	--	--
orientation toward process or product innovation	--	.18**	--
R multiple correlation	.27	.18	--
R² variance explained	.07	.03	--
N number of cases	149	423	--

Table 14. Regression analysis of the relation between demand conditions and export quote for traditional and modern industry

independent variables	tradi-tional industry	modern industry
proportional change in turnover 1988-93	--	--
change in strategic position from 1988-93	--	--
occurrence of product innovation	--	--
orientation toward process or product innovation	--	--
R multiple correlation	--	--
R² variance explained	--	--
N number of cases	--	--

Section 3. Export quote and the indicators for network features

Table 15. Regression analysis of the relation between network features and export quote

independent variables	model for total population ß-coefficients (sign. T-test)
number of economic relations	--
number of R&D relations	.26***
dependency of focal unit on suppliers	.15**
regional embeddedness	-.22***
number of suppliers of raw material	--
number of suppliers of components	.18**
number of suppliers of machines and tools	--
knowledge transfer with supply	--
number of customers	--
external influence on innovation	--
number of relations with knowledge infrastructure	--
R multiple correlation	.45
R² variance explained	.20
N number of cases	689

Table 16. Regression analysis of the relation between network features and export quote for industrial sectors

independent variables	5	6
number of economic relations	--	--
number of R&D relations	.40*	.20**
dependency of focal unit on suppliers	--	--
regional embeddedness	--	-.32***
number of suppliers of raw material	.48**	--
number of suppliers of components	--	--
number of suppliers of machines and tools	--	.28***
knowledge transfer with supply	--	--
number of customers	--	.20**
external influence on innovation	--	--
number of relations with knowledge infrastructure	--	--
R multiple correlation	.63	.58
R^2 variance explained	.41	.34
N number of cases	55	295

Table 17. Regression analysis of the relation between network features and export quote for small, medium and large industries

independent variables	<10 employees	10-99 employees	> 100 employees
number of economic relations	--	--	--
number of R&D relations	--	.21**	--
dependency of focal unit on suppliers	--	--	--
regional embeddedness	--	-.22**	--
number of suppliers of raw material	--	--	--
number of suppliers of components	--	--	--
number of suppliers of machines and tools	.37*	--	.29*
knowledge transfer with supply	--	--	--
number of customers	--	--	--
external influence on innovation	--	--	--
number of relations with knowledge infra-structure	--	--	--
R multiple correlation	.37	.32	.29
R^2 variance explained	.14	.10	.09
N number of cases	149	423	114

Table 18. Regression analysis of the relation between network features and export quote for traditional and modern industry

independent variables	tradi-tional industry	modern industry
number of economic relations	--	--
number of R&D relations	.31**	.28***
dependency of focal unit on suppliers	--	.17*
regional embeddedness	--	-.25***
number of suppliers of raw material	--	.15*
number of suppliers of components	.34**	--
number of suppliers of machines and tools	--	--
knowledge transfer with supply	--	--
number of customers	--	--
external influence on innovation	--	--
number of relations with knowledge infrastructure	--	--
R multiple correlation	.44	.49
R^2 variance explained	.19	.24
N number of cases	217	460

Notes

1. As we will show Porter considers 'better strategies' as black boxes. He neglects the link between the factors distinguished in his 'diamond' and the translation of these factors in firm strategies. In our evaluation of Porter's theory these shortcomings will be described.

2. In fact, Porter's theory can be considered to be a branch of the resource approach developed by Pfeffer and Salancik (1978), although the population ecology approach can also be recognized in Porter's theory.

3. Vaessen (1993) focuses his research on this view. One of his main questions is: How do prospective firms respond to economic conditions in poorly and richly developed production environments? The resources provided by the production environments prove to be opportunities as well as limitations for the economic performance of firms. This dual function of production environments is confirmed by the conclusions of Vaessen. One of his main conclusions is that firms are not left to the mercy of poorly developed production environments. Instead, firms differ significantly in the ways in which they exploit the resources in the environment. Firm strategy is the key variable in internalising successfully external resources. For instance, firms take action to reduce

disadvantages of the environment and, simultaneously these reductions mean additional investments and costs for the firms in question.

4. Porter used the following indicators (1990, 279-281):
- real compound annual growth in gross domestic products;
- real compound annual growth in gross domestic product per capita;
- compound annual population;
- overall labour productivity growth;
- manufacturing productivity growth;
- unemployment rates;
- net national investment.

5. Since we don't compare regions or nations the factor 'economic order' is not inserted in our analyses.

6. We consider the name of the fourth determinant of competitive advantage confusing. (Porter, 1990, 107) It suggests strategy, something like choice and action. The description, however, reveals that it regards the economic context which is conditional for strategy. So it would have been better to call this variable: 'rivalry and structure'.

7. The export quote was divided into nine categories: 0%, 1-10%, 10-20%, ..., 60-70% and 70% or more. The second indicator for competitiveness used by Porter - international investments abroad - was not inserted in our survey.

8. The indicators described were developed by the authors in their research programme 'Toward a Technical-Economical Network' (Eindhoven University of Technology, 1991). In this research programme policy research and fundamental theoretical research is done by a team of economists, sociologists and legists.

9. In the analyses the following sector were distinguished:

1 foods and allied products (SBI 21, 22);
2 textile, apparel and leather goods (SBI 22-24);
3 wood products and building materials (SBI 25 and 32)
4 paper, publishing and printing (SBI 26 and 27);
5 chemicals and allied products (SBI 29 and 31);
6 metal manufacturing, metal products, machinery, electronics and electrical appliances, transportation equipment (SBI 33-37);
7 other manufacturing (SBI 38-39);
8 business services (SBI 84).

10. The difference between traditional and modern industry is not based on the production technologies used in these sectors, but on the assumption that the products of firms in traditional industry have reached the end of the product-life-cycle. The opposite goes for products of modern industry; these are in earlier phases of the product-life-cycle (Kleinknecht and Poot, 1990).

11. We did not add this table to the annex.

12. Although Porter does not use this kind of indicator in his analyses we consider this as a valid indicator for 'factor endowment'. The number of automated processes reveals the internalization of physical, knowledge and capital resources. (Porter, 1990, 74-75).

13. A column for the consistency of ß-coefficients is left out. All the signs were consistent compared to the estimated model for the total sample.

14. In several tables in which models for sectors were estimated, sectors are lacking. If regression coefficients for a sector are not described then no variables were entered in the regression equation to predict the export quote.

References

Astley, W.G., A.H. van de Ven - Central perspectives and debates in organi
zation theory. - In: *Administrative Science Quarterly* 28 (1983), p. 245-273

Bain, J.S. - *Barriers to new competition*. - Cambridge, MA: Harvard University
Press, 1956

Boeckhout, I.J., A.W. Verkennis - Schatgraven in eigen regio. - In: *ESB* 78
(1993) no. 3914, p. 526-529

Dunnen, R. den - Knooppunt voor innovatie. - In: *ESB* 78 (1993) no. 3914, p.
536-537

Kleinknecht, A.H. and T.P. Poot - *De regionale dimensie van innovatie in de
Nederlandse industrie en dienstverlening*. - Stichting voor Economisch
Onderzoek van de Universiteit van Amsterdam, 1990

Kleinknecht, A.,T.P. Poot - Do regions matter for R&D. - In: *Regional Studies*
3 (1992)

Meeus, M.T.H., L.A.G. Oerlemans - *Technologiebeleid, innovativiteit en con
currentiekracht in Noord-Brabant. Een trendrapport ten behoeve van de
Brabant Conferentie (mei 1995)*. - TUE, Faculteit Wijsbegeerte en Maat-
schappijwetenschappen, Vakgroep Techniekdynamica, 1995

Pfeffer, J., G.R. Salancik - *The external control of organizations. A resource
dependence perspective*. - New York: Harper & Row Publishers, 1978

Porter, M. - *The competitive advantage of nations*. - Worcester: Billing & Sons
Ltd, 1990

Roos, H.B. - Eindhoven als centrum voor internationale hulpverlening. - In:
ESB 78 (1993) no. 3914, p. 538-539

Rousseau, D. - Issues of level in organizational research: Multilevel and cross-
level perspectives. - In: *Research in organizational behavior*, vol. 7:1-37 /
Eds. L.L. Cummings & B.M. Staw. Greenwich, CT: JAI Press

Scherer, F.M. - *Industrial market structure and economic performance*. -
Chicago: Rand McNally, 1970

Vaessen, P. - Small business growth in contrasting environments. - Nijmegen:
Katholieke Universiteit Nijmegen - In: *Nijmeegse Geografische Cahiers*, nr.
40, 1993

P.R. BEIJE, H.O. NUYS

CONCLUSIONS

In this closing chapter we do not intend to give a complete summary of the conclusions of all the previous chapters. We concentrate instead on some aspects which arose in several chapters. We also focus on some points we find important but which have not or not sufficiently been discussed in the book. We first pay attention to the analysis of the competitiveness of Dutch industries. Then we discuss the merits and limitations of the Porter approach itself. A few issues deserve special attention here: level of analysis, generality of the model, and market view. This is followed by an examination of the main adjustments or extensions of the 'diamond' concept according to the various empirical applications in this book. We end with some reflections on industrial policy implications of it all. But first we reflect briefly upon the Porter approach as one of many alternative views on competitiveness.

1. Analysis of competitiveness

Recently the Dutch Ministry of Economic Affairs published its first 'Test of Competitiveness' (Toets op het Concurrentievermogen, 1995). This report is the first of a series which is supposed to give an overview of the nation's current state of competitiveness. It will be repeated in the coming years. The report follows roughly Porter's idea that the competitiveness of firms in a country is determined by conditions in the national environment. However, no distinction is made between industries or clusters and the set of conditions is broader and more concerned with how the government may improve them. It is worthwhile to mention here the arguments in the report for an even broader approach. It is said that one should not merely look at the country's position on export markets, but also at the ability of firms and government to create welfare and employment in a highly competitive environment. The argument in the report is that high exports in a traditional sector, based on a favourable price-competition position, need not result in good performance in terms of welfare and employment. This seems to relate to the remarks in chapters 1 and 5 about a distinction of export markets into several classes. There it was said that high performance in a small international market will not result in substantial domestic growth of welfare and employment. Or, alternatively, a non-exporting sector in the country may be of importance to a strong exporting sector.

Coming back to the comparison of Porter and the Dutch Test of Competitiveness, the following conditions are mentioned in the last report: physical and knowledge infrastructure, fiscal infrastructure, the working of product and factor markets, and the social infrastructure which includes social security, health care, division of income, and the quality of the public administration. These conditions are somewhat different from the 'diamond' concept. Other government reports show yet other views on the factors explaining competitiveness. One is to be reminded that the earlier mentioned Dutch Porter study was carried out on behalf of the Ministry of Economic Affairs and that the report 'The Netherlands in threefold' (1992), which has also been referred to in this book, followed from a study undertaken by the Central Planning Bureau. The point here is that the new report comes up with yet another use of indicators of a nation's competitiveness. This should remind us of the fact that Porter's 'diamond' approach, although quite broad, is to be seen as one alternative among many views on competitive advantage of nations and sectors. Some views focus entirely on technological indicators (Patel and Pavitt, 1987; Archibugi and Pianta, 1992), others take a more fundamental economic approach (see, for example, Dollar (1993) in the section on issues of long-term competitive advantage of the American Economic Review), yet others use a more historical perspective (Von Tunzelmann, 1995), etc. Any approach can be said to have its limits because it has its 'narrow' perspective and disregards other perspectives. One of the limits of the 'diamond' approach is the way in which competitiveness is measured. In chapter 2, Louter and Koutstaal showed that alternative measures of competitiveness may result in different performances of industries for the country than the Porter study. Another weakness, according to these authors, is the study's 'static' character of the measurement of competitiveness. Their empirical work shows that a few Dutch industries, which do not immediately spring to mind when one thinks of the 'diamond' concept, improved their performance during the eighties. Their conclusion is that the disadvantages of Porter's indicator are that an industry is compared with other industries in the country and not with the same industry in other countries, that a non-exporting industry is automatically seen as 'non-competitive', and that the issue of import penetration is disregarded. Import penetration is no doubt more important for small than for large economies, because imports in a small economy are usually much larger as a percentage of national production than in large economies.

Chapters 6 and 7 focused entirely on the applicability of the 'diamond' concept at the regional level, while chapter 2 also looked at this point. Boekema and Van Houtum concluded that the 'diamond' concept is difficult to 'translate' into a concept able to explain competitiveness of firms in a region. There is a practical and a theoretical side to this. Practically it is difficult to acquire all the information at this level. Theoretically one of the core problems is that competitiveness of most firms in a region does not depend on exports to international markets. One should therefore make a distinction between firms in the region which do export internationally and firms which do not. For the last class of firms one probably needs another model to explain their competitiveness (see the separate section on 'generality of the model'). In their qualitative analysis Boekema and Van Houtum conclude that the Porter concept is a useful guide but that it lacks the precision to explain (differences in) performance of firms in the region in relation to networks in which they operate. It is remarkable that both Louter and Koutstaal in chapter 2, and Boekema and Van Houtum in chapter 6 come up with a criterion for competitiveness of regional firms which is quite different from Porter's criterion. Important here is that these authors tend to incorporate the future strength of the firm, which is dependent on the growth potential of the whole region. The analysis of Meeus and Oerlemans in chapter 7 is somewhat different. They also try to explain competitiveness of 'all' firms in the region, but they make a quantitative analysis of the explanatory power of the 'diamond' concept with regard to differences between firms. They look at whether the Porter concept can be used at another level of analysis. Their conclusion is that the model cannot explain competitiveness at the firm level. This brings up the question how, at the industry level, the 'diamond' factors do result in competitive advantage of (most) firms. We come back to this in the section on different levels of analysis.

Competitiveness is such a complex interplay of numerous (potential) factors that each approach necessarily oversimplifies the whole process. A particular methodological point worth mentioning here is the variety of firm strategy, of types of markets, of government involvement, etc. which makes any general approach to competitiveness of industries hazardous. Related to this is the inherent data problem. Much of the information one would like to have to assess the competitiveness of firms and industries is 'strategic' and therefore difficult to acquire.

2. Competitiveness of Dutch industries

The book presents several case-studies of competitiveness of Dutch industries and sectors and discusses the Dutch 'Porter study'. All these studies largely followed Porter's ideas, or took them at least as a starting point. The cases presented were too few in number to assess the nation's competitiveness. They can, however, indicate some strong and weak points of the economy in addition to the overall assessment of competitiveness of industries and clusters in the Dutch Porter study. We refer to chapter 1 for a presentation of the results of this study. Remarkable was the economy's strength in the agricultural/food industry cluster and the lack of strong clusters in manufacturing industry.

The alternative measure applied to OECD countries in chapter 2 confirms the general conclusion from the Dutch Porter study that most manufacturing industries do not perform very well. Two exceptions which did not come up from the last study are worth mentioning: the paper and the metal industry. These sectors improved their performance in the period 1981-1988. The study of Louter and Koutstaal also showed, however, that several Dutch industries with good export performance had far less favourable positions if one looks at value added. But then again, if one compares the country's performance in hightech industries with other small countries the score is quite satisfactory. It is concluded in chapter 2 that the 'technology mix' of the Dutch manufacturing sector is better than the Porter study suggests.

Most case-studies in the book showed that the 'diamond' factors were supplemented with additional factors. Three blocks of explanatory variables can be distinguished: In the first place the 'diamond' factors, secondly factors concerning small open economies, and thirdly factors specific to the Netherlands.

In his discussion of the 'diamond' factors in chapter 1 Nuys concluded that domestic competition and domestic-related industries seem to play a less prominent role in the 'Dutch Porter study' than in the cases presented by Porter. It was suggested that advanced factor conditions in the Netherlands were a more important factor. To some extent these conclusions were supported by the industry case-studies in the book. In the dairy cluster the success of the past decades cannot be attributed to domestic competition, according to Kamann and Strijker. Domestic-related industries do play an important role, however, but they fit into the whole public-private network of research and production which exists in this strongly regulated industry. These networks can be interpreted as part of 'advanced factor conditions' in the 'diamond' concept. In the two chapters on competitiveness of regions the importance of domestic competition was put under question too. It was argued that domestic competition is not very relevant for small open economies. Regional networks, in contrast, were argued to play a prominent role in the explanation of performance of industries, whether they are strong exporters or not. Furthermore, in chapter 5 Kuijpers and Maltha state that Porter himself puts most emphasis on geographic concentration (of related and supportive industries) and domestic competition. They conclude that their three case-studies do support this, but not unconditionally.

Which additional factors can be classified as typically Dutch or typically belonging to small open economies? In the first chapter of the book the main peculiarities of the Dutch economy have been discussed. Among them were: the country's 'delta economy', the presence of large multinational companies, the surrounding large foreign markets, and the balance between solidarity and freedom. The whole idea that corporatism may be an explanation of competitiveness relates to this last point. Another element of the last aspect are labour relations. It was concluded in chapter 1 that labour relations have positively influenced the country's competitiveness through stability and relatively slowly rising wages. Another Dutch study showed that over the period 1970-1992 labour costs per unit of product in manufacturing were considerably lower than in the USA, Germany, France, and the United Kingdom, and even lower than in Japan (Van Ark, 1994). The analysis of the dairy cluster in chapter 4 clearly showed some aspects of corporatism too.

Of the surrounding large markets Germany deserves special attention. A considerable part of all exports goes to this neighbouring economy. This brings up the question whether such strong relations between a small open economy and one of its large neighbours, in this case based mainly on geographical and economical conditions, should be treated as Porter suggests, namely that exports to neighbour countries could be misleading as an indicator of the country's competitiveness. A counter argument is that Dutch exporting firms are simply profiting from a comparative advantage in the trade with Germany. This strong relationship between The Netherlands and Germany has perhaps not been dealt with sufficiently in the book.

One aspect of the delta economy are the efficient ports and waterways, which explain why the Dutch economy is relatively specialized in the import of raw materials and bulk goods. These are processed and largely exported again, a point mentioned in chapter 5 as well. Porter would probably have argued that this specialization of the Dutch economy was largely based on favourable factor conditions, but that, because market conditions will ultimately change, one should not rely on these 'static' conditions and should upgrade continuously. We agree on this point, which was also mentioned in relation to the Dutch dairy cluster in chapter 4. We come back to it in the section on industrial policy when the 'desired' economic structure is discussed. Another aspect of the delta economy is its strong involvement with dikes and other constructions which protect the Dutch from the sea. The dredging industry, discussed in chapter 5, is no doubt an example of strong expertise in a field related to this.

A major characteristic of the Dutch economy not discussed in detail in the book is the presence of five large multinational corporations which, to give an indication of their size, together spend approximately 50% of the private R&D in the country. In industries where multinational companies play a dominant role, the success of smaller countries seems to be difficult to explain with the 'diamond' concept. The telecommunication industry, discussed in chapter 5, is perhaps such an example.

Of course many more case-studies than were presented in the book would be required to 'test' Porter's model on small open economies like The Netherlands. Nevertheless, the conclusion can be drawn that on the whole the 'diamond' is useful as a first analysis of an industry's or a region's competitiveness. It also gives room to include factors specific for the country or the region/industry. For a more thorough analysis, however, the 'diamond' concept is not sufficient as the discussion in the next section will show.

3. Strong and weak points of the 'diamond'

One of the main merits of the Porter approach compared to the 'traditional' economic approaches is its holistic character and its recognition of history and dynamics. We need not repeat what has been said on this point in the previous chapters. The 'diamond''s broadness may at the same time - not surprisingly - be its weakness. As has been put forward in the first two chapters, Auerbach and Skott (1995) argue that the analysis of each industry lacks institutional detail and, more importantly, the top exporting industries are put as an example for high performance today, although the path towards success for those industries might have depended on a historical situation which is not present any more. This point gives rise to the fundamental question of how general the Porter concept is. Is it relevant for an explanation of export performance in the next decade? Is it well suited to explain current performance in small open economies? Is the 'diamond' concept a general model which needs to be specified according to time and place? These and other points we discuss under the following headings: level of analysis, market and networks, generality of the model.

4. Level of analysis

Several contributors have discussed the proper level of analysis of competitiveness. They conclude that Porter, despite the confusing title 'competitive advantage of nations', focuses on competitiveness of industries and clusters. Porter argues that the influence of *country-specific* factors is most prominent at this level of analysis. In chapter 1 it has been stated that competitiveness of firms in an industry is reflected in their market share over time. Porter's work has been concerned with the factors of competitiveness of firms at various levels. 'Competitive strategy' (Porter, 1980) focused on how the market partly determines the strategy of the firm, 'Competitive advantage' (Porter, 1985) stressed how a single firm can do better than its competitors. The 'diamond' concept (Porter, 1990) implies that all domestic firms in an industry or cluster are influenced by national factors. It can thus be concluded more generally that Porter distinguishes three levels of factors determining a firm's profits and market share: the firm, the market, and the country. A critique of Porter 1990 is that he focuses almost exclusively on the country level and disregards the link between national factors and firm strategy. According to Meeus and Oerlemans in chapter 7 the link between *national* conditions and *firm* performance is far from evident and deserves closer examination. They suggest that environmental conditions must first be internalized by the firm before some advantage can be created based on these conditions.

If we look at the conclusions from several chapters in our book, it can be stated that the country-level of analysis itself appears to be somewhat undefined. On the one hand, small open economies, such as the Netherlands, are so dependent on larger neighbouring economies (especially Germany) that Dutch firms will be strongly influenced by *'European factors'* and not mainly by national factors. On the other hand, some industries and clusters may have regional 'diamonds' and not national. The chapters by Boekema and Van Houtum, and by Meeus and Oerlemans specifically addressed the regional level of analysis. From the regional analyses it can be concluded that three kinds of networks of firms (related to Porter's 'related and supporting' industries) may exist in

a small economy: 1. networks consisting of firms in the region, 2.
national networks which are dense enough to promote the kind of interactions suggested by Porter, and 3. international networks in which Dutch
firms participate. The third type is not discussed in the Porter book.

Another issue is the competitiveness of industries and the competitiveness of firms. Porter (1990) mentions that not all firms in a competitive
industry need to be strong exporters, but he does not explain why. Which
factors determine whether one firm 'exploits' the right conditions for the
industry and another firm not? Meeus and Oerlemans conclude that their
empirical research does not confirm that all 'diamond' factors significantly contribute to an explanation of competitiveness at the firm level. With
regard to the relation between R&D, innovative activity, and export the
study of Kleinknecht, mentioned in chapter 3, also compares the industry
and the firm level. Again, the best results follow from the analysis at the
firm level. Correlations at the industry level may be disturbed because
some firms perform R&D and many others do not, and because firms
without R&D have different technology strategies. Interesting in this
respect is Kleinknecht's conclusion from his empirical study that in an
industry with many product innovations R&D-intensity and exports are
positively correlated, while in many other industries firms may follow a
'defensive' strategy by reacting to import penetration with the purchasing
of advanced technology and equipment. In the last case the correlation
between innovation and export is less clear. As more studies come up
with better correlations at the firm level than at the industry level, the
whole idea of national factors as dominant explananda for performance at
the industry level becomes doubtful. The tradition in industrial organization theory has been to put emphasis on the industry as the proper level of
analysis. Porter added a new element to this tradition by focusing on
country conditions in addition to industrial organization elements such as
competition at the industry level. Recent results of empirical studies in
industrial organization point at a much more prominent role for explanatory factors at the firm level (see, for an overview, for example, Martin,
1992). The results of Meeus and Oerlemans put into question whether
national factors strongly influence performance at this level of analysis.

5. Market and network

Porter's emphasis on domestic competition can be seen as putting
domestic competition as a 'prerequisite' for a firm to establish an ability
to perform well on international markets. Implicit in this is the assumpti-

on that all markets in which exporting firms operate are characterized by strong competition. True as it may be that competition has been increasing in many markets, the nature and intensity of competition may vary considerably among industries. The reader is reminded of the differences between the dredging industry, telecommunications, and the dairy industry discussed in previous chapters. Kuijpers and Maltha (chapter 5) argued that markets differ in respect to the locus of production and consumption. Other aspects of the market are the speed of technological development and the technology life-cycle. In markets with rapid technological change and at the beginning of the cycle firms usually have more opportunities to build a strong position in a niche than in mature markets. More generally, markets are characterized by a large number of aspects and many, often market-specific, institutions determine the nature and extent of competition. Consequently, domestic competition may have various effects, depending on specific features of the market. An extreme case, perhaps, is the dairy cluster discussed in chapter 4. There it was stated that the market has been characterized by strong regulation and that Dutch firms have been very successful, not because there was strong competition on the domestic market, but because the cluster and the various government institutions reacted adequately to the main institutional features in this market. With regard to technology Nelson (1995, 171) puts it as follows: '... nations differ in their pace and pattern of institutional response to the birth and development of an industry, and the locus of comparative advantage is largely determined by these different kinds of national response'. The above discussion brings up the point what exactly does Porter mean by strong competition?

From industrial organization theory it is known that the best performance at the industry level may follow from competition which is not too strong and not too weak. Lawrence (1987) refers to his earlier formulated 'competitive principle' as:

(...) an industry needs to experience vigorous competition if it is to be economically strong, *either* too little *or* too much competitive pressure can lead an industry to a predictably weak economic performance characterized by its becoming inefficient and/or non-innovative. (Lawrence, 1987, 102)

A study by Mayes and Buxton (1988), which confirms the positive correlation between innovativeness and export performance, comes up with only one other significant variable: concentration. On this point they conclude:

It also appears that the firms require some degree of market power before they become export oriented, perhaps because only those firms given a respite from domestic competitive pressures can contemplate shouldering those associated with international markets. (Mayes and Buxton, 1988, 16)

This confirms the critique of Auerbach and Skott (1995) that perhaps Porter presents the situation of today - strong domestic and international competition - too much as a remedy for industries not in such a favourable position. In addition we argue that even markets with strong domestic and international competition may differ substantially with respect to the institutions 'guiding' this competition. One aspect here might be the pattern of competition as Ito and Pucik (1993, 4,5) state. They conclude in their study of the relation between R&D and export performance of Japanese manufacturing that a firm's export ratio is related to its size, but not to its R&D-intensity or to the R&D-intensity of the whole industry. A further conclusion is that follower firms have higher export ratios than market leaders, a point quite similar to Klein-knecht's conclusions discussed above. This suggests that a relation exists between the *pattern* of domestic competition and the international compe-titiveness of Japanese firms.

Related to the above can be the critical remarks of Louter and Kout-staal (chapter 2), Kamann and Strijker (chapter 4) and Boekema and Van Houtum (chapter 6) that Porter deals insufficiently with network relations. Boekema and Van Houtum suggest that participation of a firm in a network with other firms may reduce uncertainty. One main aspect of uncertainty relates to competition and market development in the future, as has been pointed out in chapter 3 by Beije. Kamann and Strijker argue that the public-private networks in the dairy cluster performed quite well until recently in the (regulated) international market. Although it should not be denied that competition plays an important role in many of today's markets, the existence of many public and private networks may be an important 'strategic asset' of a country to gain competitive advantage (Beije and Groenewegen, 1992). Porter seems to underestimate this aspect, by arguing that strategic alliances weaken competitive strength (see chapter 1). In this respect Shan and Hamilton (1991) see horizontal cooperation in a way which puts a different light on Porter's arguments:

(...) an international cooperative venture may provide the firm with access to country-specific advantages embedded in its partners. From this perspective, international cooperative relationships may be viewed as a vehicle to tap into the comparative advantages of countries. (Shan and Hamilton, 1991, 419)

This relates to the arguments of Teece (1992), mentioned in chapter 3, that increased specialization in technological competence, even within markets, forces firms to cooperate.
Most chapters recognize the role of networks, one might say 'despite' competition. Kuijper and Maltha (chapter 5) stated that a cluster cannot be successful without the existence of several interrelated networks of firms. In addition they argue that a conscious disregard by firms of cooperative agreements may result in 'structural inertia'. Related to this is the importance of types of network relations. To give another example, in chapter 1 it is mentioned that Miles and Snow (1992) extend the cluster concept by adding the important notion that if firms adopt network structures they will improve their self-renewal competence because of two unique characteristics of the network form: 'the essential relationships among components are external (and thus highly visible to all parties) and these relationships are voluntary (and thus must reflect explicit commitments)'. The above examples imply that the extent and nature of network relations co-determine cluster performance. The paradox appears that, although it is acknowledged that Porter's main contribution is the importance of the cluster of related and supported industries (Kuijper and Maltha, chapter 5, 36), many authors find the explanation of the interactions of actors in the cluster unsatisfactory.

6. How general is the 'diamond' concept?

In the last section it was argued that the Porter concept may explain competitiveness in one type of market better than in another. There is a methodological question relevant for most 'theories': how general is the theory and do factors specific to time and place have to be 'built in' in order to apply the theory to a specific case at a certain moment? From the case-studies presented in this book it can be concluded that although the 'diamond' concept is so general it can usefully be applied to various industries and regions. The main question is whether the concept really explains competitiveness of industries or if it merely serves as some 'checklist' of points which needs to be filled in specifically. Kamann and Strijker draw this last conclusion in chapter 4. Louter and Koutstaal (chapter 2) have shown how the measurement of competitiveness itself may determine whether an industry is competitive or not. A set of factors explaining a competitive industry may turn out to explain its noncompetitiveness when another measure of competitiveness is used. In addition they conclude that the model might explain any path the country follows in its development. The case-studies taught us a number of things. First, some country-specific, often historically grown, factors determining an industry's (lack of) success could not be brought into the 'diamond' concept. An example is the dairy cluster discussed in chapter 4. Second, the 'diamond' concept enabled a kind of qualitative analysis in which the various factors were specified for time and place. This quite often meant that institutional factors, inherent to the whole Porter concept, could be refined and deepened. It also meant that for some cases some 'diamond' factors turned out to be very important while others were less emphasized. Generally for the Dutch economy, the elements of domestic competition and domestic networks are less relevant than the 'diamond' concept suggests, other elements turned out to be quite useful. This leaves us with some ambiguity. On the one hand the qualitative relations between the elements can be used, but usually not all at the same time. Some emphasis is needed. On the other hand this may undermine the holistic nature of the 'diamond' concept. Kuijpers and Maltha have raised the question of relative weights of the 'diamond' factors. The Porter analyses suggest that 'the better each of the 'diamond' factors is, the better are the results'. This is far from evident, from a methodological point of view. First, there is no well-defined scale on which each factor is measured, nor is there a maximum value defined. Secondly, if one or more factors are below their maximum it is not self-evident that the other factors must be at their maximum to 'guarantee' the best overall performance. Once a single condition is below its maximum value, the best overall result might be gained in combination with other 'below maximum' conditions. An example is a 'below maximum' degree of competition, as discussed previously in relation to networks and uncertainty for individual firms.

From the various chapters it can be concluded that although the 'diamond' concept is too general and that it needs further specification and that additional theories are needed. The best example is perhaps the dairy cluster, where the dairy industry lacked domestic competition and the dairy farms work in a strongly regulated market. Kamann and Strijker concluded that the 'diamond' concept cannot explain stagnation or strong unexpected changes (bifurcations). As suggested in chapters 1 and 4, a more refined classification of types of markets is needed, dealing with size and growth rate, degree of internationalization, extent of technological change, etc. It is not unfair to say that Porter focuses too much on innovative international markets for which the 'diamond' might be a proper concept, while most industries in most countries need other concepts as a refinement of or in addition to the 'diamond' concept to explain their strength or weakness.

7. Complementary theories

In the foregoing sections it has already been suggested that corporatism and 'network theory' could be complementary theories. Strijker and Kamann conclude that more attention needs to be paid to an explanation of mental maps and nonrational behaviour to understand decision-making of firms and other actors in the networks. Meeus and Oerlemans argued that a theory is lacking which explains how firms 'internalize' favourable national conditions. Related to this is the question why some firms in an industry are successful and others not. Additional theories have to bring in the conditions under which favourable national conditions actually lead to good performance by firms in an industry (or even when specific conditions explain firm success under weak 'diamond' conditions). A smaller point is that where Porter incorporates existing theories he does so quite implicitly, without proper reference to the literature. Examples mentioned in the book are regional economics, corporate geography (chapters 2 and 6) and the economics of innovation (chapter 3).

8. Industrial policy

Perhaps the main element in Porter's explanation of competitive advantage is change. Firms need to innovate continuously and the 'diamond' factors themselves must be adjusted to changing international circumstances, especially 'advanced factor conditions'. In such a changing economy a crucial question for national government is whether the economic structure is changing in the right direction, and if firms are changing with the right speed, and if not, whether government can intervene or stimulate on both points.

Over the last two decades a shift can be seen in industrial policy from ad hoc support of individual firms and industries, often based on social considerations, towards an ex ante support of firms and organizations which focus on or contribute to technological and organizational innovation. In the Dutch case this anticipatory policy can be said to operate at two levels, the national and the regional. At the national level a *technology policy* has been developed and implemented based on three pillars: stimulating private R&D, improving the public knowledge infrastructure, and broadening society's acceptance of new technology (Ministries of Economic Affairs, Education, and Agriculture, 1995). At the regional level a *regional policy* has been implemented which increasingly focuses on improvement of the development potential of the various geographical entities. Creation of new technology and applying best-practice technology from elsewhere are the core of such a regional policy. Chapters 2 and 6 have discussed the underlying theories. The recently founded 18 innovation centres in the Netherlands can be seen as an overlap between technology and regional policy. Each centre stimulates technology transfer from the region's knowledge sources towards its small and medium sized firms.

It is fair to say that industrial policy in most OECD member countries is, like in The Netherlands, a mixture of instruments and programmes aiming at new technology creation or application at the regional and national level. Porter sees an active role for government, but compared to most contributors in this book, industrial policy is quite narrowly defined. It should consist of all kinds of measures 'securing' favourable 'diamond' conditions and continuous change of these conditions. Porter does not make a distinction between the national and regional level in this respect. Guidelines for regional policy remain implicit therefore. If, as we suggested above, Porter is focusing on a subset of exporting industries and underestimates the importance of several other classes of industries, such as regional industries with small exports but with an important role to play for an exporting cluster, he no doubt implies a narrower regional policy programme than most regional scientists will do.

With regard to technology policy Porter is more explicit. Beije (chapter 3) concluded that Porter's view on this matter can be interpreted in terms of policy aiming at radical and incremental innovation. For radical innovation Porter sees clearly an important role for the national government, but this role is not worked out well in his 'diamond' concept. With regard to incremental innovation it appears that the 'diamond' should do the work and technology policy has little domain here. It is useful to contrast this view with the main features of the discussion on industrial policy in The Netherlands in the early 1990s.

With regard to the ever changing economic structure and the role of government to influence this structure Minne (1992) states:

> (Today) many more factors determine (economic) growth and enlarge the potential room for government policy. But the high number of differenti-

ated products and the extreme complexity of interrelations, together with little quantative information on topics that really matter, automatically lead to a government which refrains from intervention. (Minne, 1992, 833, translated by the authors)

Partly because of this the exploratory study 'The Netherlands in threefold' uses three scenarios for the development of the Dutch economy in the coming decades. It is interesting that Nooteboom (1992, 243) sees generic policy instruments and infrastructures, often coinciding with a less intervening government, as insufficient to promote structural changes à la Porter. In his opinion *strategic choices* with regard to specific clusters of industries are required. It seems fair to say that he sees a Porter-like approach as a way to identify weak and strong clusters in the economy. In contrast to Porter, however, government should focus its industrial policy on a direct stimulation of strong and promising clusters of economic activity. His vision is based on a central role for specific technological fields, not for specific product groups; on the fundamental and increasing intertwining (vervlechting) of manufacturing and services; and on the undesirability of individual firm support, unless a firm creates a key-linkage in the cluster. Within or with regard to the clusters the aim of government instruments should be to stimulate R&D, improve education, promote cooperation between the various actors (Reich's network broker, mentioned in chapter 5) and abolish institutional obstacles for dynamism in the cluster. Apparently, Nooteboom sees a much more active role for government in creating more or less continuous upgrading in selected clusters. This could be related to our earlier point of institutions 'underlying' competition in markets. As Nelson pointed out, markets, technology and institutions co-evolve in an ever more complex interplay. To disregard this complex interplay bears the danger of what Roobeek (1992a) called 'technical fix', the idea that technological targets can be met by focusing all efforts on technical knowledge. In most cases the interplay with markets is recognized, but the crucial role of institutional change is underestimated. Firms increasingly operate in international networks because of this more complex interplay of technology, markets, and institutions.

With respect to the desired direction of structural economic change most participants in the industrial policy debate agree that the current strength in manufacturing, such as bulk chemicals, and in the agro-food complex must be changed into the direction of more value-added, more hightech, products (see, for example, Roobeek, 1992b). The danger exists, however, that one focuses entirely on such products, which Van Hulst

(1990) called 'structure snobbism'. We have argued that Porter also stressed such markets too much. A small country like the Netherlands has limited resources to act at the forefront of new technologies and should not disregard 'simple' sectors in which current export performance is going well or in which international trade is expected to increase considerably. Where international competition is increasingly played out in 'footloose' industries, future competitive advantage of countries becomes less clear. The future economic structure depends more and more on resources created today. As suggested above, this makes the selection of industries/clusters by firms and by government more uncertain. This uncertainty can be reduced when industrial policy is aimed at selective clusters, in which not only producers (and suppliers) but also financiers and customers believe (Wassenberg, 1992).

References

Archibugi, D. and M. Pianta - *The Technological Specialization of Advanced Countries, A report to the EEC on International science and technology activities.* - Kluwer Academic Publishers, Dordrecht and EEC, 1992

Ark, B. van - Arbeidsproduktiviteit, Arbeidskosten en Internationale Concurrentie. - *Economische Statistische Berichten* (1994) 23-11-1994, 1066-1069

Auerbach, P. and P. Skott - Michael Porter's Inquiry into the Nature and Causes of the Wealth of Nations: a Challenge to Neoclassical Economics. - In: *On Economic Institutions; Theory and Applications* / J. Groenewegen, Ch. Pitelis & Sven-Erik Sjöstrand (eds.). - EE, Aldershot, England, 1995

Beije, P.R. and J. Groenewegen - A Network Analysis of Markets. - In: *Journal of Economic Issues*, vol. 26, no.1 (1992) 87-114

Dollar, D. - *AEA Papers and Proceedings, Section on Long-term Sources of Comparative Advantage.* - vol. 83, no. 2 (1993) May, 431-435

Hulst, N. van - Hoogwaardige technologie en structuursnobisme. - In: *Economische Statistische Berichten*, 8-8-1990, 724-727

Ito, K. and V. Pucik - R&D Spending, Domestic Competition, and Export Performance of Japanese Manufacturing Firms. - In: *Strategic Management Journal* 14 (1993) 61-75

Lawrence, P.R. - Competition: A Renewed Focus for Industrial Policy. - In: D.J. Teece (ed.) / *The Competitive Challenge; strategies for industrial innovation and renewal*. - Ballinger, Cambridge (MA), 1987

Martin, S. - Advanced Industrial Economics. - Blackwell: Oxford, 1993

Mayes, D.G. and T. Buxton - *R&D Trade Performance*. - paper for the 1988 EAERIE conference at Erasmus University Rotterdam, 1988, 28 p.

Miles, R.E. and C.C. Snow - Cause of Failure in Network Organizations. - In: *California Management Review* (1992) Summer, 53-72

Ministries of Economic Affairs, Education, and Agriculture - *Kennis in Beweging ('Knowledge on the Move')* - Technology Report, The Hague, 1995

Minne, B. - Herstructurering van de Nederlandse Industrie. - In: *Econo mische Statistische Berichten*, 2-9-1992, 832-836

Centraal Planbureau - *Nederland in drievoud ('The Netherlands in threefold') : a scenario-study of the Dutch Economy 1990 - 2015*. - Den Haag, 1992

Nelson, R.R. - Co-Evolution of Industry Structure, Technology and Supporting Institutions, and the Making of Comparative Advantage. - In: *The International Journal of the Economics of Business*, vol. 2, no. 2 (1995) 171-184

Nooteboom, B. - Een Aanzet tot Industriebeleid (I); Meso-niveau. - In: *Economische Statistische Berichten*, 17-3-1993, (1993a) 240-244

Nooteboom, B. - Een Aanzet tot Industriebeleid (II); Micro-niveau. - In: *Economische Statistische Berichten*, 17-3-1993, (1993b) 245-249

Patel, P. and K. Pavitt - Is Western Europe Losing the Technological Race? - In: *Research Policy* 16, (1987) 59-85

Porter, M.E. - *Competitive Strategy: Techniques for Analyzing Industries and Competitors*. - New York: the Free Press, 1980

Porter, M.E. - *Competitive Advantage: Creating and Sustaining Superior Performance*. - New York: the Free Press, 1985

Porter, M.E. - *The Competitive Advantage of Nations*. - New York: The Free Press, 1990

Roobeek, A.J.M. - Technologie en Innovatie. -In: *Economische Statistische Berichten*, 8-4-1992 (1992a) 340-343

Roobeek, A.J.M. - Upgrading van de Industrie. - In: *Economische Statistische Berichten*, 2-9-1992 (1992b) 831

Shan, W. and W. Hamilton - Country-Specific Advantage and Internatio
  nal Cooperation. - In: *Strategic Management Journal*, vol. 12 (1991)
  419-432
Ministry of Economic Affairs - *Toets op het Concurrentievermogen (Test
  on Competitiveness)* : Executive Summary. - The Hague, 1995, June
Tunzelmann, G.N. von - Editors Introduction: Government Policy and the
  Long-run Dynamics of Competitiveness. - In: *Structural Change and
  Economic Dynamics* vol.6, no. 1 (1995) March; Special theme: Changes in Long-term Competitiveness: An Historical Perspective (Part
  One)
Wassenberg, A.F.P. - Industriepolitiek: Op Zoek naar NIeuwe Combina
  ties. - In: *Economische Statistische Berichten*, 21-7-1993 (1992) 660-
  663

CONTRIBUTORS

Paul Beije is Associate Professor of Management of Technology and Innovation at the Rotterdam School of Management of the Erasmus University Rotterdam. He wrote his PhD. thesis on 'Innovation and Information Transfer in Interorganizational Networks' in 1989. His courses focus on economics and management of innovation, both at the Management School and the Economics Faculty. He also teaches managerial economics in the MBA/MBI-executive programme at Erasmus University. His research concerns economic organization and management of innovation. He publishes regularly on this topic.

Frans Boekema is Associate Professor of Regional Economics and Economic Geography at the Faculty of Economics, Tilburg University, and is Head of the Department of Regional Economic Research of the Economic Institute Tilburg (EIT). In 1986 he completed a dissertation on local initiatives and a pilot project on regional labour market policy. He has been involved in many analyses of economic potential for regions and cities. He is also a consultant to the European Community, and national, regional and local authorities. His current research activities focus on the relationship between technology and regional economic development, and regional economic development and labour markets. He is also involved in research projects concerning cross-border regional developments and a summer school for regional managers in target-2 regions in the European Union.

Henk van Houtum is a Ph.D fellow in Regional Economics and Economic Geography at the Faculty of Economics, Tilburg University. The topic of his dissertation is 'The Economics of Borders and Border Regions.' He is a researcher of the Department of Regional Economics of the Economic Institute Tilburg (EIT). His major research topics are the measurement of economic performance, the economics of the Benelux, small and medium-sized enterprises, the economic potential of regions, European economics, and the economics of border regions.

Dirk-Jan Kamann is Associate Professor of Industrial Economics at the Department of Management and Business Administration of the Faculty of Economics, University of Groningen. His main research topics are networks, regional development and organizational culture. Apart from many articles and book contributions, he wrote 'Spatial Differentiation of the Social Impact of Technology' (1988, Avebury), 'Externe Organisatie' (1989, Charlotte Heymanns) and 'Cultuur & Strategie' (1995, Charlotte Heymanns). He also is Director of Kamann Consultancy B.V., Groningen and advisor to Kamann Karasek Management Consultants. These companies consult on strategy, management and organizational issues in the Netherlands and Central Europe.

Michael Koutstaal studied business economics at the Erasmus University of Rotterdam. At the moment, he is working as management trainee at the Postbank NV in Amsterdam.

Joost Kuijper is an public policy scientist (University of Twente, 1989) and works as senior researcher at STB-TNO, Centre for Technology and Policy Studies. In 1990 he attended a postgraduate course in European Economic Studies at the College of Europe in Brussels, Belgium. His current work is focused on strategic sector and cluster studies, with special interest in environmental issues in relation to business strategy and industrial economics. He is preparing a thesis on the economics of ecological change.

Peter Louter studied Spatial Economics at Erasmus University Rotterdam. At the moment he is working at TNO/INRO Centre of Infrastructure, Transport and Regional Development and at Erasmus University Rotterdam. His main research topics concern regional economic performance, spatial labourer markets and the relationships between infrastructure and regional economic development.

Sven Maltha is an economist (Erasmus University, 1991; Leuven University) and works as researcher at STB-TNO, Centre for Technology and Policy Studies. He is specialized in industrial organization and competitive analysis of industries. Before joining STB-TNO in 1992, he performed research at Erasmus University on the Dutch audiovisual and construction industry. Current activities are policy studies and market surveys in the field of mobile and satellite communications, telecommunications economics and industry competitive analysis in general.

Marius Meeus is Associate Professor of Technology, Policy and Sociology at the Eindhoven University of Technology, Faculty Technology Management. His research is directed at the adoption of information technology in organizations and organizational change, policy-evaluation and methodology (including problem definition, research design, data gathering methods, multivariate analysis) and economic networks.

Otto Nuys is Scientific Coordinator at SISWO, the Netherlands' Universities Institute for Coordination of Research in Social Sciences, and secretary of STIP (Studygroup for Industrial and Technology Policy). His major field of research is organization theory, especially new concepts of production and interorganizational networks.

Leon Oerlemans is Assistant Professor of Economics of Technology and Innovation at the Eindhoven University of Technology, Faculty Technology Management. His research deals with the impact of technology on regional economic development, policy-evaluation and innovation systems (economic networks).

Dirk Strijker is Assistant Professor of Regional- and Agricultural Economics at the Faculty of Economics, University of Groningen. Before that, he worked at the Agricultural Economic Research Institute (L.E.I.) in The Hague. He publishes about economic aspects of agricultural policies, regional economic issues, issues in agribusiness and rural questions. Coauthor of 'Agribusiness Complexes in the Netherlands' (the Hague, 1987) and 'Financial support to the Dutch agriculture' (Utrecht, 1994). Writes many essays in newspapers and has several official functions in and around agriculture.

278

LIST OF TABLES

280

LIST OF FIGURES